Tablecloth
IN ½ THE TIME

G000065883

General Information

Many of the products used in this pattern book can be purchased from local craft, fabric and variety stores, or from the Annie's Attic Needlecraft Catalog (see Customer Service information on page 23).

Contents

Indiana
White Daisies

FINISHED SIZE
Approximately 52 inches x 76 inches

MATERIALS
- Aunt Lydia's Fashion Crochet size 3 crochet cotton (150 yds per ball): 27 balls #201 white
- Size E/4/3.5mm crochet hook or size needed to obtain gauge
- Tapestry needle

GAUGE
29 mesh = 9½ inches

PATTERN NOTES
Weave in ends as work progresses.

Join with slip stitch as indicated unless otherwise stated.

Chain-3 at beginning of rows counts as a double crochet unless otherwise stated.

Chain-4 at beginning of rows counts as a double crochet and a chain-1 space unless otherwise stated.

SPECIAL STITCHES
Block: Dc in each of next 2 sts or dc in next ch-1 sp, dc in next dc.

Beginning mesh (beg mesh): Ch 4, dc in next dc.

Mesh: Ch 1, sk next st or sp, dc in next st.

INSTRUCTIONS
PANEL A
MAKE 3.
Row 1 (RS): Ch 62, dc in 5th ch from hook (*beg 4 sk chs count as sk a mesh*), 28 **mesh** (*see Special Stitches*), turn. (*29 mesh*)

Row 2: **Beg mesh** (*see Special Stitches*), 28 mesh, turn.

Row 3: Beg mesh, [mesh, **block** (*see Special Stitches*)] 13 times, 2 mesh, turn.

Rows 4–8: Work according to Chart A.

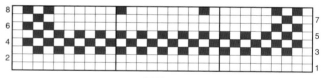

CHART A

Row 9: Beg mesh, mesh, block, 6 mesh, block, ch 10, sk next dc, dc in next dc, block, 5 mesh, block, ch 10, sk next dc, dc in next dc, block, 6 mesh, block, 2 mesh, turn.

Row 10: Beg mesh, block, mesh, block, 4 mesh, block, ch 5, sc in next ch-10 sp, ch 5, sk next 2 dc, dc in next dc, block, 3 mesh, block, ch 5, sc in next ch-10 sp, ch 5, sk next 2 dc, dc in next dc, block, 4 mesh, [block, mesh] twice, turn.

Row 11: Beg mesh, mesh, block, 4 mesh, block, ch 5, sc in next ch-5 sp, sc in next sc, sc in next ch-5 sp, ch 5, sk next 2 dc, dc in next dc, block, mesh, block, ch 5, sc in next ch-5 sp, sc in next sc, sc in next ch-5 sp, ch 5, sk next 2 dc, dc in next dc, block, 4 mesh, block, 2 mesh, turn.

Row 12: Beg mesh, block, mesh, block, 2 mesh, block, [ch 5, sc in next ch-5 sp, sc in each of next 3 sc, sc in next ch-5 sp, ch 5, sk next 2 dc,

dc in next dc, block] twice, 2 mesh, [block, mesh] twice, turn.

Row 13: Beg mesh, mesh, block, 4 mesh, [2 dc in next ch-5 sp, ch 5, sk next sc, sc in each of next 3 sc, ch 5, sk next sc, 2 dc in next ch-5 sp, dc in next dc, mesh] twice, 3 mesh, block, 2 mesh, turn.

Row 14: Beg mesh, block, mesh, block, 4 mesh, 2 dc in next ch-5 sp, ch 5, sk next sc, sc in next sc, ch 5, sk next sc, 2 dc in next ch-5 sp, dc in next dc, mesh, block, mesh, 2 dc in next ch-5 sp, ch 5, sk next sc, sc in next sc, ch 5, sk next sc, 2 dc in next ch-5 sp, dc in next dc, 4 mesh, [block, mesh] twice, turn.

Row 15: Beg mesh, mesh, block, 6 mesh, 2 dc in next ch-5 sp, ch 1, 2 dc in next ch-5 sp, dc in next dc, 2 mesh, block, 2 mesh, 2 dc in next ch-5 sp, ch 1, 2 dc in next ch-5 sp, dc in next dc, 6 mesh, block, 2 mesh, turn.

Row 16: Beg mesh, block, mesh, block, 6 mesh, block, mesh, [2 block, mesh] twice, block, 6 mesh, [block, mesh] twice, turn.

Rows 17–23: Rep rows 9–15.

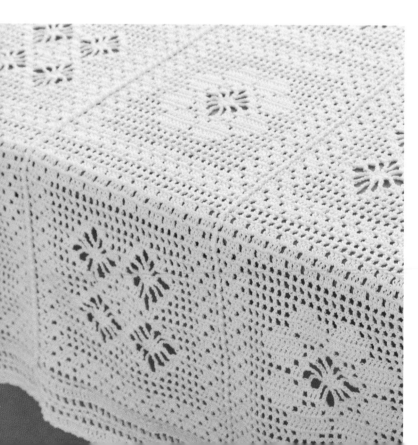

Row 24: Beg mesh, block, mesh, block, 6 mesh, block, 7 mesh, block, 6 mesh, [block, mesh] twice, turn.

Rows 25–41: Work according to Chart B.

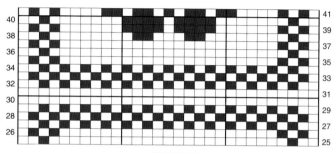

CHART B

Row 42: Beg mesh, mesh, block, 4 mesh, 4 blocks, 2 mesh, block, ch 10, sk next dc, dc in next dc, block, 2 mesh, 4 blocks, 4 mesh, block, 2 mesh, turn.

Row 43: Beg mesh, block, mesh, block, 3 mesh, 4 blocks, mesh, block, ch 5, sc in next ch-10 sp, ch 5, sk next 2 dc, dc in next dc, block, mesh, 4 blocks, 3 mesh, [block, mesh] twice, turn.

Row 44: Beg mesh, mesh, block, 5 mesh, 2 blocks, mesh, block, ch 5, sc in next ch-5 sp, sc in next sc, sc in next ch-5 sp, ch 5, sk next 2 dc, dc in next dc, block, mesh, 2 blocks, 5 mesh, block, 2 mesh, turn.

Row 45: Beg mesh, block, mesh, block, 6 mesh, block, ch 5, sc in next ch-5 sp, sc in each of next 3 sc, sc in next ch-5 sp, ch 5, sk next 2 dc, dc in next dc, block, 6 mesh, [block, mesh] twice, turn.

Row 46: Beg mesh, mesh, block, 5 mesh, 2 blocks, mesh, 2 dc in next ch-5 sp, ch 5, sk next sc, sc in each of next 3 sc, ch 5, sk next sc, 2 dc in next ch-5 sp, dc in next dc, mesh, 2 blocks, 5 mesh, block, 2 mesh, turn.

Row 47: Beg mesh, block, mesh, block, 3 mesh, 4 blocks, mesh, 2 dc in next ch-5 sp, ch 5, sk next sc, sc in next sc, ch 5, sk next sc, 2 dc in next ch-5 sp, dc in next dc, mesh, 4 blocks, 3 mesh, [block, mesh] twice, turn.

Row 48: Beg mesh, mesh, block, 4 mesh, 4 blocks, 2 mesh, 2 dc in next ch-5 sp, ch 1, 2 dc in next ch-5 sp, dc in next dc, 2 mesh, 4 blocks, 4 mesh, block, 2 mesh, turn.

Rows 49–59: Work according to Chart C.

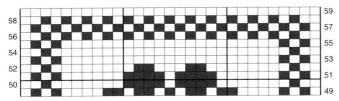

CHART C

Rows 60–175: [Rep rows 2–59 consecutively] twice.

Row 176: Beg mesh, 28 mesh. Fasten off.

PANEL B
MAKE 2.
Rows 1 & 2: Rep rows 1 and 2 of Panel A.

Rows 3–12: Work according to Chart D.

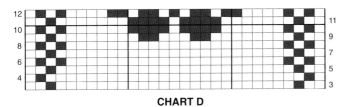

CHART D

Rows 13–19: Rep rows 42–48 of Panel A.

Row 20: Beg mesh, block, mesh, block, 4 mesh, 2 blocks, mesh, 2 blocks, mesh, block, mesh, 2 blocks, mesh, 2 blocks, 4 mesh, [block, mesh] twice, turn.

Rows 21–30: Work according to Chart E.

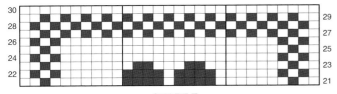

CHART E

Rows 31–146: [Rep rows 2–59 of Panel A consecutively] twice.

Rows 147–176: Rep rows 2–31 of Panel A. At end of last row, fasten off.

ASSEMBLY
Arrange Panels according to assembly diagram. Hold first 2 Panels with WS tog and long edge at top; working through both Panels at same time, join cotton in end of first row at left-hand left end of Panels. Ch 1, work **reverse sc** (see Fig. 1) sc in same sp, working left to right, work [ch 2, reverse sc in next row] across edge. Fasten off. Join rem Panels in same manner.

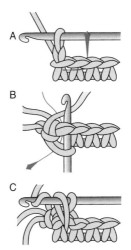

Fig. 1
Reverse Single Crochet

BORDER
Rnd 1 (RS): With RS facing, **join** (see Pattern Notes) cotton in any ch-2 sp, **ch 3** (see Pattern Notes), dc in same sp, [2 dc in next sp] around, working (2 dc, ch 2, 2 dc) in each corner, join in 3rd ch of beg ch-3.

Rnd 2: Sl st in next ch-1 sp, **ch 4** (see Pattern Notes), sk next dc, [dc in next dc, ch 1, sk next st] around, working (dc, ch 4, dc) in each corner, join in 3rd ch of beg ch-4.

Rnd 3: Sl st in next ch-1 sp, **ch 3** (counts as a hdc and a ch-1 sp), sk next dc, [hdc in next ch-1 sp, ch 1, sk next dc] around, working (hdc, ch 3, hdc) in each corner ch-4 sp, join in 2nd ch of beg ch-3.

Rnd 4: Sl st in next ch-1 sp, ch 4, sk next hdc, [dc in next ch-1 sp, ch 1, sk next hdc] around, working (dc, ch 4, dc) in each corner ch-3 sp, join in 3rd ch of beg ch-4.

Rnd 5: Sl st in next ch-1 sp, ch 3, dc in same sp, 2 dc in each rem ch-1 sp around, working (2 dc, ch 3, 2 dc) in each corner ch-4 sp, join in 3rd ch of beg ch-4.

Rnd 6: Ch 1, working left to right, reverse sc in same ch as joining, sk next 2 dc, *work reverse sc in next dc, ch 2, sk next 2 dc, rep from * around, join in beg reverse sc. Fasten off. ∎

Louisiana Golden Stems

SKILL LEVEL

INTERMEDIATE

FINISHED SIZE

Approximately 53 inches in diameter

MATERIALS

- Aunt Lydia's Fashion Crochet size 3 crochet cotton (150 yds per ball): 19 balls #226 natural
- Size E/4/3.5mm crochet hook or size needed to obtain gauge
- Tapestry needle

GAUGE

Rnds 1–7 = 4½ inches

PATTERN NOTES

Weave in ends as work progresses.

Join with slip stitch as indicated unless otherwise stated.

Chain-3 at beginning of rnds counts as first double crochet unless otherwise stated.

SPECIAL STITCHES

Beginning half shell (beg half shell): Ch 3, dc in indicated sp.

Half shell: 2 dc in indicated sp.

Beginning shell (beg shell): Ch 3, (dc, ch 2, 2 dc) in indicated sp.

Shell: (2 dc, ch 2, 2 dc) in indicated sp.

Beginning half double shell (beg half double shell): Ch 3, (dc, ch 2, dc) in indicated sp.

Double shell: (Shell, ch 2, 2 dc) in indicated sp.

Cluster (cl): Yo, draw up lp in indicated ch-3 sp, draw up lp in each of next 2 ch-3 sps, [yo, draw through 3 lps on hook] twice.

Small cluster (small cl): Yo, draw up lp in each of next 2 indicated sts, yo, draw through 3 lps on hook, yo and draw through 2 lps on hook.

INSTRUCTIONS
CENTER

Rnd 1 (RS): Ch 6, **join** (see Pattern Notes) in first ch to form a ring, **ch 3** (see Pattern Notes), 23 dc in ring, join in 3rd ch of beg ch-3. (24 dc)

Rnd 2: Ch 1, sc in same ch as joining, **fpdc** (see Stitch Guide) around next dc, *sc in next dc, fpdc around next dc, rep from * around, join in beg sc. (12 fpdc, 12 sc)

Rnd 3: Ch 1, sc in same ch as joining, 2 sc in next st, *sc in next sc, 2 sc in next st, rep from * around, join in beg sc. (36 sc)

Rnd 4: Ch 1, sc in each sc around, join in beg sc.

Rnd 5: Ch 1, sc in same sc, sc in next sc, 2 sc in next sc, *sc in each of next 2 sc, 2 sc in next sc, rep from * around, join in beg sc. (48 sc)

Rnd 6: Ch 1, sc in same sc, [**fptr** (see Stitch Guide) around first fpdc on rnd 2, sc in each of next 3 sts] 11 times, sc in each of last 2 sc, join in beg sc. (12 fptr, 36 sc)

Rnd 7: Ch 1, sc in same sc, *ch 3, sk next st, sc in next st, rep from * around, ch 2, join with hdc in beg sc. (24 ch sps)

Rnd 8: Beg half shell (see Special Stitches) in sp formed by joining hdc, sc in next ch-3 sp, ch 3, sc in next ch-3 sp, *shell (see Special Stitches) in next ch-3 sp, sc in next ch-3 sp, ch 3, sc in

next ch-3 sp, rep from * 6 times, **half shell** (*see Special Stitches*) in same sp as beg ch-3, ch 1, sc in 3rd ch of beg ch-3. (*8 shells, 8 ch sps*)

Rnd 9: Beg half shell in sp formed by joining sc, ch 3, sc in next sc, (sc, ch 3, sc) in next ch-3 sp, sc in next sc, ch 3, *shell in ch-2 sp of next shell, ch 3, sc in next sc, (sc, ch 3, sc) in next ch-3 sp, sc in next sc, ch 3, rep from * 6 times, half shell in same sp as beg ch-3, ch 1, join with sc in 3rd ch of beg ch-3. (*8 shells, 24 ch sps*)

Rnd 10: Beg half shell in sp formed by joining sc, *ch 3, 2 sc in next ch-3 sp, (sc, ch 3, sc) in next ch-3 sp, 2 sc in next ch-3 sp, ch 3 **, shell in ch-2 sp of next shell, rep from * around, ending last rep at **, half shell in same sp as beg ch-3, ch 1, join with sc in 3rd ch of beg ch-3.

Rnd 11: Beg half double shell (*see Special Stitches*) in sp formed by joining sc, ch 2, dc in same sp, *ch 3, 2 sc in next ch-3 sp, (sc, ch 3, sc) in next ch-3 sp, 2 sc in next ch-3 sp, ch 3 **, **double shell** (*see Special Stitches*) in ch-2 sp of next shell, rep from * around, ending last rep at **, half shell in same sp as beg ch-3, ch 1, join with sc in 3rd ch of beg ch-3. (*8 double shells, 24 ch sps*)

Rnd 12: Beg half shell in sp formed by joining sc, ch 3, shell in next ch-2 sp, *ch 3, 2 sc in next ch-3 sp, (sc, ch 3, sc) in next ch-3 sp 2 sc in next ch-3 sp, ch 3 **, shell in ch-2 sp of next shell, ch 3, shell in next ch-2 sp, rep from * around, ending last rep at **, half shell in same sp as beg ch-3, ch 1, join with sc in 3rd ch of beg ch-3. (*16 shells, 56 ch sps*)

Rnd 13: Beg half shell in sp formed by joining sc, *ch 3, sc in next ch-3 sp, ch 3, shell in ch-2 sp of next shell, ch 3, 2 sc in next ch-3 sp, (sc, ch 3, sc) in next ch-3 sp, 2 sc in next ch-3 sp, ch 3 **, rep from * around, ending last rep at **, half shell in same sp as beg ch-3, ch 1, join with sc in 3rd ch of beg ch-3. (*16 shells, 40 ch-3 sps*)

Rnd 14: Beg half shell in sp formed by joining sc, *ch 3, 2 sc in next ch-3 sp, sc in next sc, 2 sc in next ch-3 sp, ch 3, shell in ch-2 sp of next shell, ch 3, 2 sc in next ch-3 sp, (sc, ch 3, sc) in next ch-3 sp, 2 sc in next ch-3 sp, ch 3 **, shell in ch-2 sp of next shell, rep from * around, ending

last rep at **, half shell in same sp as beg ch-3, ch 1, join with sc in 3rd ch of beg ch-3.

Rnd 15: Beg half shell in sp formed by joining sc, *ch 3, 2 sc in next ch-3 sp, ch 5, 2 sc in next ch-3 sp, ch 3, shell in ch-2 sp of next shell, ch 3, 2 sc in next ch-3 sp, (sc, ch 3, sc) in next ch-3 sp, 2 sc in next ch-3 sp, ch 3 **, shell in ch-2 sp of next shell, rep from * around, ending last rep at **, ch 3, half shell in same sp as beg ch-3, ch 1, join with sc in 3rd ch of beg ch-3. (*16 shells, 8 ch-5 sps, 32 ch-3 sps*)

Rnd 16: Beg half shell in sp formed by joining sc, *ch 3, 2 sc in next ch-3 sp, ch 3, (sc, ch 3, sc) in next ch-5 sp, ch 3, 2 sc in next ch-3 sp, ch 3, half shell in ch-2 sp of next shell, ch 1, **cl** (*see Special Stitches*) in next 3 ch-3 sps **, half shell in ch-2 sp of next shell, rep from * around, ending last rep at **, join in 3rd ch of beg ch-3.

Rnd 17: Beg half shell in same ch as joining, *ch 3, 2 sc in next ch-3 sp, ch 3, sc in next ch-3 sp, ch 3, shell in next ch-3 sp, ch 3, 2 sc in next ch-3 sp, ch 3, 2 sc in next ch-3 sp, ch 3, half shell in next ch-1 sp **, ch 2, sk next cl, half shell in next dc, rep from * around, ending last rep at **, ch 1, join with sc in 3rd ch of beg ch-3. (*8 shells, 16 half shells, 48 ch-3 sps*)

Rnd 18: Beg half shell in sp formed by joining sc, ch 3, 2 sc in next ch-3 sp, (sc, ch 3, sc) in next ch-3 sp, 2 sc in next ch-3 sp, ch 3, shell in ch-2 sp of next shell, ch 3, 2 sc in next ch-3 sp, (sc, ch 3, sc) in next ch-3 sp, 2 sc in next ch-3 sp, ch 3 **, shell in next ch-2 sp, rep from * around, ending last rep at **, half shell in same sp as beg ch-3, ch 1, join with sc in 3rd ch of beg ch-3. (*16 shells, 48 ch-3 sps*)

Rnd 19: Beg half shell in sp formed by joining sc, *ch 3, 2 sc in next ch-3 sp, (sc, ch 3, sc) in next ch-3 sp, 2 sc in next ch-3 sp, ch 3 **, shell in ch-2 sp of next shell, rep from * around, ending last rep at **, half shell in same sp as beg ch-3, ch 1, join with sc in 3rd ch of beg ch-3.

Rnd 20: Beg half shell in sp formed by joining sc, *ch 3, 2 sc in next ch-3 sp, (sc, ch 3, sc) in next ch-3 sp, 2 sc in next ch-3 sp, ch 3 **, double shell in ch-2 sp of next shell, rep from * around, ending last rep at **, shell in same sp as beg ch-3, ch 1, join with sc in 3rd ch of beg ch-3. (*16 double shells, 48 ch-3 sps*)

Rnd 21: Beg half shell in sp formed by joining sc, *ch 3, 2 sc in next ch-3 sp, (sc, ch 3, sc) in next ch-3 sp, 2 sc in next ch-3 sp, ch 3, shell in ch-2 sp of next double shell, ch 3 **, shell in next ch-2 sp, rep from * around, ending last rep at **, half shell in same sp as beg ch-3, ch 1, join with sc in 3rd ch of beg ch-3. (*32 shells, 64 ch-3 sps*)

Rnd 22: Beg half shell in sp formed by joining sc, *ch 3, 2 sc in next ch-3 sp, (sc, ch 3, sc) in next ch-3 sp, 2 sc in next ch-3 sp, ch 3, shell in ch-2 sp of next shell, ch 3, sc in next ch-3 sp, ch 3 **, shell in ch-2 sp of next shell, rep from * around, ending last rep at **, half shell in same sp as beg ch-3, ch 1, join with sc in 3rd ch of beg ch-3. (*32 shells, 80 ch sps*)

Rnd 23: Beg half shell in sp formed by joining sc, *ch 3, 2 sc in next ch-3 sp, (sc, ch 3, sc) in next ch-3 sp, 2 sc in next ch-3 sp, ch 3, shell in ch-2 sp of next shell, ch 3, 2 sc in next ch-3 sp, sc in next sc, 2 sc in next ch-3 sp, ch 3 **, shell in ch-2 sp of next shell, rep from * around, ending last rep at **, half shell in same sp as beg ch-3, ch 1, join with sc in 3rd ch of beg ch-3.

Rnd 24: Beg half shell in sp formed by joining sc, ch 3, 2 sc in next ch-3 sp, (sc, ch 3, sc) in next ch-3 sp, 2 sc in next ch-3 sp, ch 3, shell in ch-2 sp of next shell, ch 3, 2 sc in next ch-3 sp, ch 5, 2 sc in next ch-3 sp, ch 3, shell in ch-2 sp of next shell, ch 3, 2 sc in next ch-3 sp, (sc, ch 3, sc) in next ch-3 sp, 2 sc in next ch-3 sp, ch 3 **, shell in ch-2 sp of next shell, rep from * around, ending last rep at **, half shell in same sp as beg ch-3, ch 1, join with sc in 3rd ch of beg ch-3. (*32 shells, 128 ch-3 sps*)

Rnd 25: Beg half shell in sp formed by joining sc, *cl in next 3 ch-3 sps, shell in ch-2 sp of next shell, ch 3, 2 sc in next ch-3 sp, ch 3, (sc, ch 3, sc) in next ch-5 sp, ch 3, 2 sc in next ch-3 sp, ch 3 **, shell in ch-2 sp of next shell, rep from * around, ending last rep at **, half shell in same sp as beg ch-3, ch 1, join with sc in 3rd ch of beg ch-3.

Rnd 26: *Sc in ch-2 sp of next shell, [ch 3, sc in next ch-3 sp] 5 times, ch 3, sc in ch-2 sp of next shell, rep from * around, join in joining sc. (*96 sc, 96 ch-3 sps*)

Rnd 27: Ch 2, dc in next sc, *[3 dc in next ch-3 sp, dc in next sc] 6 times, **small cl** (*see Special Stitches*) in next 2 sc, rep from * around; join in first dc. (*24 cls, 360 dc*)

Rnd 28: Ch 3, *fpdc around next st, dc in each of next 2 sts, rep from * around to last 2 sts, fpdc around next st, dc in last st, join in 3rd ch of beg ch-3. (*384 sts*)

Rnd 29: Ch 3, *fpdc around next st, dc in each of next 2 dc, rep from * around to last fpdc, fpdc around last fpdc, dc in last dc, join in 3rd ch of beg ch-3.

Rnd 30: Ch 1, sc in same ch as joining, *ch 3, sk next 2 sts, sc in next st, rep from * around, join in beg sc. (*128 ch-3 sps*)

Rnd 31: Sl st in next ch of next ch-3 sp, **beg shell** (*see Special Stitches*) in same ch-3 sp, ch 3, 2 sc in next ch-3 sp, (sc, ch 3, sc) in next ch-3 sp, 2 sc in next ch-3 sp, ch 3 **, shell in next ch-3 sp, rep from * around, ending last rep at **, join in 3rd ch of beg ch-3. (*32 shells, 96 ch-3 sps*)

Rnd 32: Beg shell in sp formed by joining sc, *ch 3, 2 sc in next ch-3 sp, (sc, ch 3, sc) in next ch-3 sp, 2 sc in next ch-3 sp, ch 3 **, shell in ch-2 sp of next shell, rep from * around, ending last rep at **, join in 3rd ch of beg ch-3.

Rnd 33: Sl st in next dc, sl st in next ch-2 sp, beg half shell in sp formed by joining sc, *ch 3, 2 sc in next ch-3 sp, (sc, ch 3, sc) in next ch-3 sp, 2 sc in next ch-3 sp, ch 3 **, shell in ch-2 sp of next shell, rep from * around, ending last rep at **, half shell in same sp as beg ch-3, ch 1, join with sc in 3rd ch of beg ch-3.

Rnd 34: Beg half shell in sp formed by joining sc, ch 2, 2 dc in same sp, *ch 3, 2 sc in next ch-3 sp, (sc, ch 3, sc) in next ch-3 sp, 2 sc in next ch-3 sp, ch 3 **, double shell in ch-2 sp of next shell, rep from * around, ending last rep at **, half shell in same sp as beg ch-3, ch 1, join with sc in 3rd ch of beg ch-3. (*32 double shells, 96 ch-3 sps*)

Rnd 35: Beg half shell in sp formed by joining sc, *ch 3, 2 sc in next ch-3 sp, (sc, ch 3, sc) in next ch-3 sp 2 sc in next ch-3 sp, ch 3, shell in ch-2 sp of next shell, ch 3 **, shell in next ch-2 sp, rep from * around, ending last rep at **, half shell in same sp as beg ch-3, ch 1, join with sc in 3rd ch of beg ch-3. *(64 shells, 128 ch-3 sps)*

Rnd 36: Beg half shell in sp formed by joining sc, *ch 3, 2 sc in next ch-3 sp, (sc, ch 3, sc) in next ch-3 sp, 2 sc in next ch-3 sp, ch 3, shell in ch-2 sp of next shell, ch 3, sc in next ch-3 sp, ch 3 **, shell in ch-2 sp of next shell, rep from * around, ending last rep at **, half shell in same sp as beg ch-3, ch 1, join with sc in 3rd ch of beg ch-3. *(64 shells, 160 ch-3 sps)*

Rnd 37: Beg half shell in sp formed by joining sc, *ch 3, 2 sc in next ch-3 sp, (sc, ch 3, sc) in next ch-3 sp, 2 sc in next ch-3 sp, shell in ch-2 sp of next shell, ch 3, 2 sc in next ch-3 sp, sc in next sc, 2 sc in next ch-3 sp, ch 3 **, shell in ch-2 sp of next shell, rep from * around, ending last rep at **, half shell in same sp as beg ch-3, ch 1, join with sc in 3rd ch of beg ch-3.

Rnd 38: Beg half shell in sp formed by joining sc, *ch 3, 2 sc in next ch-3 sp, (sc, ch 3, sc) in next ch-3 sp, 2 sc in next ch-3 sp, ch 3, shell in ch-2 sp of next shell, ch 3, 2 sc in next ch-3 sp, ch 5, 2 sc in next ch-3 sp, ch 3 **, shell in ch-2 sp of shell, rep from * around, ending last rep at **, ch 3, half shell in same sp as beg ch-3, ch 1, join with sc in 3rd ch of beg ch-3. *(64 shells, 64 ch-5 sps, 160 ch-3 sps)*

Rnd 39: Beg half shell in sp formed by joining sc, *cl, half shell in ch-2 sp of next shell, ch 3, 2 sc in next ch-3 sp, ch 3, (sc, ch 3, sc) in next ch-5 sp, ch 3, 2 sc in next ch-3 sp, ch 3 **, half shell in ch-2 sp of next shell, rep from * around, ending last rep at **, join in 3rd ch of beg ch-3.

Rnd 40: Sl st in next dc, sl st in next cl, beg shell in same cl, *ch 3, [sc in next ch-3 sp, ch 3] twice, shell in next ch-3 sp, ch 3, [sc in next ch-3 sp, ch 3] twice **, shell in next cl, rep from * around, ending last rep at **, join in 3rd ch of beg ch-3. *(64 shells, 192 ch-3 sps)*

Rnd 41: Sl st in next dc, sl st in next ch-2 sp, beg shell in same sp, *ch 3, 2 sc in next ch-3 sp, (sc, ch 3, sc) in next ch-3 sp, 2 sc in next ch-3 sp, ch 3 **, shell in ch-2 sp of next shell, rep from * around, ending last rep at **, join in 3rd ch of beg ch-3.

Rnd 42: Rep rnd 41.

Rnd 43: Sl st in next dc, sl st in next ch-2 sp, beg half shell in same sp, *ch 3, 2 sc in next ch-3 sp, (sc, ch 3, sc) in next ch-3 sp, 2 sc in next ch-3 sp, ch 3 **, double shell in ch-2 sp of next shell, rep from * around, ending last rep at **, shell in same sp as beg ch-3, ch 1, join with sc in 3rd ch of beg ch-3. *(64 double shells, 192 ch-3 sps)*

Rnd 44: Beg half shell in sp formed by joining sc, *ch 3, 2 sc in next ch-3 sp, (sc, ch 3, sc) in next ch-3 sp, 2 sc in next ch-3 sp, ch 3, shell in ch-2 sp of next shell, ch 3 **, shell in ch-2 sp of next shell, rep from * around, ending last rep at **, half shell in same sp as beg ch-3, ch 1, join with sc in 3rd ch of beg ch-3. *(128 shells, 256 ch-3 sps)*

Rnd 45: Beg half shell in sp formed by joining sc, *ch 3, 2 sc in next ch-3 sp, (sc, ch 3, sc) in next ch-3 sp, 2 sc in next ch-3 sp, ch 3, shell in ch-2 sp of next shell, ch 3, sc in next ch-3 sp, ch 3 **, shell in ch-2 sp of next shell, rep from * around, ending last rep at **, half shell in same sp as beg ch-3, ch 1, join with sc in 3rd ch of beg ch-3. *(128 shells, 320 ch-3 sps)*

Rnd 46: Beg half shell in sp formed by joining sc, *ch 3, 2 sc in next ch-3 sp, (sc, ch 3, sc) in next ch-3 sp, 2 sc in next ch-3 sp, ch 3, shell in ch-2 sp of next shell, ch 3, 2 sc in next ch-3 sp, sc in next sc, 2 sc in next ch-3 sp, ch 3 **, shell in ch-2 sp of next shell, rep from * around, ending last rep at **, half shell in same sp as beg ch-3, ch 1, join with sc in 3rd ch of beg ch-3.

Rnd 47: Beg half shell in sp formed by joining sc, *ch 3, 2 sc in next ch-3 sp, (sc, ch 3, sc) in next ch-3 sp, 2 sc in next ch-3 sp, ch 3, shell in ch-2 sp of next shell, ch 3, 2 sc in next ch-3 sp, ch 5, 2 sc in next ch-3 sp, ch 3 **, shell in ch-2 sp of next shell, rep from * around, ending last rep at **, half shell in same sp as beg ch-3, ch 1, join with sc in 3rd ch of beg ch-3. *(128 shells, 64 ch-5 sps, 320 ch-3 sps)*

Rnd 48: Beg half shell in sp formed by joining sc, *cl *(see Special Stitches)* in next 3 ch-3 sps, half shell in ch-2 sp of next shell, 2 sc in next ch-3 sp, (sc, ch 3, sc) in next ch-3 sp, 2 sc in next ch-3 sp, ch 3 **, half shell in ch-2 sp of next shell, rep from * around, ending last rep at **, join in 3rd ch of beg ch-3. *(128 half shells, 64 cls, 320 ch-3 sps)*

BORDER

Rnd 1: Ch 1, sc in same ch as joining, ch 4, sk next cl, sc in next dc, ch 4, [sc in next ch-3 sp, ch 4] 4 times, sk next cl, sc in next dc, ch 4, [sc in next ch-3 sp, ch 4] 5 times, rep from * around, join in beg sc. *(384 ch-4 sps)*

Rnd 2: Sl st in ch-4 sp, ch 1, sc in same sp, ch 4, *sc in next ch-4 sp, ch 4, rep from * around, join in beg sc.

Rnd 3: Sl st in next ch-4 sp, ch 1, sc in same sp, shell in next sc, [sc in next ch-4 sp, ch 4] 3 times **, sc in next ch-4 sp, rep from * around, ending last rep at **, join in beg sc. *(96 shells, 288 ch-4 sps)*

Rnd 4: Sl st in each of next 2 dc, sl st in next ch-2 sp, ch 1, sc in same sp, ch 4, *sc in next ch sp, ch 4, rep from * around, join in beg sc. *(384 ch-4 sps)*

Rnd 5: Sl st in next ch-4 sp, ch 1, sc in same sp, ch 4, sc in next ch-4 sp, *shell in next sc, sc in next ch-4 sp **, [ch 4, sc in next ch-4 sp] 3 times, rep from * around, ending last rep at **, ch 4, sc in next ch-4 sp, ch 4, join in beg sc. *(96 shells, 288 ch-4 sps)*

Rnd 6: Sl st in next ch-4 sp, ch 1, sc in same sp, ch 4, *sc in next ch sp, ch 4, rep from * around, join in beg sc.

Rnd 7: Sl st in next ch-4 sp, **ch 4** *(see Pattern Notes)*, [dc, ch 1] 4 times in same sp, *sc in next ch-4 sp, ch 1, [dc, ch 1] 5 times in next ch-4 sp, rep from * around, join in beg sc, fasten off. ∎

Illinois Thistle Seed

SKILL LEVEL

INTERMEDIATE

FINISHED SIZE

Approximately 54 inches x 82 inches

MATERIALS

- Aunt Lydia's Fashion Crochet size 3 crochet cotton (150 yds per ball):
  26 balls #226 natural
- Size E/4/3.5mm crochet hook or size needed to obtain gauge
- Tapestry needle
- Stitch markers

GAUGE

Triangle = 5 inches along side

PATTERN NOTES

Weave in ends as work progresses.

Join with slip stitch as indicated unless otherwise stated.

Chain-3 at beginning of rounds counts as a double crochet unless otherwise stated.

SPECIAL STITCHES

Beginning shell (beg shell): Ch 3, (dc, ch 2, 2 dc) in indicated sp.

Shell: (2 dc, ch 2, 2 dc) in indicated sp.

Beginning cluster (beg cl): Ch 3, holding back last lp of each dc on hook, 2 dc in indicated st, yo, draw through 3 lps on hook, yo and draw through rem 2 lps on hook.

Cluster (cl): Holding back last lp of each dc on hook, 3 dc in indicated st, yo, draw through 3 lps on hook, yo and draw through rem 2 lps on hook.

INSTRUCTIONS
FIRST TRIANGLE

Rnd 1 (RS): Ch 5, **join** (see Pattern Notes) in first ch to form a ring, **beg shell** (see Special Stitches) in ring, ch 3, [**shell** (see Special Stitches) in ring, ch 3] twice, join in 3rd ch of beg ch-3. (3 shells, 3 ch-3 sps)

Rnd 2: Sl st in next dc, sl st in next ch-2 sp, beg shell in same sp, *ch 3, (sc, ch 3, sc) in next ch-3 sp, shell in ch-2 sp of next shell, rep from * once, ch 3, (sc, ch 3, sc) in next ch-3 sp, join in 3rd ch of beg ch-3. (3 shells, 6 sc, 6 ch-3 sps)

Rnd 3: Sl st in next dc, sl st in next ch-2 sp, beg shell in same sp, *ch 3, [sc in next ch-3 sp, ch 3] 3 times **, shell in ch-2 sp of next shell, rep from * twice ending last rep at **, join in 3rd ch of beg ch-3. (3 shells, 9 sc, 12 ch-3 sps)

Rnd 4: Sl st in next dc, sl st in next ch-2 sp; (**beg cl**—see Special Stitches, in same sp, ch 3, **cl**—see Special Stitches, ch 5, cl, ch 3, cl) in same sp (corner), ch 3, [sc in next ch-3 sp, ch 3] 4 times **, (cl, ch 3, cl, ch 5, cl, ch 3, cl) in ch-2 sp of next shell (corner), rep from * twice ending last rep at **, join in beg cl. Fasten off.

2ND TRIANGLE

Rnds 1–3: Rep rnds 1–3 of First Triangle.

Rnd 4: Sl st in next dc, sl st in next ch-2 sp, (beg cl, ch 3, cl, ch 5, cl, ch 3, cl) in same sp (corner), ch 3, [sc in next ch-3 sp, ch 3] 4 times, (cl, ch 3, cl) in ch-2 sp of next shell, ch 2, hold previous Triangle with WS facing and carefully matching sts, sl st in corresponding ch-5 sp on previous Triangle, ch 2, cl in same sp on working triangle, ch 1, sl st in next ch-3 sp on previous Triangle, ch 1, cl in same sp on working triangle (joined corner), [ch 1, sl st in corresponding ch-3 sp on previous Triangle, ch 1, sc in next ch-3 sp on working

triangle] 4 times, ch 1, sl st in corresponding ch-3 sp on previous Triangle, ch 1, cl in ch-2 sp of next shell on working triangle, ch 1, sl st in corresponding sp on previous Triangle, ch 1, cl in same ch-2 sp on working triangle, ch 2, sl st in next ch-5 sp on previous Triangle, ch 2, cl in same ch-2 sp on working triangle (*joined corner*), ch 3, [sc in next ch-3 sp, ch 3] 4 times, join in beg cl. Fasten off.

REMAINING TRIANGLES
Referring to assembly diagram for placement, work remaining triangles same as 2nd Triangle, joining 1 or 2 sides in same manner.

BORDER
Note: Mark 6 corners as noted on assembly diagram. Move markers after each rnd.

Rnd 1 (RS): Hold piece with RS facing, join cotton in marked corner sp indicated on assembly diagram, ch 1, (sc, ch 4, sc) in same sp (*corner*), working across next side and sk joinings, *ch 3, [sc in next ch-3 sp, ch 3] across to next marked corner **, (sc, ch 4, sc) in marked corner (*corner*), rep from * around ending last rep at **, join in beg sc.

Rnd 2: Sl st in next ch-4 sp, (sc, ch 4, sc) in same sp (*corner*), *ch 3, [sc in next ch-3 sp, ch 3] across to next corner ch-4 sp **, (sc, ch 4, sc) in corner ch-4 sp (*corner*), rep from * around, ending last rep at **, join in beg sc.

Rnd 3: Sl st in next ch-4 sp, (sc, ch 4, sc) in same sp (*corner*), *ch 4, [sc in next ch-3 sp, ch 4] across to next corner ch-4 sp **, (sc, ch 4, sc) in corner ch-4 sp (*corner*), rep from * around, ending last rep at **, join in beg sc.

Rnd 4: Sl st in next ch-4 sp, (sc, ch 4, sc) in same sp *(corner)*, *ch 4, [sc in next ch-4 sp, ch 4] across to next corner ch-4 sp **, (sc, ch 4, sc) in corner ch-4 sp *(corner)*, rep from * around, ending last rep at **, join in beg sc.

Rnds 5–7: Rep rnd 4. At end of last rnd, fasten off.

Rnd 8: With RS facing, join cotton in first corner ch-4 sp on rnd 7, ch 1, (sc, ch 4, sc) in same sp *(corner)*, *[ch 4, sc in next ch-4 sp] 3 times, (cl, ch 4, cl) in next sc, sc in next ch-4 sp, rep from * 12 times, ch 4, (sc, ch 4, sc) in marked sp *(corner)*, ch 4, sc in next ch-4 sp, (cl, ch 4, cl) in next sc, sc in next ch-4 sp, **[ch 4, sc in next ch-4 sp] 3 times, (cl, ch 4, cl) in next sc, sc in next ch-4 sp, rep from ** 11 times, [ch 4, sc in next ch-4 sp] twice, ch 4, (sc, ch 4, sc) in next marked corner ch-4 sp *(corner)*, ***[ch 4, sc in next ch-4 sp] 3 times, (cl, ch 4, cl) in next sc, sc in next ch-4 sp, rep from *** 18 times, [ch 4, sc in next ch-4 sp] twice, ch 4, (sc, ch 4, sc) in next marked corner ch-4 sp *(corner)*, ****[ch 4, sc in next ch-4 sp] 3 times, (cl, ch 4, cl) in next sc, sc in next ch-4 sp, rep from **** 12 times, ch 4, (sc, ch 4, sc) in next marked corner ch-4 sp *(corner)*, ch 4, sc in next ch-4 sp, (cl, ch 4, cl) in next sc, sc in next ch-4 sp, *****[ch 4, sc in next ch-4 sp] 3 times, (cl, ch 4, cl) in next sc, sc in next ch-4 sp, rep from ***** 11 times, [ch 4, sc in next ch-4 sp] twice, ch 4, (sc, ch 4, sc) in next marked corner ch-4 sp *(corner)*, ******[ch 4, sc in next ch-4 sp] 3 times, (cl, ch 4, cl) in next sc, sc in next ch-4 sp, rep from ***** 18 times, [ch 4, sc in next ch-4 sp] twice, ch 4, join in beg sc.

Rnd 9: Sl st in next ch-4 sp, (beg cl, {ch 3, cl}) 3 times in same sp, *ch 1, sc in next ch-4 sp, [ch 4, sc in next ch-4 sp] twice, ch 1**; [cl, ch 3] 3 times in next corner ch-4 sp, cl in same sp, rep from * around, ending last rep at **, join in beg cl.

Rnd 10: Sl st in next ch-3 sp, ch 3, dc in same sp, (sl st, ch 3, dc) in each rem ch-3 sp and in each ch-4 sp around, join in joining sl st. Fasten off. ∎

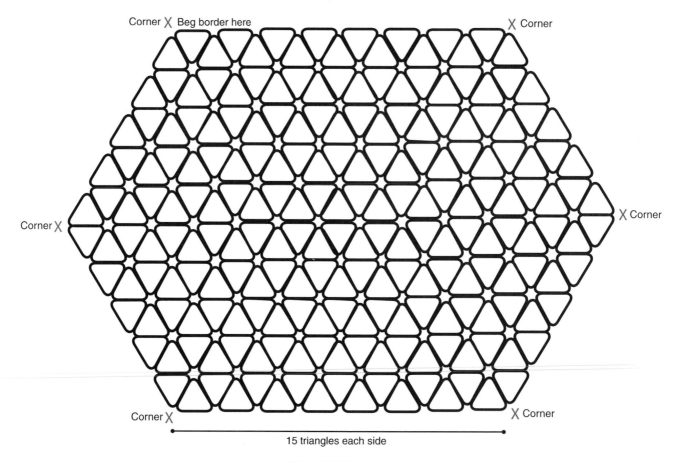

Corner X Beg border here   X Corner

Corner X   X Corner

Corner X   X Corner

← 15 triangles each side →

Illinois Thistle Seed
Assembly Diagram

Kansas Lacy Pineapples

FINISHED SIZE
Approximately 54 inches x 72 inches

MATERIALS
- Aunt Lydia's Fashion Crochet size 3 crochet cotton (150 yds per ball): 17 balls #201 white
- Size E/4/3.5mm crochet hook or size needed to obtain gauge
- Tapestry needle

GAUGE
Motif = 4½ inches along size

PATTERN NOTES
Weave in ends as work progresses.

Join with slip stitch as indicated unless otherwise stated.

Chain-3 at beg of rows counts as a dc unless otherwise stated.

SPECIAL STITCHES
Beginning shell (beg shell): Ch 3, (dc, ch 2, 2 dc) in indicated sp.

Shell: (2 dc, ch 2, 2 dc) in indicated sp.

Beginning pineapple (beg pineapple): (Dc, ch 1) 6 times in indicated sp, dc in same sp.

INSTRUCTIONS
CENTER
Foundation row: Ch 25, **shell** (*see Special Stitches*) in 6th ch from hook (*beg 5 sk chs count as 2 sk chs and a dc*), ch 3, sk next 2 chs, sc in next ch, [ch 5, sk next 4 chs, sc in next ch] twice, ch 3, sk next 2 chs, shell in next ch, sk next 2 chs, dc in last ch, turn.

Row 1: Ch 3 (*see Pattern Notes*), shell in ch-2 sp of next shell, [ch 5, sc in next ch-5 sp] twice, ch 5, shell in ch-2 sp of next shell, dc in next ch of beg 5 sk chs, turn.

Row 2: Ch 3, shell in ch-2 sp of next shell, ch 3, [sc in next ch-5 sp, ch 5] twice, ch 3, shell in ch-2 sp of shell, dc in last dc, turn.

Row 3: Ch 3, shell in ch-2 sp of next shell, [ch 5, sc in next ch-5 sp] twice, ch 5, shell in ch-2 sp of next shell, dc in 3rd ch of beg ch-3, turn.

Rows 4–21: [Rep rows 2 and 3 alternately] 9 times.

Row 22: Ch 3, shell in ch-2 sp of next shell, sc in next ch-5 sp, (2 dc, ch 1, 2 dc) in next sc, sc in next ch-5 sp, shell in ch-2 sp of next shell, dc in 3rd ch of beg ch-3. Fasten off.

EDGING
Rnd 1 (RS): Hold Center with RS facing and starting ch at top, join cotton in unused lp of starting ch at base of first dc, ch 3, (2 dc, ch 1, 2 dc) in unused lp of ch at base of next shell, sk next ch, sc in next ch, [(2 dc, ch 1, 2 dc) in sp formed by next 4 sk chs] twice, (2 dc, ch 1,

2 dc) in unused lp at base of next shell, (dc, ch 5, sc) in sp formed by beg 5 sk chs of starting ch, working across next side, ch 5, sc in top of dc at end of next row, *ch 5, sk next row, sc in end of next row, ch 5, sc in 3rd ch of beg ch-3 of next row, ch 5, sk next row, sc in end of next row, ch 5, sc in top of dc at end of next row, rep from * twice, ch 5, sk next row, sc in end of next row, ch 5, sc in 3rd ch of beg ch-3 of next row, ch 5, working across next side, sk next shell, [sc in next sc, ch 5, sk next 4 dc] twice, sc in next sc, ch 5, sk next shell, dc in next dc, ch 5, working across next side, sk row 22, sc in end of next row, **ch 5, sk next row, sc in 3rd ch of beg ch-3 of next row, ch 5, sc in end of next row, ch 5, sk next row, sc in top of dc at end of next row, ch 5, sc in end of next row, rep from ** twice, ch 5, sk next row, sc in top of dc at end of next row, ch 5, sc in end of next row, ch 5, working across beg of rnd, sc in 3rd ch of beg ch-3, ch 5, sc in next sc, ch 5, sk next 2 dc, ch-1 sp and next dc, sc in next dc, ch 5, sc in next dc, ch 5, sk next 3 dc, **join** (see Pattern Notes) in next dc.

Rnd 2: Ch 1, (sc, ch 5, sc) in same ch as joining (corner), *[ch 5, sc in next ch-5 sp] 16 times, ch 5, (sc, ch 5, sc) in next sc (corner), [ch 5, sc in next ch-5 sp] 4 times, ch 5 **, (sc, ch 5, sc) in next sc (corner), rep from * once, ending rep at **, join in beg sc. Fasten off.

Note: Mark first corner made.

BODY

Rnd 1 (RS): Hold piece with RS facing and marked corner in upper right-hand corner, join cotton in first ch-5 sp to right of marked corner, ch 1, sc in same sp, ch 5, sc in marked corner ch-5 sp (corner), working across side, *[ch 5, sc in next ch-5 sp] twice, [dc, ch 1] 6 times in next ch-5 sp, dc in same sp (pineapple base), sc in next ch-5 sp, rep from * 3 times, ch 5, sc in next ch-5 sp, ch 5, sc in next corner ch-5 sp (corner), [ch 5, sc in next ch-5 sp] twice, [dc, ch 1] 6 times in next ch-5 sp, dc in same sp (pineapple base), [sc in next ch-5 sp, ch 5] twice, sc in next corner ch-5 sp (corner), **[ch 5, sc in next ch-5 sp] twice, [dc, ch 1] 6 times in next ch-5 sp, dc in same sp (pineapple base), sc in next ch-5 sp, rep from ** 3 times, ch 5, sc in next ch-5 sp, ch 5, sc in next corner ch-5 sp (corner), [ch 5, sc in next ch-5 sp] twice, [dc, ch 1] 6 times in next

ch-5 sp, dc in same sp (pineapple base), sc in next ch-5 sp, ch 5, sc in next ch-5 sp, ch 5, join in beg sc. (10 pineapple bases)

Rnd 2: Ch 3, 2 dc in same sc as joining, sc in next ch-5 sp, shell in next corner sc (corner), *sc in next ch-5 sp, 3 dc in next sc, sc in next ch-5 sp, ch 3, [sc in next ch-1 sp, ch 3] 6 times, rep from * 3 times, sc in next ch-5 sp, 3 dc in next sc, sc in next ch-5 sp, shell in next corner sc (corner), sc in next ch-5 sp, 3 dc in next sc, sc in next ch-5 sp, ch 3, [sc in next ch-1 sp, ch 3] 6 times, sc in next ch-5 sp, 3 dc in next sc, sc in next ch-5 sp, shell in next corner sc (corner), **sc in next ch-5 sp, 3 dc in next sc, sc in next ch-5 sp, ch 3, [sc in next ch-1 sp, ch 3] 6 times, rep from ** 3 times, sc in next ch-5 sp, 3 dc in next sc, sc in next ch-5 sp, shell in next corner sc (corner), sc in next ch-5 sp, 3 dc in next sc, sc in next ch-5 sp, ch 3, [sc in next ch-1 sp, ch 3] 6 times, sc in next ch-5 sp, join in 3rd ch of beg ch-3.

Rnd 3: Sl st in next dc, sl st in next ch-2 sp, beg shell in same sp, ch 2, (shell, ch 2, shell) in ch-2 sp of next corner shell (corner), ch 2, *shell in 2nd dc of next 3-dc group, ch 3, [sc in next ch-3 sp, ch 3] 5 times, rep from * 3 times, shell in 2nd dc of next 3-dc group, ch 2, (shell, ch 2, shell) in ch-2 sp of next corner shell (corner), ch 2, shell in 2nd dc of next 3-dc group, ch 3, [sc in next ch-3 sp, ch 3] 5 times, shell in 2nd dc of next 3-dc group, ch 2, (shell, ch 2, shell) in ch-2 sp of next shell (corner), ch 2, **shell in 2nd dc of next 3-dc group, ch 3, [sc in next ch-3 sp, ch 3] 5 times, rep from ** 3 times, shell in 2nd dc of next 3-dc group, ch 2, (shell, ch 2, shell) in ch-2 sp of next corner shell (corner), ch 2, shell in 2nd dc of next 3-dc group, ch 3, [sc in next ch-3 sp, ch 3] 5 times, join in 3rd ch of beg ch-3.

Rnd 4: Sl st in next dc, sl st in next ch-2 sp, beg shell in same sp, ch 3, shell in each of next 3 ch-2 sps, ch 3, *shell in ch-2 sp of next shell, ch 3, [sc in next ch-3 sp, ch 3] 4 times, rep from * 3 times, shell in ch-2 sp of next shell, ch 3, shell in ch-2 sp of each of next 3 shells, ch 3, shell in ch-2 sp of next shell, ch 3, [sc in next ch-3 sp, ch 3] 4 times, shell in ch-2 sp of next shell, ch 3, shell in ch-2 sp of each of next 3 shells, ch 3, **shell in ch-2 sp of next shell, ch 3, [sc in next ch-3 sp, ch 3] 4 times, rep from ** 3 times, shell in ch-2 sp of next shell, ch 3, shell in each

of next 3 ch-2 sp, ch 3, shell in ch-2 sp of next shell, ch 3, [sc in next ch-3 sp, ch 3] 4 times, join in 3rd ch of beg ch-3.

Rnd 5: Sl st in next dc, sl st in next ch-2 sp, beg shell in same sp, ch 3, [shell in ch-2 sp of next shell, ch 3] 4 times, *[sc in next ch-3 sp, ch 3] 3 times, shell in ch-2 sp of next shell, rep from * 3 times, [shell in ch-2 sp of next shell, ch 3] 4 times, [sc in next ch-3 sp, ch 3] 3 times, [shell in ch-2 sp of next shell, ch 3] 5 times, **[sc in next ch-3 sp, ch 3] 3 times, shell in ch-2 sp of next shell, ch 3, rep from ** 3 times, [shell in ch-2 sp of next shell, ch 3] 4 times, [sc in next ch-3 sp, ch 3] 3 times, join in 3rd ch of beg ch-3.

Rnd 6: Sl st in next dc, sl st in next ch-2 sp, (beg shell, ch 2, 2 dc) in same sp, ch 3, shell in next ch-2 sp of next shell, ch 3, (shell, ch 2, 2 dc) in ch-2 sp of next shell, ch 3, shell in ch-2 sp of next shell, ch 3, *(shell, ch 2, 2 dc) in ch-2 sp of next shell, ch 3, [sc in next ch-3 sp, ch 3] twice, rep from * 3 times, [(shell, ch 2, 2 dc) in ch-2 sp of next shell, ch 3, shell in ch-2 sp of next shell, ch 3] twice, (shell, ch 2, 2 dc) in ch-2 sp of next shell, ch 3, [sc in next ch-3 sp, ch 3] twice, [(shell, ch 2, 2 dc) in ch-2 sp of next shell, ch 3, shell in ch-2 sp of next shell, ch 3] twice, **(shell, ch 2, 2 dc) in ch-2 sp of next shell, ch 3, [sc in next ch-3 sp, ch 3] twice, rep from ** 3 times, [(shell, ch 2, 2 dc) in ch-2 sp of next shell, ch 3, shell in ch-2 sp of next shell, ch 3] twice, (shell, ch 2, 2 dc) in ch-2 sp of next shell, ch 3, [sc in next ch-3 sp, ch 3] twice, join in 3rd ch of beg ch-3.

Rnd 7: Sl st in next dc, sl st in next ch-2 sp, beg shell in same sp, shell in next ch-2 sp, [ch 3, shell in ch-2 sp of next shell, ch 3, shell in each of next 2 ch-2 sps] twice, *ch 3, sc in next ch-3 sp, ch 3, shell in each of next 2 ch-2 sps, rep from * 3 times, [ch 3, shell in ch-2 sp of next shell, ch 3, shell in each of next 2 ch-2 sps] twice, ch 3, sc in next ch-3 sp, ch 3, shell in each of next 2 ch-2 sps, [ch 3, shell in ch-2 sp of next shell, ch 3, shell in ch-2 sp of each of next 2 shells] twice, **ch 3, sc in next ch-3 sp, ch 3, shell in each of next 2 ch-2 sps, rep from ** 3 times, [ch 3, shell in ch-2 sp of next shell, ch 3, shell in each of next 2 ch-2 sps] twice, ch 3, sc in next ch-3 sp, ch 3, join in 3rd ch of beg ch-3.

Rnd 8: Sl st in next dc, sl st in next ch-2 sp, beg shell in same sp, ch 3, *shell in ch-2 sp of next shell, ch 3, rep from * around, join in 3rd ch of beg ch-3.

Rnd 9: Sl st in next dc, sl st in next ch-2 sp, *ch 5, sk next 2 dc, sc in next ch sp, rep from * around, join in first ch of beg ch-5.

Note: On following rnd, mark first corner made.

Rnd 10: Sl st in next 2 chs, [ch 5, sc in next ch-5 sp] 6 times, ch 5, (sc, ch 5, sc) in next ch-5 sp (corner), [ch 5, sc in next ch-5 sp] 28 times, ch 5, (sc, ch 5, sc) in next ch-5 sp (corner), [ch 5, sc in next ch-5 sp] 16 times, ch 5, (sc, ch 5, sc) in next ch-5 sp (corner), [ch 5, sc in next ch-5 sp] 28 times, ch 5, (sc, ch 5, sc) in next ch-5 sp (corner), [ch 5, sc in next ch-5 sp] 9 times, ch 5, join in first ch of beg ch-5. Fasten off.

Rnd 11: Hold piece with RS facing, join cotton in first ch-5 sp to right of marked corner, ch 1, sc in same sp, ch 5, sc in marked corner ch-5 sp (corner), *[ch 5, sc in next ch-5 sp] twice, [dc, ch 1] 6 times in next ch-5 sp, dc in same sp (pineapple base), sc in next ch-5 sp, rep from * 6 times, ch 5, sc in next ch-5 sp, ch 5, sc in next corner ch-5 sp (corner), **[ch 5, sc in next ch-5 sp] twice, [dc, ch 1] 6 times in next ch-5 sp, dc in same sp (pineapple base), sc in next ch-5 sp, rep from ** 3 times, ch 5, sc in next corner ch-5 sp (corner), ***[ch 5, sc in next ch-5 sp] twice, [dc, ch 1] 6 times in next ch-5 sp, dc in same sp (pineapple base), sc in next ch-5 sp, rep from *** 6 times, ch 5, sc in next ch-5 sp, ch 5, sc in next corner ch-5 sp (corner), ****[ch 5, sc in next ch-5 sp] twice, [dc, ch 1] 6 times in next ch-5

sp, dc in same sp (pineapple base), sc in next ch-5 sp, rep from **** 3 times, ch 5, join in beg sc. (22 pineapples bases)

Rnd 12: Ch 3, 2 dc in same sc as joining, sc in next ch-5 sp, shell in next corner sc (corner), *sc in next ch-5 sp, 3 dc in next sc, sc in next ch-5 sp, ch 3, [sc in next ch-1 sp, ch 3] 6 times, rep from * 6 times, sc in next ch-5 sp, 3 dc in next sc, sc in next ch-5 sp, shell in next corner sc (corner), **sc in next ch-5 sp, 3 dc in next sc, sc in next ch-5 sp, ch 3, [sc in next ch-1 sp, ch 3] 6 times, rep from ** 3 times, sc in next ch-5 sp, 3 dc in next sc, sc in next ch-5 sp, shell in next corner sc (corner), ***sc in next ch-5 sp, 3 dc in next sc, sc in next ch-5 sp, ch 3, [sc in next ch-1 sp, ch 3] 6 times, rep from *** 6 times, sc in next ch-5 sp, 3 dc in next sc, sc in next ch-5 sp, shell in next corner sc (corner), ****sc in next ch-5 sp, 3 dc in next sc, sc in next ch-5 sp, ch 3, [sc in next ch-1 sp, ch 3] 6 times, rep from **** 3 times, sc in next ch-5 sp, join in 3rd ch of beg ch-3.

Rnd 13: Sl st in next dc, beg shell in same sp, ch 2, (shell, ch 2, shell) in ch-2 sp of next corner shell (corner), ch 2, *shell in 2nd dc of next 3-dc group, ch 3, [sc in next ch-3 sp, ch 3] 5 times, rep from * 6 times, shell in 2nd dc of next 3-dc group, ch 2, (shell, ch 2, shell) in ch-2 sp of next corner shell (corner), ch 2, **shell in 2nd dc of next 3-dc group, ch 3, [sc in next ch-3 sp, ch 3] 5 times, rep from ** 3 times, shell in 2nd dc of next 3-dc group, ch 2, (shell, ch 2, shell) in ch-2 sp of next shell (corner), ch 2, ***shell in 2nd dc of next 3-dc group, ch 3, [sc in next ch-3 sp, ch 3] 5 times, rep from *** 6 times, shell in 2nd dc of next 3-dc group, ch 2, (shell, ch 2, shell) in ch-2 sp of next corner shell (corner), ch 2, ****shell in 2nd dc of next 3-dc group, ch 3, [sc in next ch-3 sp, ch 3] 5 times, rep from **** 3 times, join in 3rd ch of beg ch-3.

Rnd 14: Sl st in next dc, sl st in next ch-2 sp, beg shell in same sp, ch 3, shell in each of next 3 ch-2 sps, ch 3, *shell in ch-2 sp of next shell, ch 3, [sc in next ch-3 sp, ch 3] 4 times, rep from * 6 times, shell in ch-2 sp of next shell, ch 3, shell in ch-2 sp of each of next 3 shells, ch 3, **shell in ch-2 sp of next shell, ch 3, [sc in next ch-3 sp, ch 3] 4 times, rep from ** 3 times, shell in ch-2 sp of next shell, ch 3, shell in ch-2 sp of each of next 3 shells, ch 3, ***shell in ch-2 sp of next shell, ch 3, [sc in next ch-3 sp, ch 3] 4 times, rep from *** 6 times, shell in ch-2 sp of next shell, ch 3, shell in each of next 3 ch-2 sps, ch 3, ****shell in ch-2 sp of next shell, ch 3, [sc in next ch-3 sp, ch 3] 4 times, rep from * 3 times, join in 3rd ch of beg ch-3.

Rnd 15: Sl st in next dc, sl st in next ch-2 sp, beg shell in same sp, ch 3, [shell in ch-2 sp of next shell, ch 3] 4 times, *[sc in next ch-3 sp, ch 3] 3 times, shell in ch-2 sp of next shell, ch 3, rep from * 6 times, [shell in ch-2 sp of next shell, ch 3] 4 times, **[sc in next ch-3 sp, ch 3] 3 times, shell in ch-2 sp of next shell, ch 3, rep from ** 3 times, [shell in ch-2 sp of next shell, ch 3] 4 times, ***[sc in next ch-3 sp, ch 3] 3 times, shell in ch-2 sp of next shell, ch 3, rep from *** 6 times, [shell in ch-2 sp of next shell, ch 3] 4 times, ****[sc in next ch-3 sp, ch 3] 3 times, shell in ch-2 sp of next shell, ch 3, rep from **** 3 times, join in 3rd ch of beg ch-3.

Rnd 16: Sl st in next dc, sl st in next ch-2 sp, (beg shell, ch 2, 2 dc) in same sp, ch 3, shell in next ch-2 sp of next shell, ch 3, (shell, ch 2, 2 dc) in ch-2 sp of next shell, ch 3, shell in ch-2 sp of next shell, ch 3, *(shell, ch 2, 2 dc) in ch-2 sp of next shell, ch 3, [sc in next ch-3 sp, ch 3] twice, rep from * 6 times, [(shell, ch 2, 2 dc) in ch-2 sp of next shell, ch 3, shell in ch-2 sp of next shell, ch 3] twice, **(shell, ch 2, 2 dc) in ch-2 sp of next shell, ch 3, [sc in next ch-3 sp, ch 3] twice, rep from ** 3 times, [(shell, ch 2, 2 dc) in ch-2 sp of next shell, ch 3, shell in ch-2 sp of next shell, ch 3] twice, ***(shell, ch 2, 2 dc) in ch-2 sp of next shell, ch 3, [sc in next ch-3 sp, ch 3] twice, rep from *** 6 times, [(shell, ch 2, 2 dc) in ch-2 sp of next shell, ch 3, shell in ch-2 sp of next shell, ch 3] twice, ****(shell, ch 2, 2 dc) in ch-2 sp of next shell, ch 3, [sc in next ch-3 sp, ch 3] twice, rep from **** 3 times, join in 3rd ch of beg ch-3.

Rnd 17: Sl st in next dc, sl st in next ch-2 sp, beg shell in same sp, ch 1, shell in next ch-2 sp, [ch 3, shell in ch-2 sp of next shell, ch 3, shell in ch-2 sp of next shell, ch 1, shell in next ch-2 sp] twice, *ch 3, sc in next ch-3 sp, ch 3, shell in ch-2 sp of next shell, ch 1, shell in next ch-2 sp, rep from * 6 times, [ch 3, shell in ch-2 sp of next shell, ch 3, shell in ch-2 sp of next shell, ch 1, shell in next ch-2 sp] twice, **ch 3, sc in next ch-3 sp, ch 3, shell in ch-2 sp of next shell, ch 1, shell in next ch-2 sp, rep from ** 3 times, [ch 3, shell in ch-2 sp of next shell, ch 3, shell in ch-2 sp of next shell, ch 1, shell in next ch-2 sp] twice, ***ch 3, sc in next ch-3 sp, ch 3, shell in ch-2 sp of next shell, ch 1, shell in next ch-2 sp, rep from *** 6 times, [ch 3, shell in ch-2 sp of next shell, ch 3, shell in ch-2 sp of next shell, ch 1, shell in next ch-2 sp] twice, ****ch 3, sc in next ch-3 sp, ch 3, shell in ch-2 sp of next shell, ch 1, shell in next ch-2 sp, rep from **** twice, ch 3, sc in next ch-3 sp, ch 3, join in 3rd ch of beg ch-3.

Rnd 18: Sl st in next dc, sl st in next ch-2 sp, beg shell in same sp, ch 3, *shell in ch-2 sp of next shell, ch 3, rep from * around, join in 3rd ch of beg ch-3.

Rnd 19: Sl st in next dc, sl st in next ch-2 sp, *ch 5, sk next 2 dc, sc in next ch sp, rep from * around, join in first ch of beg ch-5.

Note: On following rnd, mark first corner made.

Rnd 20: Sl st in next 2 chs, [ch 5, sc in next ch-5 sp] 6 times, ch 5, (sc, ch 5, sc) in next ch-5 sp *(corner)*, [ch 5, sc in next ch-5 sp] 40 times, ch 5, (sc, ch 5, sc) in next ch-5 sp *(corner)*, [ch 5, sc in next ch-5 sp] 28 times, ch 5, (sc, ch 5, sc) in next ch-5 sp *(corner)*, [ch 5, sc in next ch-5 sp] 40 times, ch 5, (sc, ch 5, sc) in next ch-5 sp *(corner)*, [ch 5, sc in next ch-5 sp] 21 times, ch 5, join in first ch of beg ch-5. Fasten off.

Rnd 21: Hold piece with RS facing, join cotton in first ch-5 sp to right of marked corner, ch 1, sc in same sp, ch 5, sc in marked corner ch-5 sp *(corner)*, *[ch 5, sc in next ch-5 sp] twice, [dc, ch 1] 6 times in next ch-5 sp, dc in same sp *(pineapple base)*, sc in next ch-5 sp, rep from * 9 times, ch 5, sc in next ch-5 sp, ch 5, sc in next corner ch-5 sp *(corner)*, **[ch 5, sc in next ch-5 sp] twice, [dc, ch 1] 6 times in next ch-5 sp, dc in same sp *(pineapple base)*, sc in next ch-5 sp, rep from ** 6 times, ch 5, sc in next ch-5 sp, ch 5, sc in next corner ch-5 sp *(corner)*, ***[ch 5, sc in next ch-5 sp] twice, [dc, ch 1] 6 times in next ch-5 sp, dc in same sp *(pineapple base)*, sc in next ch-5 sp, rep from *** 9 times, ch 5, sc in next ch-5 sp, ch 5, sc in next corner ch-5 sp *(corner)*,

****[ch 5, sc in next ch-5 sp] twice, [dc, ch 1] 6 times in next ch-5 sp, dc in same sp *(pineapple base)*, sc in next ch-5 sp, rep from **** 6 times, ch 5, join in beg sc. *(34 pineapple bases)*

Rnd 22: Beg shell in same sc as joining, sc in next ch-5 sp, shell in next corner sc *(corner)*, *sc in next ch-5 sp, shell in next sc, sc in next ch-5 sp, ch 3, [sc in next ch-1 sp, ch 3] 6 times, rep from * 9 times, sc in next ch-5 sp, shell in next sc, sc in next ch-5 sp, shell in next corner sc *(corner)*, **sc in next ch-5 sp, shell in next sc, sc in next ch-5 sp, ch 3, [sc in next ch-1 sp, ch 3] 6 times, rep from ** 3 times, sc in next ch-5 sp, shell in next sc, sc in next ch-5 sp, shell in next corner sc *(corner)*, ***sc in next ch-5 sp, shell in next sc, sc in next ch-5 sp, ch 3, [sc in next ch-1 sp, ch 3] 6 times, rep from *** 9 times, sc in next ch-5 sp, shell in next sc, sc in next ch-5 sp, shell in next corner sc *(corner)*, ****sc in next ch-5 sp, shell in next sc, sc in next ch-5 sp, ch 3, [sc in next ch-1 sp, ch 3] 6 times, rep from **** 6 times, sc in next ch-5 sp, join in 3rd ch of beg ch-3.

Rnd 23: Sl st in next dc, beg shell in same sp, ch 2, (shell, ch 2, shell) in ch-2 sp of next corner shell *(corner)*, ch 2, *shell in 2nd dc of next 3-dc group, ch 3, [sc in next ch-3 sp, ch 3] 5 times, rep from * 9 times, shell in ch-2 sp of next shell, ch 2, (shell, ch 2, shell) in ch-2 sp of next corner shell *(corner)*, ch 2, **shell in ch-2 sp of next shell, ch 3, [sc in next ch-3 sp, ch 3] 5 times, rep from ** 6 times, shell in ch-2 sp of next shell, ch 2, (shell, ch 2, shell) in ch-2 sp of next corner shell *(corner)*, ch 2, ***shell in ch-2 sp of next shell, ch 3, [sc in next ch-3 sp, ch 3] 5 times, rep from *** 9 times, shell in ch-2 sp of next shell, ch 2, (shell, ch 2, shell) in ch-2 sp of next corner shell *(corner)*, ch 2, ****shell in ch-2 sp of next shell, ch 3, [sc in next ch-3 sp, ch 3] 5 times, rep from **** 6 times, join in 3rd ch of beg ch-3.

Rnd 24: Sl st in next dc, sl st in next ch-2 sp, beg shell in same sp, ch 3, shell in each of next 3 ch-2 sps, ch 3, *shell in ch-2 sp of next shell, ch 3, [sc in next ch-3 sp, ch 3] 4 times, rep from * 9 times, shell in ch-2 sp of next shell, ch 3, shell in ch-2 sp of each of next 3 shells, ch 3, **shell in ch-2 sp of next shell, ch 3, [sc in next ch-3 sp, ch 3] 4 times, rep from ** 6 times, shell in ch-2 sp of next shell, ch 3, shell in ch-2 sp of each of

next 3 shells, ch 3, ***shell in ch-2 sp of next shell, ch 3, [sc in next ch-3 sp, ch 3] 4 times, rep from *** 9 times, shell in ch-2 sp of next shell, ch 3, shell in each of next 3 ch-2 sps, ch 3, ****shell in ch-2 sp of next shell, ch 3, [sc in next ch-3 sp, ch 3] 4 times, rep from * 6 times, join in 3rd ch of beg ch-3.

Rnd 25: Sl st in next dc, sl st in next ch-2 sp, beg shell in same sp, ch 3, [shell in ch-2 sp of next shell, ch 3] 4 times, *[sc in next ch-3 sp, ch 3] 3 times, shell in ch-2 sp of next shell, ch 3, rep from * 9 times, [shell in ch-2 sp of next shell, ch 3] 4 times, **[sc in next ch-3 sp, ch 3] 3 times, shell in ch-2 sp of next shell, ch 3, rep from ** 6 times, [shell in ch-2 sp of next shell, ch 3] 4 times, ***[sc in next ch-3 sp, ch 3] 3 times, shell in ch-2 sp of next shell, ch 3, rep from *** 9 times, [shell in ch-2 sp of next shell, ch 3] 4 times, ****[sc in next ch-3 sp, ch 3] 3 times, shell in ch-2 sp of next shell, ch 3, rep from **** 6 times, join in 3rd ch of beg ch-3.

Rnd 26: Sl st in next dc, sl st in next ch-2 sp, (beg shell, ch 2, 2 dc) in same sp, ch 3, shell in next ch-2 sp of next shell, ch 3, (shell, ch 2, 2 dc) in ch-2 sp of next shell, ch 3, shell in ch-2 sp of next shell, ch 3, *(shell, ch 2, 2 dc) in ch-2 sp of next shell, ch 3, [sc in next ch-3 sp, ch 3] twice, rep from * 9 times, [(shell, ch 2, 2 dc) in ch-2 sp of next shell, ch 3, shell in ch-2 sp of next shell, ch 3] twice, **(shell, ch 2, 2 dc) in ch-2 sp of next shell, ch 3, [sc in next ch-3 sp, ch 3] twice, rep from ** 6 times, [(shell, ch 2, 2 dc) in ch-2 sp of next shell, ch 3, shell in ch-2 sp of next shell, ch 3] twice, ***(shell, ch 2, 2 dc) in ch-2 sp of next shell, ch 3, [sc in next ch-3 sp, ch 3] twice, rep from *** 9 times, [(shell, ch 2, 2 dc) in ch-2 sp of next shell, ch 3, shell in ch-2 sp of next shell, ch 3] twice, ****(shell, ch 2, 2 dc) in ch-2 sp of next shell, ch 3, [sc in next ch-3 sp, ch 3] twice, rep from **** 6 times, join in 3rd ch of beg ch-3.

Rnd 27: Sl st in next dc, sl st in next ch-2 sp, beg shell in same sp, ch 1, shell in next ch-2 sp, [ch 3, shell in ch-2 sp of next shell, ch 3, shell in each of next 2 ch-2 sps] twice, *ch 3, sc in next ch-3 sp, ch 3, shell in ch-2 sp of next shell, ch 1, shell in next ch-2 sps, rep from * 9 times, [ch 3, shell in ch-2 sp of next shell, ch 3, shell in each of next 2 ch-2 sps] twice, **ch 3, sc in next ch-3 sp, ch 3, shell in ch-2 sp of next shell, ch 1, shell in next ch-2 sp, rep from ** 6 times, [ch 3, shell in ch-2 sp of next shell, ch 3, shell in ch-2 sp of next shell, ch 1, shell in next ch-2 sp] twice, ***ch 3, sc in next ch-3 sp, ch 3, shell in ch-2 sp of next shell, ch 1, shell in next ch-2 sp, rep from *** 9 times, [ch 3, shell in ch-2 sp of next shell, ch 3, shell in ch-2 sp of next shell, ch 1, shell in next ch-2 sp] twice, ****ch 3, sc in next ch-3 sp, ch 3, shell in ch-2 sp of next shell, ch 1, shell in next ch-2 sp, rep from **** 5 times, ch 3, sc in next ch-3 sp, ch 3, join in 3rd ch of beg ch-3.

Rnd 28: Sl st in next dc, sl st in next ch-2 sp, beg shell in same sp, ch 3, *shell in ch-2 sp of next shell, ch 3, rep from * around, join in 3rd ch of beg ch-3.

Rnd 29: Sl st in next dc, sl st in next ch-2 sp, *ch 5, sk next 2 dc, sc in next ch sp, rep from * around, join in first ch of beg ch-5.

Note: On following rnd, mark first corner made.

Rnd 30: Sl st in next 2 chs, [ch 5, sc in next ch-5 sp] 6 times, ch 5, (sc, ch 5, sc) in next ch-5 sp *(corner)*, [ch 5, sc in next ch-5 sp] 40 times, ch 5, (sc, ch 5, sc) in next ch-5 sp *(corner)*, [ch 5, sc in next ch-5 sp] 28 times, ch 5, (sc, ch 5, sc) in next ch-5 sp *(corner)*, [ch 5, sc in next ch-5 sp] 40 times, ch 5, (sc, ch 5, sc) in next ch-5 sp *(corner)*, [ch 5, sc in next ch-5 sp] 21 times, ch 5, join in first ch of beg ch-5. Fasten off.

Rnd 31: Hold piece with RS facing, join cotton in first ch-5 sp to right of marked corner, ch 1, sc in same sp, ch 5, sc in marked corner ch-5 sp *(corner)*, *[ch 5, sc in next ch-5 sp] twice, [dc, ch 1] 6 times in next ch-5 sp, dc in same sp *(pineapple base)*, sc in next ch-5 sp, rep from * 9 times, ch 5, sc in next ch-5 sp, ch 5, sc in next corner ch-5 sp *(corner)*, **[ch 5, sc in next ch-5 sp] twice, [dc, ch 1] 6 times in next ch-5 sp, dc in same sp *(pineapple base)*, sc in next ch-5 sp, rep from ** 6 times, ch 5, sc in next ch-5 sp, ch 5, sc in next corner ch-5 sp *(corner)*, ***[ch 5, sc in next ch-5 sp] twice, [dc, ch 1] 6 times in next ch-5 sp, dc in same sp *(pineapple base)*, sc in next ch-5 sp, rep from *** 9 times, ch 5, sc in next ch-5 sp, ch 5, sc in next corner ch-5 sp *(corner)*, ****[ch 5, sc in next ch-5 sp] twice, [dc, ch 1] 6

times in next ch-5 sp, dc in same sp *(pineapple base)*, sc in next ch-5 sp, rep from **** 6 times, ch 5, join in beg sc. *(34 pineapple bases)*

Rnd 32: Beg shell in same sc as joining, sc in next ch-5 sp, shell in next corner sc *(corner)*, *sc in next ch-5 sp, shell in next sc, sc in next ch-5 sp, ch 3, [sc in next ch-1 sp, ch 3] 6 times, rep from * 9 times, sc in next ch-5 sp, shell in next sc, sc in next ch-5 sp, shell in next corner sc *(corner)*, **sc in next ch-5 sp, shell in next sc, sc in next ch-5 sp, ch 3, [sc in next ch-1 sp, ch 3] 6 times, rep from ** 3 times, sc in next ch-5 sp, shell in next sc, sc in next ch-5 sp, shell in next corner sc *(corner)*, ***sc in next ch-5 sp, shell in next sc, sc in next ch-5 sp, ch 3, [sc in next ch-1 sp, ch 3] 6 times, rep from *** 9 times, sc in next ch-5 sp, shell in next sc, sc in next ch-5 sp, shell in next corner sc *(corner)*, ****sc in next ch-5 sp, shell in next sc, sc in next ch-5 sp, ch 3, [sc in next ch-1 sp, ch 3] 6 times, rep from **** 6 times, sc in next ch-5 sp, join in 3rd ch of beg ch-3.

Rnd 33: Sl st in next dc, beg shell in same sp, ch 2, (shell, ch 2, shell) in ch-2 sp of next corner shell *(corner)*, ch 2, *shell in 2nd dc of next 3-dc group, ch 3, [sc in next ch-3 sp, ch 3] 5 times, rep from * 9 times, shell in ch-2 sp of next shell, ch 2, (shell, ch 2, shell) in ch-2 sp of next corner shell *(corner)*, ch 2, **shell in ch-2 sp of next shell, ch 3, [sc in next ch-3 sp, ch 3] 5 times, rep from ** 6 times, shell in ch-2 sp of next shell, ch 2, (shell, ch 2, shell) in ch-2 sp of next shell *(corner)*, ch 2, ***shell in ch-2 sp of next shell, ch 3, [sc in next ch-3 sp, ch 3] 5 times, rep from *** 9 times, shell in ch-2 sp of next shell, ch 2, (shell, ch 2, shell) in ch-2 sp of next corner shell *(corner)*, ch 2, ****shell in ch-2 sp of next shell, ch 3, [sc in next ch-3 sp, ch 3] 5 times, rep from **** 6 times, join in 3rd ch of beg ch-3.

Rnd 34: Sl st in next dc, sl st in next ch-2 sp, beg shell in same sp, ch 3, shell in each of next 3 ch-2 sps, ch 3, *shell in ch-2 sp of next shell, ch 3, [sc in next ch-3 sp, ch 3] 4 times, rep from * 9 times, shell in ch-2 sp of next shell, ch 3, shell in ch-2 sp of each of next 3 shells, ch 3, **shell in ch-2 sp of next shell, ch 3, [sc in next ch-3 sp, ch 3] 4 times, rep from ** 6 times, shell in ch-2 sp of next shell, ch 3, shell in ch-2 sp of each of next 3 shells, ch 3, ***shell in ch-2 sp of next shell, ch 3, [sc in next ch-3 sp, ch 3] 4 times, rep from *** 9 times, shell in ch-2 sp of next shell, ch 3, shell in each of next 3 ch-2 sps, ch 3, ****shell in ch-2 sp of next shell, ch 3, [sc in next ch-3 sp, ch 3] 4 times, rep from * 6 times, join in 3rd ch of beg ch-3.

Rnd 35: Sl st in next dc, sl st in next ch-2 sp, beg shell in same sp, ch 3, [shell in ch-2 sp of next shell, ch 3] 4 times, *[sc in next ch-3 sp, ch 3] 3 times, shell in ch-2 sp of next shell, ch 3, rep from * 9 times, [shell in ch-2 sp of next shell, ch 3] 4 times, **[sc in next ch-3 sp, ch 3] 3 times, shell in ch-2 sp of next shell, ch 3, rep from ** 6 times, [shell in ch-2 sp of next shell, ch 3] 4 times, ***[sc in next ch-3 sp, ch 3] 3 times, shell in ch-2 sp of next shell, ch 3, rep from *** 9 times, [shell in ch-2 sp of next shell, ch 3] 4 times, ****[sc in next ch-3 sp, ch 3] 3 times, shell in ch-2 sp of next shell, ch 3, rep from **** 6 times, join in 3rd ch of beg ch-3.

Rnd 36: Sl st in next dc, sl st in next ch-2 sp, (beg shell, ch 2, 2 dc) in same sp, ch 3, shell in next ch-2 sp of next shell, ch 3, (shell, ch 2, 2 dc) in ch-2 sp of next shell, ch 3, shell in ch-2 sp of next shell, ch 3, *(shell, ch 2, 2 dc) in ch-2 sp of next shell, ch 3, [sc in next ch-3 sp, ch 3] twice, rep from * 9 times, [(shell, ch 2, 2 dc) in ch-2 sp of next shell, ch 3, shell in ch-2 sp of next shell, ch 3] twice, **(shell, ch 2, 2 dc) in ch-2 sp of next shell, ch 3, [sc in next ch-3 sp, ch 3] twice, rep from ** 6 times, [(shell, ch 2, 2 dc) in ch-2 sp of next shell, ch 3, shell in ch-2 sp of next shell, ch 3] twice, ***(shell, ch 2, 2 dc) in ch-2 sp of next shell, ch 3, [sc in next ch-3 sp, ch 3] twice, rep from *** 9 times, [(shell, ch 2, 2 dc) in ch-2 sp of next shell, ch 3, shell in ch-2 sp of next shell, ch 3] twice, ****(shell, ch 2, 2 dc) in ch-2 sp of next shell, ch 3, [sc in next ch-3 sp, ch 3] twice, rep from **** 6 times, join in 3rd ch of beg ch-3.

Rnd 37: Sl st in next dc, sl st in next ch-2 sp, beg shell in same sp, ch 1, shell in next ch-2 sp, [ch 3, shell in ch-2 sp of next shell, ch 3, shell in each of next 2 ch-2 sp] twice, *ch 3, sc in next ch-3 sp, ch 3, shell in ch-2 sp of next shell, ch 1, shell in next ch-2 sp, rep from * 9 times, [ch 3, shell in ch-2 sp of next shell, ch 3, shell in each of next 2 ch-2 sps] twice, **ch 3, sc in next ch-3 sp, ch 3, shell in ch-2 sp of next shell, ch 1, shell

in next ch-2 sp, rep from ** 6 times, [ch 3, shell in ch-2 sp of next shell, ch 3, shell in ch-2 sp of next shell, ch 1, shell in next ch-2 sp] twice, ***ch 3, sc in next ch-3 sp, ch 3, shell in ch-2 sp of next shell, ch 1, shell in next ch-2 sp, rep from *** 9 times, [ch 3, shell in ch-2 sp of next shell, ch 3, shell in ch-2 sp of next shell, ch 1, shell in next ch-2 sp] twice, ****ch 3, sc in next ch-3 sp, ch 3, shell in ch-2 sp of next shell, ch 1, shell in next ch-2 sp, rep from **** 5 times, ch 3, sc in next ch-3 sp, ch 3, join in 3rd ch of beg ch-3.

Rnd 38: Sl st in next dc, sl st in next ch-2 sp, beg shell in same sp, ch 3, *shell in ch-2 sp of next shell, ch 3, rep from * around, join in 3rd ch of beg ch-3.

BORDER

Rnd 1: Sl st in next dc, sl st in next ch-2 sp, [ch 5, sc in next ch sp] 6 times, ch 5, (sc, ch 5, sc) in next ch-3 sp (corner), [ch 5, sc in next ch sp] 63 times, ch 5, (sc, ch 5, sc) in next ch-3 sp (corner), [ch 5, sc in next ch sp] 51 times, ch 5, (sc, ch 5, sc) in next ch-3 sp (corner), [ch 5, sc in next ch sp] 63 times, ch 5, (sc, ch 5, sc) in next ch-3 sp (corner), [ch 5, sc in next ch sp] 44 times, ch 5, join in first ch of beg ch-5.

Rnd 2: Sl st in each of next 2 chs, ch 5, [sc in next ch-5 sp, ch 5] across to next corner ch-5 sp, (sc, ch 5, sc) in corner ch-5 sp (corner), *ch 5, [sc in next ch-5 sp, ch 5] across to next corner ch-5 sp, (sc, ch 5, sc) in corner ch-5 sp (corner), rep from * twice, ch 5, [sc in next ch-5 sp, ch 5] across to beg ch-5, join in first ch of beg ch-5.

Rnd 3: Sl st in each of next 2 chs, ch 3, [shell in next ch-5 sp, ch 3, sc in next ch-5 sp, ch 3] twice, shell in next ch-5 sp, ch 3, sc in next ch-5 sp, ch 3, (sc, ch 5, sc) in next corner ch-5 sp (corner), *ch 3, sc in next ch-5 sp, ch 3, [shell in next ch-5 sp, ch 3, sc in next ch-5 sp, ch 3] across to next corner, (sc, ch 5, sc) in corner ch-5 sp (corner), rep from * twice, ch 3, [sc in next ch-5 sp, ch 3, shell in next ch-5 sp, ch 3] across to beg ch-3, join in first ch of beg ch-3.

Rnd 4: Sl st in each of next 2 chs, sl st in each of next 2 dc, sl st in next ch-2 sp, beg shell in same sp, ch 5, [shell in ch-2 sp of next shell, ch 5] twice, (shell, ch 2, 2 dc) in next corner ch-5 sp *(corner)*, *ch 5, [shell in ch-2 sp of next shell, ch 5] across to next corner, (shell, ch 2, 2 dc) in next corner ch-5 sp *(corner)*, rep from * twice, ch 5, [shell in ch-2 sp of next shell, ch 5] across to beg shell, join in 3rd ch of beg ch-3.

Rnd 5: Sl st in next dc, sl st in next ch-2 sp, beg shell in same sp, [ch 2, sc in next ch-5 sp, ch 2, shell] twice, ch 2, sc in next ch-5 sp, shell in ch-2 sp of next shell, ch 1 *(corner)*, shell in next ch-2 sp, *sc in next ch-5 sp, [ch 2, shell in ch-2 sp of next shell, ch 2, sc in next ch-5 sp] across to next corner, shell in ch-2 sp of next shell, ch 1 *(corner)*, shell in next ch-2 sp, rep from * twice, sc in next ch-5 sp, [ch 2, shell in ch-2 sp of next shell, ch 2, sc in next ch-5 sp] across to beg shell, ch 2, join in 3rd ch of beg ch-3.

Rnd 6: Sl st in next dc, sl st in next ch-2 sp, beg shell in same sp, [ch 3, shell in ch-2 sp of next shell] 3 times, ch 3 *(corner)*, shell in ch-2 sp of next shell, *[ch 3, shell in ch-2 sp of next shell] across to next corner ch-1 sp, ch 3 *(corner)*, sk corner ch-1 sp, shell in ch-2 sp of next shell, rep from * twice, [ch 3, shell in ch-2 sp of next shell] across to beg shell, ch 3, join in 3rd ch of beg ch-3.

Rnd 7: Sl st in next dc, sl st in next ch-2 sp, beg shell in same sp, *[ch 1, sc in next ch-3 sp, ch 1, shell in ch-2 sp of next shell] across to next corner ch-3 sp, ch 1, shell in corner ch-3 sp *(corner)*, ch 1, shell in ch-2 sp of next shell, rep from * 3 times, ch 1, sc in next ch-3 sp, ch 1, [shell in ch-2 sp of next shell, ch 1, sc in next sc, ch 1] across to beg shell, join in 3rd ch of beg ch-3.

Rnd 8: Sl st in next dc, sl st in next ch-2 sp, beg shell in same sp, *ch 3, [shell in ch-2 sp of next shell, ch 3] across to next corner shell, (shell, ch 2, 2 dc) in ch-2 sp of corner shell *(corner)*, rep from * 3 times, ch 3, [shell in ch-2 sp of next shell, ch 3] across to beg shell, join in 3rd ch of beg ch-3.

Rnd 9: Sl st in next dc, sl st in next ch-2 sp, beg shell in same sp, [ch 1, sc in next ch-5 sp, ch 1, shell] 3 times, ch 1, sc in next ch-5 sp, shell in ch-2 sp of next shell, ch 3 *(corner)*, shell in next ch-2 sp, *sc in next ch-5 sp, [ch 1, shell in ch-2 sp of next shell, ch 1, sc in next ch-5 sp] across to next corner, shell in ch-2 sp of next shell, ch 3 *(corner)*, shell in next ch-2 sp, rep from * twice, sc in next ch-5 sp, [ch 1, shell in ch-2 sp of next shell, ch 1, sc in next ch-5 sp] across to beg shell, ch 2, join in 3rd ch of beg ch-3.

Rnd 10: Sl st in next dc, sl st in next ch-2 sp, beg shell in same sp, *[ch 3, shell in ch-2 sp of next shell] across to next corner ch-3 sp, shell in corner ch-3 sp *(corner)*, ch 3, shell in ch-2 sp of next shell, rep from * 3 times, [ch 3, shell in ch-2 sp of next shell] across to beg shell, ch 3, join in 3rd ch of beg ch-3.

Rnd 11: Sl st in next dc, sl st in next ch-2 sp, beg shell in same sp, ch 1, sc in next ch-3 sp, ch 1, *shell in ch-2 sp of next shell, ch 1, sc in next ch-3 sp, ch 1, rep from * around to beg shell, join in 3rd ch of beg ch-3. Fasten off. ∎

TOLL-FREE ORDER LINE or to request a free catalog (800) LV-ANNIE (800) 582-6643
Customer Service (800) AT-ANNIE (800) 282-6643, **Fax** (800) 882-6643
Visit anniesattic.com

We have made every effort to ensure the accuracy and completeness of these instructions.
We cannot, however, be responsible for human error, typographical mistakes or variations in individual work.

ISBN: 978-1-59635-223-0

Printed in USA   1 2 3 4 5 6 7 8 9

Stitch Guide

For more complete information, visit **FreePatterns.com**

ABBREVIATIONS

beg	begin/begins/beginning
bpdc	back post double crochet
bpsc	back post single crochet
bptr	back post treble crochet
CC	contrasting color
ch(s)	chain(s)
ch-	refers to chain or space previously made (i.e. ch-1 space)
ch sp(s)	chain space(s)
cl(s)	cluster(s)
cm	centimeter(s)
dc	double crochet (singular/plural)
dc dec	double crochet 2 or more stitches together, as indicated
dec	decrease/decreases/decreasing
dtr	double treble crochet
ext	extended
fpdc	front post double crochet
fpsc	front post single crochet
fptr	front post treble crochet
g	gram(s)
hdc	half double crochet
hdc dec	half double crochet 2 or more stitches together, as indicated
inc	increase/increases/increasing
lp(s)	loop(s)
MC	main color
mm	millimeter(s)
oz	ounce(s)
pc	popcorn(s)
rem	remain/remains/remaining
rep(s)	repeat(s)
rnd(s)	round(s)
RS	right side
sc	single crochet (singular/plural)
sc dec	single crochet 2 or more stitches together, as indicated
sk	skip/skipped/skipping
sl st(s)	slip stitch(es)
sp(s)	space(s)/spaced
st(s)	stitch(es)
tog	together
tr	treble crochet
trtr	triple treble
WS	wrong side
yd(s)	yard(s)
yo	yarn over

Chain—ch: Yo, pull through lp on hook.

Slip stitch—sl st: Insert hook in st, pull through both lps on hook.

Single crochet—sc: Insert hook in st, yo, pull through st, yo, pull through both lps on hook.

Front post stitch—fp: Back post stitch—bp: When working post st, insert hook from right to left around post st on previous row.

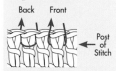

Front loop—front lp Back loop—back lp

Front Loop   Back Loop

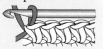

Half double crochet— hdc: Yo, insert hook in st, yo, pull through st, yo, pull through all 3 lps on hook.

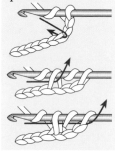

Double crochet—dc: Yo, insert hook in st, yo, pull through st, [yo, pull through 2 lps] twice.

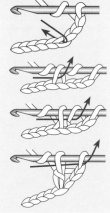

Change colors: Drop first color; with 2nd color, pull through last 2 lps of st.

Treble crochet—tr: Yo twice, insert hook in st, yo, pull through st, [yo, pull through 2 lps] 3 times.

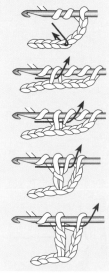

Double treble crochet—dtr: Yo 3 times, insert hook in st, yo, pull through st, [yo, pull through 2 lps] 4 times.

Single crochet decrease (sc dec): (Insert hook, yo, draw lp through) in each of the sts indicated, yo, draw through all lps on hook.

Example of 2-sc dec

Half double crochet decrease (hdc dec): (Yo, insert hook, yo, draw lp through) in each of the sts indicated, yo, draw through all lps on hook.

Example of 2-hdc dec

Double crochet decrease (dc dec): (Yo, insert hook, yo, draw loop through, draw through 2 lps on hook) in each of the sts indicated, yo, draw through all lps on hook.

Example of 2-dc dec

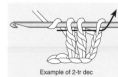

Example of 2-tr dec

Treble crochet decrease (tr dec): Holding back last lp of each st, tr in each of the sts indicated, yo, pull through all lps on hook.

US		UK
sl st (slip stitch)	=	sc (single crochet)
sc (single crochet)	=	dc (double crochet)
hdc (half double crochet)	=	htr (half treble crochet)
dc (double crochet)	=	tr (treble crochet)
tr (treble crochet)	=	dtr (double treble crochet)
dtr (double treble crochet)	=	ttr (triple treble crochet)
skip	=	miss

ABOUT
MARY

FR. DAVID VINCENT MECONI, SJ

Cover design by Caroline Green

ISBN: 978-1-5051-1614-4

Published in the United States by

TAN Books
PO Box 269
Gastonia, NC 28053
www.TANBooks.com

Printed in the United States of America

To Bob and Doris,
who have lived only
to love Jesus through Mary

Introduction

Over two thousand years ago, a beautiful Jewish baby girl named Miriam was born to her parents, whom Sacred Tradition names Ann and Joachim. Little did anyone then know how special this graced girl would be. Little did anyone realize how countless churches, devotions, schools, and cities would one day be named after this little Mary. From St. Mary Grade School in Paw Paw, Michigan, to the Queen of Apostles Seminary in Moscow, innumerable places of learning are proud to take the name of the Seat of Wisdom. From the snowy Cathedral of the Nativity of the Blessed Virgin Mary in Juneau, Alaska, to the current ashes of the main transept of Notre Dame Cathedral in France, there are more places of worship named after Our Lady than any other human person on earth. But as these pages set out to playfully remind us, there are also times and seasons, animals and plants, and of course, apparitions, devotions, and spiritualities which all pivot around Mary, the Mother of God.

Even though 101 facts fill these pages, and even though a million more could be added, all truths about Mary are ultimately about Jesus Christ and the Triune God. For Mary is the one human person who alone can boast that her entire identity is Christ, her entire mission maternal. The Catholic Church therefore dotes on this Mother, the Mother of all of our souls "in the order of grace" (*Lumen Gentium* §61). The Catholic Church thinks deeply about this woman, because coming to know her more intimately is the singular way to enjoy an authentic and living awareness of her Son as well. As the only person present at both the Savior of the world's birth as well as his death (Fact 6), Mary offers the world a most unique lens through which to view the Lord and his life. In short, every Marian doctrine and devotion can be summarized by her own words recorded in John's Gospel, "Do whatever he tells you" (Jn 2:5).

This is how the Triune God has arranged it from all time. No miserly dictator jealous of other instances of holiness, the loving Father revels in seeing his life reflected in and through his saints. The instant God chose to create, he chose not to be everything, but instead arranged the universe so he would be "all in all" (1 Cor 15:28 NABRE). St. Ignatius of Loyola, the founder of the Jesuits, took this as one of his central mottos, "To find God in all things," and so we must. This is how Sacred Scripture can tell us that all generations will call Mary blessed (Lk 1:48). For this is the praise of the New Eve, the second woman to be immaculately conceived, and whose sinless life gives praise to God. Christians throughout the ages have known that Mary was conceived instantaneously without sin, saved like the rest of us by the Lamb of Sacrifice on Calvary, but in a singular and most unique way, from the moment of her conception.

This is how the first Christian theologians wanted to write about Mary and present her to the world. Every cell of her being is for Christ. She is his first real disciple. She is his Mother, the Mother of God, and that is why someone like Proclus of Constantinople (d. 446) can preach on Mary's birthday that:

> The mystery of the God who becomes man,
> the divinization of humanity assumed by the

Word, represents the most supreme good that Christ has granted us, the revelation of the divine plan and the defeat of every presumptuous human self-sufficiency. God's coming among us, as the brilliant light and clear and visible divine reality, is the great and marvelous divine gift bestowed upon us. Today's celebration honors the birth of the Mother of God. But the true meaning and purpose of this event is the incarnation of the Word. In fact, Mary is herself born, nursed and raised to be the Mother of the King of the Ages, of God (Discourse 1).

This is a humanity that God in his perfect humility chose to need. Think of the colossal nature of that moment, of a Divine Person waiting upon the "yes" of a young woman, the one human who could grant God access into his own good creation.

The immaculateness of Mary regathers all of humanity back into herself. Just as all humans were once "in" Eve as the first mother of the human race, all have been regathered into Mary as the new Mother of the Christian people. Whereas sin and death divide, obedience and true life unite. Mary was created without sin, not of course from any merit of her own. Instead, she was kept free from sin because fourteen or fifteen years from the time of her being immaculately conceived, her "yes" would hand all of humanity over to her Son who would assume the fullness of human nature into his own divine personhood. At that moment the New Adam becomes all of us and we are invited to become him. How else would this be true: "as you did it to one of the least of these my brethren, you did it to me" (Mt 25:40)? How else would this be true: "Saul, Saul, why do you persecute me?" (Acts 9:4)?

Following from the beginning of Mary's immaculate conception is found also her finale, the assumption. If death is the unnatural separation of body and soul, the result of our divine disobedience, would one without sin need to undergo this deadly divide between body and soul? As one who was brought into being by means of a graced perfection, and through grace also remained free from the contagion of sin, the Church has always taught that Mary never had to experience the decay of the grave. This is how the Anglican poet John Donne (d. 1631) can call Mary "our tainted nature's solitary boast," as she is what we all too shall one day become, but even now Christ asks us to look to her to maternal care as we make our way home. "Behold, your mother" (Jn 19:27). There is no holier woman, there can be no holier human person in the history of humankind.

These pages are meant to be occasions of delight as well as insight. For Mary's own joy in holding the world's Savior from the first moment of his earthly existence has proven to be an invitation to theologians, lyricists, and artists throughout the centuries, expressed in poetry and paint, mosaic and music. Finally, the first real Ark, the first real Tabernacle, the first real Monstrance is able to be known, encountered, befriended. As such, these pages are alive with the joys and sorrows of real motherhood, the freeing truths of divine doctrine, and the examples and encouragement to become bearers of Christ as well.

1

Mary became a new mother to humanity

The first woman met in Sacred Scripture is, of course, Eve, "mother of all living" (Gn 3:20). By the second century, Mary is already being referred to as the "New Eve" because she was brought into being to bring about a new covenant, fixing what the first man and woman fractured. This sense of Mary's repairing what Eve broke inaugurated Mariology as a form of Christian devotion. From *Eva* comes the salutation *Ave Maria* ("Hail Mary"), from being duped by one fallen angel arises the obedience to the good angel Gabriel, from fruit disobediently picked from a forbidden tree, we realize the compliant fruit of Mary's womb giving life from an eternal tree, the wood of Christ's cross, and so on.

2

Mary is referenced at the first proclamation of Jesus's coming

The entire Christian message first shines through God's promise to the devil that the Lord "will put enmity between you and the woman, and between your seed and her seed; he shall bruise your head, and you shall bruise his heel" (Gn 3:15). Since the mid-second century, this verse has been known as "The First Gospel," the *Protoevangelium*, since it is the first proclamation of Christ's coming. It foreshadows how Satan may be able to nip at Mary's heal, but her children, Christ and his Church, will crush the enemy's head. St. Paul concludes his letter to the Romans by invoking this ancient promise, "Then the God of peace will soon crush Satan under your feet. The grace of our Lord Jesus Christ be with you" (Rom 16:20).

(*opposite*) The Immaculate Conception, Giovanni Battista Tiepolo, Public domain via Wikimedia Commons

There are many foreshadowings of Mary in the Old Testament

3

"Christians therefore read the Old Testament in the light of Christ crucified and risen. . . . The New Testament lies hidden in the Old and the Old Testament is unveiled in the New" (*Catechism of the Catholic Church* §129). As such, Christians see in the women of the Old Testament, foreshadowings of Mary. For example, Abraham's wife, Sarah, has traditionally stood as the first realization of how faith in God's power to perform the miraculous overcomes physical barrenness (Gn 18:9–15; Lk 1:26–34). No wonder the Old Testament titles "Daughter of Zion" and "Chosen Daughter of Israel" were applied to Mary within the first few centuries of Christianity.

The term "full of grace" has profound theological implications

4

The Greek word *kecharitomene* is the type of participle that says this one is favored because she is totally receptive to God's grace, thus the Latin equivalent, *gratia plena*, refers to a woman fully replete with divine favor. This angelic greeting in the Gospel of Luke (1:28) thus contains the Church's first teaching on Mary, one who is uniquely saved, uniquely sinless. This is why Vatican II teaches, "Adorned from the first instant of her conception with the radiance of an entirely unique holiness, the Virgin of Nazareth is greeted, on God's command, by an angel messenger as 'full of grace'" (Vatican II, *Lumen Gentium* §56).

(*opposite*) The Annunciation, Fra Angelico, public domain via Wikimedia Commons

(*above*) The Birth of the Virgin, Erasmus Quellinus II (1607–1678), oil on canvas, Museo de Prado

5 Our Lady's birthday is celebrated on September 8

Based on the stories recorded in the second-century *Protoevangelium of James* and the later *Pseudo-Gospel of Matthew*, St. Ann's conceiving of Mary was first commemorated in the East, going back to the early 600s, on December 9. Miraculous stories of Mary's birth and life as a young girl captivated Christian readers, and liturgical celebrations followed. When this feast of St. Ann's pregnancy was brought westward, it was moved to December 8 and was renamed the Feast of the Immaculate Conception of the Blessed Virgin Mary. While disagreement remained on what "Immaculate" might mean theologically, the date of December 8 was set, and the celebration of Mary's birthday thus followed nine months later on September 8. Along with Mary's, the Church only celebrates two other birthdays: Jesus's and John the Baptist's.

Mary was the only person present at both the birth and death of Jesus

6

Seldom considered is that Mary was the only one present at both the birth and death of our Lord. Joseph and some shepherds, and the Magi some time later, were the only ones who took witness to Jesus's first moments on earth. With Joseph passing some time during the life of Christ and with Scripture giving no indication that those same shepherds or Wise Men were there on Calvary, Mary remained, thus further solidifying her life's story as inextricable and unexplainable from the life of Christ and the mysteries of his entire life.

(*below*) Jesus Christ and virgin Mary bronze statue. On background the cross. Photo by KYNA STUDIO / Shutterstock

7

St. Luke devotes more time to Mary's story than the other Gospel authors

As a trained medical doctor turned Evangelist, St. Luke shows more interest in the process of motherhood, childbirth, and femininity in general than any of the other Gospel authors. This is perhaps why only in Luke's Gospel do we receive information on the Annunciation (Lk 1:26–38), the Visitation to Elizabeth (vv. 39–45), her beautiful song of praise in the Magnificat (vv. 46–56), the naming of Jesus and his Presentation in the Temple (Lk 2:21–40), as well as instances where womanhood is celebrated in unblushing ways, for example, "Blessed is the womb that bore you, and the breasts that you sucked!" (Lk 11:27).

8

Luke the Evangelist was the first person to paint an icon of the Blessed Virgin Mary

The sixth-century historian Theodorus the Lector wrote two important works chronicling the years from Christianity's legalization (AD 313) to the reign of Emperor Justin I (AD 518). Here, Theodorus detailed the pilgrimage of Empress Eudocia (d. 460) to Jerusalem in 438, telling how she discovered the Hodegetria (meaning one who points the way) style of icon, depicting Mary as pointing to her Son, Jesus, as the Way himself. On this icon was inscribed, "written by the holy Evangelist Luke," and is thus said to be the first ever depiction of the Blessed Virgin Mary.

(*opposite*) St. Luke painting the Virgin, Simone Cantarini (1612–1648), oil on canvas

9 Isaiah prophesized and many Church Fathers taught that Mary experienced no pain during childbirth

When Old Testament prophets envisioned what the Messiah's reign would look like, they believed that the ancient curse of Eve's pain in childbirth would be undone, the new promise being: "Before she was in labor, she gave birth; before her pain came upon her, she was delivered of a son" (Is 66:7). Many of the early Church Fathers saw this as a prediction that Mary the Mother of God would give birth to Jesus miraculously without pain or corruption of her body: "Only Jesus came to light through a new way of being born. . . . In fact, his birth alone occurred without labor pains, and he alone began to exist without sexual relations" (Gregory of Nyssa, *On the Song of Songs* §13).

(*above*) The Nativity, John Singleton Copley (1738–1815), oil on canvas, Museum of Fine Arts, Boston

The Marian iconography style known as Panagia means "The Woman who is All Holy"

A nother popular style of Marian icon is the Panagia, meaning "The Woman who is All Holy" (from *pan*, "all," and *hagios*, meaning "holy" in Greek). Here Mary is facing the viewer wholly visible and transparent, with her hands aloft usually in the *orans* position, one of the most ancient expressions of Christian prayer. A medallion in the middle of Mary's body shows the Christ Child within her, depicting the great paradox of an ancient hymn: "He whom the entire universe could not contain was contained within your womb, O *Theotokos*."

(*right*) Our Lady of the Great Panagiya Images, anonymous, tempera on wood, Tretyakov Gallery

(*above*) Basilica del Santuario di Loreto, Massimo Roselli, public domain via Wikimedia Commons

11 There is a legend that claims angels carried Mary's home to Italy

In Loreto, Italy stands a house-turned-shrine, the home of *Our Lady of Loreto*, where Mary is claimed to have lived. Pious legend tells the story of the house where Mary was born and where she conceived Jesus Christ at the annunciation. The legend states that after the Muslim conquest of Jerusalem in 1291, a band of angels swooped down and transported Mary's girlhood home safely to Loreto. The Church has never officially commented on this incredible enterprise, but the past few popes (Paul VI, John Paul II, Benedict XVI, and Francis) have all made pilgrimages to this hallowed home.

March 25 is seen as the date of the Annunciation because it marked the spring equinox

The Annunciation has been celebrated on March 25 since the third century, although not fixed as a feast until the Council of Toledo in 656. For early Christians, March 25 marked the spring equinox, the day God said, "Let there be light" (Gn 1:3). This was therefore seen as the most fitting day for God to recreate the world with the Annunciation and Mary's "let it be done to me" (Lk 1:38). An obscure third-century Latin work, *On the Computing of Easter*, captured another popular devotion by arguing that March 25 was also the original Good Friday, as Christ entered both this world and the underworld as the New Adam to defeat death and bring true life.

(*left*) Crozier with the Annunciation, champlevé enamel on gilded copper, early 13th century, Louvre Museum, photo by Marie-Lan Nguyen (2012), public domain via Wikimedia Commons

13 There are many reasons for why Christmas is celebrated on December 25

This became the date of Jesus's birth by 336. First, because it fell nine months after the Church's earlier celebration of the Annunciation. Second, it conveniently was able to consecrate the pagan feast of Saturnalia (December 17–23), a time of debauched drunkenness. Third, it fell at the time of the winter solstice when Romans invoked the *Deus Sol Invictus* to return (Emperor Aurelian made worship of this Unconquerable Sun God compulsory in 270). Fourth, it was the birthday of the Persian deity Mithras, so important to the Roman army. Concerning the connection to the winter solstice, St. Augustine once said, "So in bending down to pick us up, he chose the smallest day, but the one from which light starts increasing" (*Sermon* 192.3).

(*Below*) Wise men and the Christmas star by MarcelClemens / Shutterstock

(*above*) Hannah's Song, woodcut for "Die Bibel in Bildern", 1860, Julius Schnorr von Carolsfeld (1794–1872, public domain via Wikimedia Commons

The Magnificat was prefigured by Hannah's own song of praise

14

After Gabriel's departure at the Annunciation, Mary leaves "in haste" (Lk 1:39) to visit her relative Elizabeth who lived in Ain Karim, a small town in Judea, nearly eighty miles from Nazareth. Here it becomes clear that young Mary loved to sing her Bible stories, echoing the Song of Hannah (1 Sm 2:1–10) in her beloved Magnificat (Lk 1:46–55). Both blessed with new life, each woman's soul glorified God (1 Sm 2:1; Lk 1:46), assuring the world that God would not stop there, but would fulfill even further-ranging promises of dispersing the arrogant (1 Sm 2:3; Lk 1:51) and exalting the humble (1 Sm 2:7; Lk 1:52).

(*above*) Ruined Byzantine Kathisma church on the southern outskirts of Jerusalem, Israel, photo by Bukvoed (2019), Wikimedia Commons

15 An archeological dig uncovered a spot where Joseph and Mary were said to have rested on the way to Bethlehem

Under the road between Jerusalem and Bethlehem, excavators in 1992 found ancient ruins of an octagonal church, the Kathisma, the Place of the Seat, built in 456 by the wealthy widow Ikelia. It is on this spot where a second-century legend reports that Mary had to stop and sit as she and Joseph traveled to the City of David to be enrolled for that year's census (Lk 2:4). Here at Kathisma, the pious Ikelia also began a new tradition still practiced today: monks attached to the church would process with white candles to commemorate the purification of Mary forty days after the birth of Jesus, known today as Candlemas (February 2).

The Magi who visited at the Nativity had symbolic significance

16

The first Gentiles to make an appearance in the New Testament are the "wise men from the East" (Mt 2:1–12), traveling to honor Mother Mary's newborn son. Although neither numbered or named in Scripture, Origen (d. c. 250) argued there were three magi because they were the fulfillment of Abraham's three mysterious visitors in Genesis 26:26–31. Additionally, each gift they would have placed in Mary's hands represents the "triple office" of her Son: frankincense for Christ's priesthood, gold for his kingship, and the embalming resin of myrrh for his prophetic death.

(*below*) The Prophecy of Isaiah (fresco), Roman, (2nd century AD), Catacombs of Priscilla, Rome, Italy, Alinari / Bridgeman Images

17

The Seven Sorrows Devotion stems in part from Christ's presentation at the Temple

The Feast of the Presentation, or Candlemas, recalls the Jewish custom of a mother bringing her child to the Temple for ritual purification (Lv 12:2–8). While there, both Anna and Simeon, two aged and devout children of Israel, are allured by the Christ Child, and in beholding him, they prophesized to Our Lady that he would be "a sign that that is spoken against, (and a sword will pierce through your own soul also), that thoughts out of many hearts may be revealed" (Lk 2:34–35), a line which would develop into the Seven Sorrows of Mary Devotion.

18

All seven of Mary's sorrows are found in Scripture

Early in the Church's life, a devotion arose to Our Lady of Sorrows. These sorrows had traditionally been interpreted as Mary's way of participating in the sufferings of her Son in a way that only a mother could. The Seven Sorrows of Mary are Simeon's prophecy that a sword would pierce her Immaculate Heart (Lk 2:35), the flight into Egypt (Mt 2:13–23), the loss of the Child Jesus in the Temple (Lk 2:41–52), meeting Jesus on the Via Dolorosa (suggested at Lk 23:28), his crucifixion (Mt 27:50), Mary receiving Christ from the cross (Jn 19:31–37), and his burial by Joseph of Arimathea (Mt 27:59–60).

(*opposite*) Virgin of the Seven Sorrows, Master of the Female Half-Lengths, late 16th century, public domain via Wikimedia Commons

(*above*) Rest on the Flight into Egypt, Luc-Olivier Merson (1846–1920), 1880, Museum of Fine Arts, Boston, public domain via Wikimedia Commons

19 The flight into Egypt points to prophesies and events found in the Old Testament

One of the more celebrated scenes of Our Lady and Lord's life is their flight into Egypt. Other than being a necessity to avoid Herod's wrath in the killing of all baby boys (Mt 2:13), the trip also came to represent other mystical truths. Scripturally, it was how the Father fulfilled Hosea's prophecy: "Out of Egypt I called my Son" (Hos 11:1). Still more, it pointed to the Exodus. The Church Fathers saw Egypt as the center of human wisdom, which the Jews took when they "despoiled the Egyptians" (Ex 12:36). Christ returning there as the King of the Jews and as the true font and fullness of wisdom proves how God is always and everywhere faithful to his promises.

Miraculous legends surround two popular pilgrimage sights associated with the Holy Family's flight into Egypt

While traveling from Bethlehem into the Egyptian desert, two sites are still revered for offering solace to the Holy Family. South of where the Lord was born, the Chapel of Milk dates back to the fifth century and is built where Mary first stopped to nurse Jesus. A drop of her breast milk spilled, creating a beautiful white patina on the floor of the cave. Traveling farther, the Holy Family stopped to rest under the *Matareyah*, Mary's Tree (still standing in northern Cairo), which offered invaluable shade from the Egyptian sun. Here, the Infant Christ caused water to spring forth, enabling Our Lady to drink and, as legend has it, to catch up on the family laundry.

(*below*) Saint Peter's Basilica and square in Vatican City, Rome, Italy. Photo © Sopotnicki / Shutterstock

21

Jesus had no blood brothers and sisters

As the spouse of the Holy Spirit, no orthodox Christian can claim that Mary had other children apart from Jesus. To think otherwise is a blasphemy started with early heretics who also denied the full divinity (consubstantiality with the Father) of Christ, resurfacing with many of the Protestant reformers devaluing the gift of celibacy. Yet the Greek term *Aeiparthenos* ("Ever Virgin") for Mary is ancient, and the terms for "brothers and sisters" in the New Testament are very Asiatic ways of describing close kin and even trustworthy allies. The Church's position is that Mary was, of course, a virgin before the Annunciation, during Christ's birth, in that her bodily integrity was preserved, and until her dormition (cf., *Lumen Gentium* §57).

The events at the wedding at Cana reflect Mary's prime mission

Jesus's first recorded miracle was accomplished at his mother's intercession: "They have no wine" (Jn 2:3). Her final words in Scripture summarize all of Marian theology: "Do whatever he tells you" (Jn 2:5). The wedding at Cana (Jn 2:2–12) thus represents how the wills of Jesus and Mary are in perfect communion, her only mission being to bring others to God: "At Cana, the Mother of Christ presents herself as the spokeswoman of her Son's will, pointing out those things which must be done so that the salvific power of the Messiah may be manifested. . . . Her faith evokes his first 'sign' and helps to kindle the faith of the disciples" (St. John Paul II, *Mater Redemptoris* §22).

(*below*) Les weddings de Cana (The wedding at Cana) Painting by Bernardo Strozzi (1581-1644) 17th century Private Collection, Luisa Ricciarini / Bridgeman Images

23

Some traditions claim Mary spent her last years in Turkey

After the Crucifixion, John cared for Mary, who was now widowed with no other children (Jn 19:27). It is said that he took her to a tiny lodging outside Ephesus in Turkey, known today as "Meryem Ana Evi" (Mother Mary's House). It was unearthed based on the visions of the German Augustinian nun Anne Catherine Emmerich (1774–1824), who miraculously reported: "Mary's dwelling was on a hill to the left of the road from Jerusalem, some three and a half hours from Ephesus. . . . Narrow paths lead southwards to a hill near the top of which is an uneven plateau, some half hour's journey." This house was finally discovered in 1892 by French archeologists.

24

Saturday is often seen as a Marian day within the Church

Traditionally, Saturday is seen as Our Lady's Day. It is considered the day God finished creating, therefore becoming the day also representing the fulfillment of his new creation in Mary. Saturday is also the day Mary alone had to console the Church between Jesus's death on Good Friday and his resurrection on Easter Sunday. The Englishman Alcuin (d. 804) is responsible for orchestrating Marian votive Masses and prayers for exclusive use on Saturdays. In 1096, Pope Urban II exhorted the Church to pray the Liturgy of the Hours on Saturdays in honor of the Blessed Mother. The month of May is also dedicated to Mother Mary, and the month of October is a special time for Our Lady of the Rosary.

25 The first Marian apparition is said to have occurred before she was assumed into heaven

The first apparition in Church history occurred in the year 40. In order to bolster his hope in converting the pagans, the Virgin Mary appeared to St. James the Great in Zaragoza, Spain. The vision gave rise to a new title and devotion, Our Lady of the Pillar, because Our Lady appeared to James standing on a pillar of jasper held aloft by two angels. It is the only reported Marian apparition reported before her assumption into heaven.

(*below*) Francisco de Goya, El apóstol Santiago y sus discípulos adorando a la Virgen del Pilar, 1775-1780, Museo de Zaragoza, public domain in the United States via Wikimedia Commons

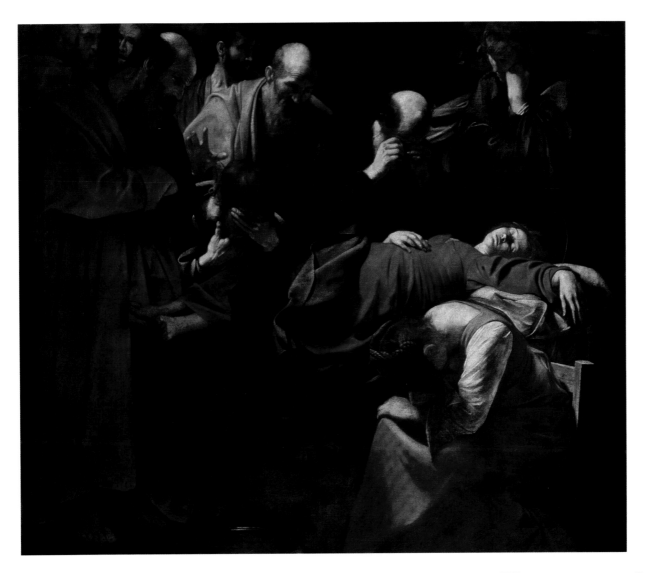

(*above*) Death of the Virgin, Caravaggio (1571–1610), oil on canvas, public domain via Wikimedia Commons

The Catholic Church has no official teaching on whether Mary died or not 26

Legends differ, but most state that Mary simply "fell asleep" at the end of her life. This is Mary's dormition, thus celebrating that "when the course of her earthly life was finished, [Mary] was taken up body and soul into heavenly glory, and exalted by the Lord as Queen over all things . . . 'in your Dormition you did not leave the world, O Mother of God, but were joined to the source of Life. You conceived the living God and, by your prayers, will deliver our souls from death'" (CCC [*Catechism of the Catholic Church*] §966). The earliest known account of Mary's passing from this earth is from the late third or early fourth century, "The Book of Mary's Repose."

The site where the Assumption is said to have occurred is revered by Christians and Muslims

27

The oldest (nearly) intact church in Jerusalem is Mary's Church of the Assumption, most of which dates back to the early fifth century, marking the place where legend holds Mary was lifted into heaven. This site is not only beloved by Christians. After the Islamic conquest of Jerusalem in the twelfth century, Saladin built a niche over the place where Muslims believe Muhammad once witnessed a light shining over his "sister Mary." Two relics from the Church of the Assumption remain: a cincture as well as a shroud Mary discarded upon being assumed, housed today in the Church of Our Lady of Blachernae in Istanbul.

The first biography of Mary was produced in the seventh century

28

Maximus the Confessor (d. 662) almost surely wrote the first biography of Mary. Gleaning all the ancient stories and stitching them together into a unified narrative, Maximus composed a comprehensive account of Mary's life, from her immaculate conception to her glorious assumption. Included are many wonderful details: Joseph's initial psychological turmoil in understanding Mary's pregnancy, Mary as the storyteller guiding the apostles in the writing of the Gospels, and how Mary kept constant vigil at Christ's tomb and was thus the one to whom he fittingly first appeared—a fact the Gospels suppress "so no one would take as reason for disbelief that the vision of the Resurrection was first reported by his mother."

(*opposite*) The Assumption of the Virgin, 1516-18 (oil on canvas), Titian (Tiziano Vecellio) (c.1488-1576) / Italian, Santa Maria Gloriosa dei Frari, Venice, Italy, Bridgeman Images

29 The earliest depiction of the Blessed Mother we still have is from second-century Syria

Mary's beauty has inspired countless pieces of artwork. One of the first was discovered within the famous Church at Dura-Europos. Here Mary is depicted drawing water from her well when the Angel Gabriel appears to her, evidenced by two divine rays beaming into her womb. By the third century, the Roman catacombs were also painting more and more portraits of the Virgin and the Christ Child in various scriptural scenes.

(*above*) Mural in the Doura Europos House Church (235 CE), Pictures from History / Bridgeman Images

The world's oldest recorded Marian prayer is the *Sub Tuum Praesidium*

Faithful Christians pray not *to* Mary but *through* her, as God is the ultimate provider of our petitions. Nonetheless, Christians have been praying with Mary for a very long time. The oldest known Marian prayer is the *Sub Tuum Praesidium*:

Beneath your compassion,
We take refuge, O Mother of God:
do not despise our petitions in time of trouble:
but rescue us from dangers,
only pure, only blessed one.

We possess one little scrap of the Rylands Papyrus, dating back to c. 250, on which we can still read a version of *Sub Tuum*, where *Theotokos*, a term which sparked the Council of Ephesus in 431, first appears.

(*right*) Rylands Greek P457 Recto, Rylandsimaging, public domain via Wikimedia Commons

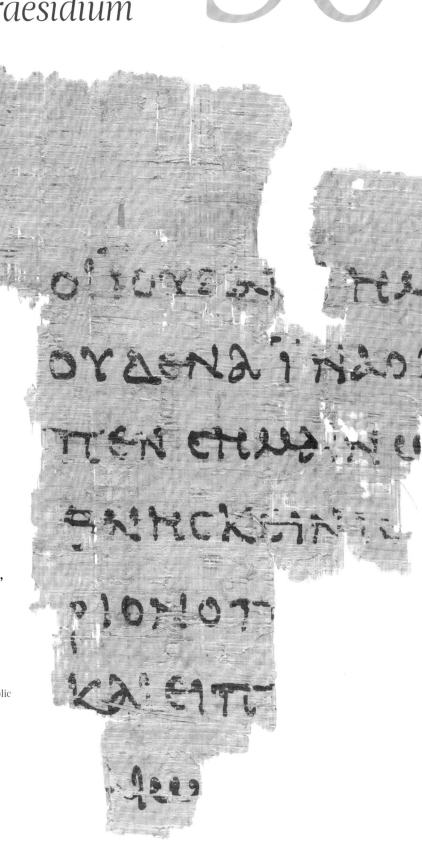

31

A miraculous snowfall led to the construction of a prominent Marian landmark

In the fourth century, a patrician couple told Pope Liberius (352–366) about a dream they had in which Mary desired a church to be built where she would soon miraculously indicate. On the sweltering morning of August 5, 352 (some calculations have 358), Romans woke up to a beautiful blanket of snow on the Esquiline Hill. Here, the Basilica of St. Mary Major was built, invoking a new devotion: Our Lady of Snows. It is also known as Saint Mary of the Crib because its rear side altar houses wooden slats from the creche from Bethlehem.

(*right*) The Foundation of Santa Maria Maggiore, Masolino da Panicale (1383–1447), public domain via Wikimedia Commons

(*above*) Saint Proclus, Archbishop of Constantinople, Shamshin, Petr Mikhailovich (1811-95) / Russian, Photo © Fine Art Images / Bridgeman Images

Early Church theologians found Mary's womb to be a divine "workshop"

32

The Eastern Fathers tended to praise God for making Mary's womb a type of workplace where the Father toiled to weld humanity and divinity together. For instance, Basil of Caesarea (d. 379) asked his congregants, "But what is the workshop of this order of salvation? The body of a Holy Virgin" (*Generation of Christ* §5). The officiating bishop at the Council of

Ephesus, Proclus of Constantinople (d. 446), likened Mary's womb to a loom where God and man were woven together: "O Virgin, unmarried Maid, incorrupt Mother, where did you get the wool to clothe the Master of the world? Where did you discover the uterine loom on which you wove this seamless garment?" (*Homily* 4.2).

33 Mary's "yes" to God brought about the greatest paradox humanity has ever known

Ephrem the Syrian (d. 373) was a tremendous poet, known as the "Harp of the Holy Spirit." He put to song one of the great paradoxes of Mary's "yes"—namely, that as a mortal creature, she could offer Life himself only death, could give God who is Power only weakness, could reduce the Infinite to one very small: "A wonder is your Mother, the Lord entered and became a servant /

He entered able to speak and in her was reduced to silence / He entered as One thundering but now a voice that is silent / He descended the Shepherd of all, but a Lamb he became" (*Hymns on the Nativity*, 11.6).

(*below*) Portrait of Saint Ephrem the Syrian (Nisibis, 306-Edessa, 373), Syrian theologian. Doctor of the Church. Painting by Giuseppe Franchi (1565-1628), oil on canvas, © Veneranda Biblioteca Ambrosiana/Mondadori Portfolio, Bridgeman Images

(*above*) Saint Mary (the Blessed Virgin) with the Christ Child, Saint Jerome and Saint Francis of Assisi. Etching by A.G. Faldoni, 1724, after A.M. Zanetti, Iconographic Collections, public domain via Wikimedia Commons.

The Church Fathers had a strong devotion to the Mother of God

34

The great polyglot and biblical commentator St. Jerome (d. 420) enjoyed a beautiful devotion to Our Lady, once comparing her to Easter: "As the Virgin Mary, Mother of the Lord, holds the first place among all women, so, among all other days, Easter is the mother of all days." Jerome wasn't the only Church Father to venerate Mary. St. Irenaeus of Lyon (d. 202) was arguably the first true Mariologist and was the first to establish Mary as the New Eve. St. Justin Martyr, St. Ambrose, and St. Ephraem have also all written glowingly about Our Lady, as have many other Fathers.

35 The great St. Augustine did not try to explain Mary's sinlessness

St. Augustine (d. 430) did not dare judge Mary's sinlessness. Against the Pelagian sect's belief that humans could be naturally perfect without Christ, Augustine stressed the fallenness of every man and woman. But when it came to the awesome possibility of an inherently sinless Mother of God, the usually loquacious Augustine fell silent: "Let us then leave aside the Holy Virgin Mary. . . . I do not want to raise here any question about her when we are dealing with sin. After all, how do we know what wealth of grace was given to her in order to conquer sin completely, since she merited to conceive and bear the One who certainly had no sin?" (*Nature and Grace* 36.42).

(*right*) Saint Augustine statue holding a burning heart in hand, Charles bridge in Prague,Czech Republic, photo by Maran Garai/Shutterstock

Cyril of Alexandria argued passionately that Mary was the Mother of God

One of the great Church Fathers, Cyril of Alexandria (d. 444), produced a list of *12 Anathemas* which helped the early Church think theologically about Mary's motherhood. Setting the stage for the Council of Ephesus, these anathemas are first found in a letter to the heresiarch Nestorius who wrongly taught that Jesus was both a divine person and a human person, Mary giving birth only to the latter. Cyril began his list of errors—worthy of excommunication—with this warning: "If anyone does not confess that Emmanuel is God in truth, and therefore that the Holy Virgin is the Mother of God (for she bore in a fleshly way the Word of God become flesh), let him be anathema."

(*below*) Sant Salvador de Khora - Pintures de l'absis, photo by Josep Renalias, public domain via Wikimdia Commons

(*above*) Theotokos Hodegetria, Bysantic icon, 16th century, anonymous, public domain via Wikimedia Commons

37 The Council of Ephesus declared the dogma of the *Theotokos*

In 431, the Church held her third ecumenical council. Strategically held in Ephesus, where Marian piety was very popular, the Council of Ephesus officially declared Mary to be *Theotokos*, truly the Mother of God (Latin, *Mater Dei*). As archbishop of Constantinople, Nestorius refused to let anyone invoke Mary as the "Mother of God," but only the "Mother of Jesus." How can an eternal Son be born of a human? But in her wisdom, the Church knew that the ancient devotion of calling upon Mary as *Theotokos* was correct because Jesus is God and Mary is his mother. She is, of course, not the mother of the Father or mother of the Holy Spirit but of the Son-now-made flesh.

The term *Mediatrix* first appeared in the sixth century

Upon threat of being removed from his office as archdeacon of a small town in Cilicia, in modern-day Turkey, Theophilus of Adana (d. 538) asked the devil to destroy the new bishop. Satan agreed, if only Theophilus would renounce Christ and the Blessed Virgin. He did so but later came to his senses and invoked Mary's aid, at which point she appeared to him and assured that through her mediation he had obtained forgiveness: "The Lord has heard your prayers and grants your petitions through me." In this sixth-century story, over forty distinct titles are used for Mary, with *Mediatrix* appearing for the first time, emphasizing how Christ never works independently from the interceding presence of his mother.

(*right*) Virgin Mary statue, photo by Tanakorn Moolsarn/Shutterstock

One hymn to the Blessed Virgin forbids sitting while it is being sung

39

Standard by the middle of the 600s, the *Akathist Hymn* was written for the Annunciation, the Eastern feast of the *Theotokos*, and is accordingly directed to Gabriel, God's "invincible champion." So named because reverence for Mary's "yes" mandates there be *no sitting* (*a-*, negating in Greek, and *kathist* being the Greek for sitting or for chair, from where the term "cathedral" comes) while it is being sung.

Romanus the Melodist (d. 556) is considered its author, which so beautifully opens: "Queen of the Heavenly Host, Defender of our souls, we thy servants offer to thee songs of victory and thanksgiving, for thou, O Mother of God, hast delivered us from dangers. But as thou hast invincible power, free us from conflicts of all kinds that we may cry to thee: Rejoice, unwedded Bride!"

Islam holds Mary in high esteem

40

The only *sura*, or section, in the Koran named after a woman is dedicated to Mary. Many elements from the Gospels and the *Protoevangelium of James* found their way into this portion of the Koran: Mary takes a very early vow of virginity, she is visited by Gabriel as a young woman to give birth to Jesus, she then spends her life as one who speaks on the Lord's behalf, and she is one of the few humans not "pricked" by Satan at birth but spends her life as one who speaks on behalf of God, as a *nabiyya* or prophetess. This esteem given to Mary extends to the Hagia Sophia, where several beautiful images of her can still be seen.

(*opposite*) Mosaic in the interior of Hagia Sophia showing the Virgin Mary with Child Jesus Pantocrator, photo by Andre Telles/Shutterstock

41 The Agiosoritissa icon symbolically depicts Mary's role as intercessor for humanity

The Agiosoritissa icon is one of the few styles typically presenting Mary without the Christ Child. It is so called after the Church of the Holy Urn (*Hagia Soros*) in Constantinople where Mary's cincture is housed. The Agiosoritissa icon is also known as the "Madonna Advocate" icon because Mary is purposefully portrayed interceding between the faithful who gaze upon her and her Son who is intentionally out of the picture above her.

(*above*) Hagiosoritissa, Santa Maria Maggiore, public domain via Wikimedia Commons

42 The Church places the date for the Assumption in August

By the middle of the seventh century, Christians were liturgically celebrating Mary's bodily assumption into heaven at Masses falling in mid-August. Understanding how early Christians consecrated otherwise pagan feast days and stamped an indelible Christian mark upon them, some scholars have argued that August was originally chosen as the month of Mary's assumption because it was also when non-Christians around the Mediterranean celebrated the pagan goddess Isis, "the mother god," who was esteemed for being the divine mother of the pharaoh and the mother of the Egyptian deity Horus.

(*opposite*) Bogolubskaya, Workshop of Kremlin armoury, photo by shakko, public domain via Wikimedia Commons

43 The term *hyperdulia* was coined at the Second Council of Nicaea

In 787, the Second Council of Nicaea was convened to address the use of icons in Christian worship. During these proceedings, a new term describing our relationship to Mary entered the Christian vocabulary. Whereas *latria* in Greek means "worship" and is reserved for the three Divine Persons only, we are to have *dulia*, or "reverence," for all other holy people—saints and angels. Yet when it comes to Our Lady, the term *hyperdulia*, meaning "deep-" or "super-veneration," was canonized as the most proper term for our loving honor of Mary.

(*below*) Second Council of Nicaea, 787. After a 9th Century miniature. Illustration for Weltgeschichte Fur Das Volk by Otto von Corvin and Wilhelm Held (Verlag und Druck von Otto Spamer, 1880). Digitally cleaned image. © Look and Learn / Bridgeman Images

(*above*) Cherry tree orchard, photo by Serguei Levykin/Shutterstock

There is a legend of a cherry tree venerating Our Lady

44

In the seventh-century Pseudo-Gospel of Matthew, a story is told which caught peoples' imaginations for several generations. As Mary and Joseph were traveling to Bethlehem for the census, Mary stopped to rest under a date tree, which bowed down to offer the mother of its Creator shade and sustenance. In sixteenth-century England, this story became the basis of the Cherry Tree Carol. Here, Joseph is still confused about Mary's mysterious pregnancy, and so the cherry tree bends down to provide Mary with the fruit Joseph is too stubborn to get: "O then bespoke Joseph / With words so unkind, / 'Let him pluck thee a cherry / That brought thee with child.' / Then bow'd down the highest tree / Unto our Lady's hand."

45 Some of the most prominent Marian hymns are attributed to a crippled monk

Two standard Marian hymns were composed by an eleventh-century monk who, suffering from cerebral palsy and spinal bifida since childhood, could hardly speak but was blessed with the gift of music. The *Salve Regina* and the *Alma Redemptoris Mater* (as well as the *Veni, Sancte Spiritus*), are all attributed to St. Hermann the Cripple (d. 1054).

Too burdensome to care for, his parents gave him over to the Benedictine monks in Reichenau where chanting captured his soul. His *Salve Regina* became so popular that the Carmelites began to sing it instead of proclaiming John's Prologue after Mass. St. Pius V later mandated that it be sung after Vespers between Trinity Sunday and the First Sunday of Advent.

(*below*) Veringenstadt Hermanus Contractus, photo by Th. Fink Veringen, public domain via Wikimedia Commons

A mosaic in Rome depicts the unique scene of Jesus hugging his mother

The apse mosaic in the sanctuary of Santa Maria in Trastevere is unique in that it is possibly the only depiction of Christ seated with his arm lovingly draped around Mother Mary's shoulder. In her hand is a scroll with a most beautifully fitting verse from the Song of Songs: "O that his left hand were under my head, and that his right hand embraced me!" (Sg 2:6).

Christ holds a line recorded in Jacob of Voragine's *Golden Legend* (c. 1260) which he speaks to Mary upon her assumption into heaven: "Come, my chosen one, and I shall put you on my throne."

(*below*) Corontation of the Virgin from main Apse of Santa Maria in Trastevere church from 13th-century by Pietro Cavallini, photo by Renata Sedmakova/Shutterstock

(*above*) Digitalis purpurea (Foxglove) flowers, photo by NadyaRa/Shutterstock

47 Many different kinds of flowers take their name from Mary

In Scripture, we read of Mary being like a flower: "I am a rose of Sharon, a lily of the valleys" (Sg 2:1). Likewise, Konrad of Würzburg (d. 1287) wrote, "You are a living paradise of gloriously colored flowers," and Dante (d. 1321) called her "the Rose in which the Word became incarnate." Medieval monasteries cared for their Marian gardens with great skill

and many flowers came to be named after the Creator's own mother: Marigolds, Lady's Mantle (alchemilla), Our Lady's Gloves (foxgloves), Mary's Bedstraw (ragwort), and Madonna Lilies. By the twelfth century, numerous Rose Legends abounded, uniting various types of roses with moments in Mary's life.

England has a rich history of venerating the Blessed Virgin

England has long been known as the land of "Our Lady's Dowry," a title appearing as early as the middle of the eleventh century, due to the English defense and love of Mary. In 1061, Our Lady of Walsingham became a popular pilgrimage site when visions directed local citizens to construct a replica of Mary's house from where she was assumed. Geoffery Chaucer's (d. 1400) "Prioress Tale" is full of stories of Our Lady's protecting her children against the forces of evil, and Shakespeare (d. 1616) acknowledged the power of the Rosary: "When holy and devout religious men / Are at their beads, 'tis hard to draw them thence, / So sweet is zealous contemplation" (*Richard III*, Act 3, Scene 7).

(*below*) Portrait of Shakespeare - Cobbe portrait, public domain via Wikimedia Commons

49 Aristotle's teachings provided understanding on the practice Marian veneration

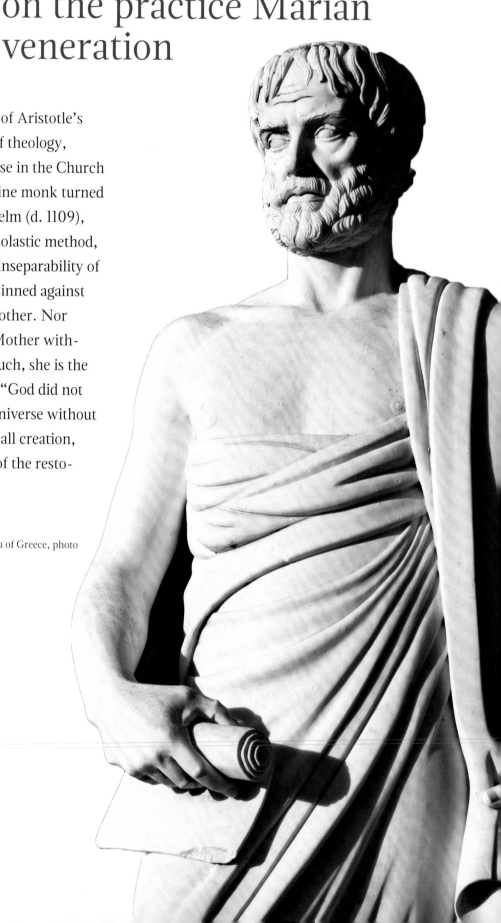

With the rediscovery of Aristotle's works, new ways of theology, preaching, and praying arose in the Church around 1100. The Benedictine monk turned bishop of Canterbury, Anselm (d. 1109), is the forerunner of the scholastic method, and his writings stress the inseparability of Jesus and Mary: "When I sinned against the Son, I distressed the Mother. Nor could I have offended the Mother without injuring the Son." As such, she is the Mother of life made anew: "God did not want to restore the fallen universe without Mary: God is the Father of all creation, while Mary is the Mother of the restoration of all creation."

(*right*) Aristotle statue located at Stageira of Greece, photo by Panos Karas/Shutterstock

(*above*) Apparition of The Virgin to St Bernard, 1486, Filippino Lippi (1457–1504), oil on panel, public domain via Wikimedia Commons

St. Bernard of Clairvaux was one of Mary's greatest champions

Known today as the *Doctor Mellifluus*, the "honey-dripping doctor," for his sweet preaching, Bernard of Clairvaux (d. 1153) was also a great monastic reformer, a holy abbot, and preacher of the Second Crusade. But he preferred to call himself *Beatae Mariae capellanus*, "Blessed Mary's little chaplain." In Dante's *Paradiso*, Mary calls Bernard her *fedel Bernardo*, her "faithful Bernard" (XXXI.102). His homilies are astounding examples of Marian devotion, and the closing words of the *Salve Regina*, "O clement, O loving, O sweet Virgin Mary," are attributed to him. Bernard ensured that every Cistercian abbey be dedicated to Our Lady of the Assumption.

51 One of Mary's many titles is Mediatrix of all Grace

Although Mary had been invoked as Mediatrix since the sixth century, Paul the Deacon (d. 799) emerges as the first in the West to reflect theologically on what Mary as the *Mediatrix of All Grace* really meant, setting off a new Marian emphasis in the Church. St. Anselm defended this title as taking nothing away from Christ's uniquely divine mediation, and after the widespread influence of Bernard of Clairvaux, Mary's dispensing the grace that comes only from her Son became a theological standard. In 1894, Pope Leo XIII even declared, "The recourse we have to Mary in prayer follows upon the office she continuously fills by the side of the throne of God as Mediatrix of Divine grace" (*On the Rosary*), and Vatican II's *Lumen Gentium* calls her "Advocate, Auxiliatrix, Adjutrix, and Mediatrix" (§62).

(*below*) Monastery of St Bernard de Clairvaux, photo by RossbetReynet, public domain via Wikimedia Commons

(*above*) Praying the rosary, photo by StockPhotosArt/Shutterstock

An ancient prayer known as the Servite Rosary focuses on the Seven Sorrows of Mary

52

Seven cloth merchants from Tuscany banded together in 1233 to found the Servite Order, or the Order of the Servants of Mary. This early group of priests also took on an order of brothers as well as a women's order. The unifying devotion of all Servites is Our Lady of Sorrows, depicting their prayer life of that moment of trust under the cross of Christ. The Chaplet of Seven Sorrows, also known as the Servite Rosary, is thus a meditation on the sacred wounds of Jesus. This special rosary is also referred to as the Seven Swords Rosary, invoking the prophecy of Simeon found in the Gospel of Luke (2:34–35).

53 St. Simon Stock spread the devotion of wearing the Brown Scapular

After the monks of Mount Carmel left Jerusalem for Europe, the Englishman St. Simon Stock (d. 1265) was elected prior general and fostered a devotion to the Carmelite scapular (from the Latin for "shoulder"), a piece of cloth worn by monks over their habit. Tradition states that the Blessed Virgin appeared to him and gave him the Brown Scapular. For those lay people who wanted to unite their lives and prayers to the local Carmel, the Brown Scapular became a way of tangibly associating their daily activities with monastic piety. The prayer of lay investiture begins, "Receive this Scapular, a sign of your special relationship with Mary, the Mother of Jesus, whom you pledge to imitate. May it be a reminder to you of your dignity as a Christian, in serving others and imitating Mary."

(*left*) Mary's altar (left side altar) at the parish church Our Lady in Zedlitzdorf, photo by Johann Jaritz, public domain via Wikimedia Commons

Dominicans hang rosaries from their hip to emulate medieval soldiers who wore swords

Mary became known as Our Lady of the Rosary after appearing to the founder of the Dominicans, St. Dominic, in 1208 in the Church of Prouille, France. Here she presented him with a rosary and taught him how to pray it as the equivalent of his medieval sword, an even mightier weapon against heresy and division. To this day, Dominicans, friars and sisters alike, wear their rosaries where a medieval soldier would have worn his sword.

(*below*) Dominican monks, detail of the monastic habit, photo by Pigama/Shutterstock

55

A rosary has 150 Hail Mary beads because it was originally meant to replace the chanting of the 150 Psalms

The Rosary was originally called the Psalter of the Blessed Virgin Mary because the 150 Hail Mary beads were meant to replace the 150 psalms, which were too difficult for the laity to memorize. Various Popes such as Pius XII and Paul VI have called the Rosary the "epitome of the whole Gospel" of Jesus Christ (CCC §971), as it captures the key scenes of Christ's saving work through the eyes of the person who loved him most on earth, his Blessed Mother. While the earliest concept of praying the Rosary was actually with small stones, the faithful eventually began to tie knots into pieces of rope and string, until St. Dominic's vision of Mary led to the style of rosary we think of today.

56

The Joyful Mysteries can be prayed for specific virtues

The earliest moments of Jesus's earthly life are captured in the fittingly-named Joyful Mysteries. These are usually prayed on Mondays and Saturdays, with the fruit being a more intimate awareness of the Son of God's becoming human through Mary's "yes," and her maternal protection of this divinely fragile life. Each of these scriptural mysteries can be prayed to obtain a particular virtue:

- The Annunciation for Humility (Lk 1:26–38)
- The Visitation for Love of Neighbor (Lk 1:39–56)
- The Nativity for Love of Poverty (Mt 1:18–25)
- The Presentation in the Temple for Obedience (Lk 2:22–39)
- The Finding in the Temple for Joy (Lk 2:41–51)

(*opposite*) The Presentation in the Temple by Master of the Prado Adoration of the Magi, between 1470 and 1480, oil on panel, National Gallery of Art, public domain via Wikimedia Commons

(*above*) Mosaic depiction of Christ's body being in the arms of the Virgin Mary, photo by Kyna Studio/Shutterstock

57 The Sorrowful Mysteries can be prayed for specific aids in overcoming sin

On Tuesdays and Fridays, the faithful are encouraged to pray the Sorrowful Mysteries. Here, the emphasis is on the love of Christ for us sinners as expressed in his passion and death on the cross. Each of these scriptural mysteries can be prayed for specific aids in overcoming sin:

- The Agony in the Garden for True Contrition (Mt 26:36–56)
- The Scourging at the Pillar for Mortification (Mt 27:26)
- The Crowning with Thorns for Courage to Love our Enemies (Mt 27:27–31)
- The Carrying of the Cross for Patience Amidst Trial (Mt 27:32)
- The Crucifixion and Death for the Gift of Perseverance (Mt 27:33–56)

The Glorious Mysteries are prayed for a stronger devotion to the Mother of God

The events that changed humanity forever are captured in the Glorious Mysteries, traditionally prayed on Sunday and Wednesday. Christ is raised on the third day and then labors to bring the rest of his Mystical Body into heaven, beginning with his sinless mother and thus crowning her Queen of Heaven and of Earth. These five mysteries can be prayed to obtain the theological virtues, eternal life, and a stronger devotion to the Mother of God:

- The Resurrection for the Gift of Faith (Jn 20:1–29)
- The Ascension for the Gift of Hope (Lk 24:36–53)
- The Descent of the Holy Spirit for Charity (Acts 2:1–41)
- The Assumption for Eternal Happiness (Ps 132:8; 1 Cor 15:23)
- The Coronation of Mary for True Devotion to Mary (Rv 12:1)

(*below*) Alsace, Bas-Rhin, Église Saint-Martin de Wilwisheim, © Ralph Hammann - Wikimedia Commons

Pope Pius V formulized the method of praying the Rosary while meditating on the mysteries

59

A papal bull in 1569 (*Consueuerunt Romani Pontifices*) by Pope Pius V, a Dominican, set the Rosary into the configuration of three sets of mysteries—the Joyful, the Sorrowful, and the Glorious—to meditate on. This fairly new method of prayer, Pius V wrote, "which is called the Rosary, or Psalter of the Blessed Virgin Mary, in which the same most Blessed Virgin is venerated by the angelic greeting repeated one hundred and fifty times, that is, according to the number of the Davidic Psalter, and by the Lord's Prayer with each decade. Interposed with these prayers are certain meditations showing forth the entire life of Our Lord Jesus Christ, thus completing the method of prayer devised by the Fathers of the Holy Roman Church."

Pope John Paul II introduced the Luminous Mysteries in 2002

60

On the twenty-fifth anniversary of his pontificate (October 16, 2002), John Paul II promulgated an apostolic letter to introduce five new mysteries, which he dubbed the Luminous. Filling out key moments of Christ's saving acts, these Thursday mysteries are to be prayed as the "revelation of the Kingdom now present in the very person of Jesus" (*Rosarium Virginis Mariae* §21). Like the Joyful, Sorrowful, and Glorious, these mysteries can be prayed for specific intentions:

- Jesus's Baptism for our own baptismal vocation to holiness (Mt 3:13–16)
- The Wedding Feast at Cana for Mary's intercession in all things (Jn 2:1–11)
- Jesus's Proclamation of the Kingdom for personal conversion (Mk 1:14–15)
- The Transfiguration for all healing (Mt 17:1–8)
- The Institution of the Eucharist for our love of the sacrament (Mt 26)

(*opposite*) Madonna of the Rosary, circa 1607 Caravaggio (1571–1610), Kunsthistorisches Museum, public domain via Wikimedia Commons

61 St. Thomas Aquinas saw Mary as a vital channel of God's grace

One of the greatest Catholic minds is the Angelic Doctor, the patron of Catholic education, St. Thomas Aquinas (d. 1274). Raised on the principles of Scholasticism, Thomas stressed Mary as the one human so close to Jesus she could naturally communicate his own saving presence. Thomas's Mariology thus stressed her divine motherhood as the way grace is made accessible to all of Christ's disciples: "The Blessed Virgin Mary obtained such a fullness of grace, so that she contained within herself the One who is full of every grace, and giving birth to him, she in some way made grace reach everyone" (*Summa Theologiae* III.27, a.5).

(*right*)Saint Thomas Aquinas by Abraham Van Diepenbeek (1596-1675). Museum of fine arts in Valenciennes. Photo by Adam Jan Figel/Shutterstock

St. Thomas Aquinas did not subscribe to the doctrine of the Immaculate Conception

62

As reliable a guide as Thomas Aquinas is in all matters philosophical and theological, he did not see how the Blessed Mother could be conceived without sin, arguing that this would exempt her from being saved by Christ at least at some point in her life. In this way, Thomas got the Immaculate Conception wrong, but for all the right reasons, saying, "If the soul of the Blessed Virgin had never incurred the stain of original sin, this would be derogatory to the dignity of Christ, by reason of His being the universal Savior of all . . . But the Blessed Virgin did indeed contract original sin, but was cleansed therefrom before her birth from the womb" (*Summa Theologiae* III.27, a.2).

(*below*) La Inmaculada Concepción, circa 1712, Antonio Palomino (1655–1726), Museo del Prado, public domain via Wikimedia Commons

63 John Duns Scotus helped to theologically explain the doctrine of the Immaculate Conception

The Scotsman, Oxonian, and Franciscan friar John Duns Scotus (d. 1308) is known today as "the Subtle Doctor" because of his ability to make fine distinctions lost on others. He is also known as "the Marian Doctor" because of his early promotion of the Immaculate Conception, rightly arguing that Mary's sinlessness was most fitting for God's own mother, and that she was saved proleptically (that is, in advance or in anticipation of) from the sacrifice of her Son on the cross. Teaching at the University of Paris, he so brilliantly defended the doctrine of the Immaculate Conception that the university made this the official position of its faculty of theology in 1307.

(*below*) John Duns, aka Duns Scotus, c. 1266-1308. Important philosopher-theologian of the High Middle Ages. From Enciclopedia Ilustrada Segui, published c. 1900, Bridgeman Images

Dante depicts Mary as helping souls reach heaven in his *Divine Comedy*

64

Dante Alighieri (d. 1321), one of the greatest poets to ever live, ends his *Divine Comedy* with the beatific vision and Mary's central role in aiding souls to heavenly bliss. As the one who houses all our desires (*albergo del nostro disiro*), she is the fulfillment of all intimacy, regaining what Eve lost: "The wound that Mary healed with balm so sweet" (*Paradiso* XXXII.4). She is the Great

Lady of Heaven whose presence increases its holiness: "So shall I wheel, Lady of Heaven, till / you follow your great Son to the highest sphere / and, by your presence, make it holier still." She is the Queen whose "encircling melody of flame / revealed itself; and all the other lamps / within that Garden rang out Mary's name" (XXIII.106-111).

65 One of the most famous Marian icons has two scars on her right cheek

The most famous of all the Marian images in the Hodegetria style is Our Lady of Częstochowa in northern Poland. The earliest legend surrounding this icon is that St. Luke drew it while visiting Mary, and St. Helena brought it back from Jerusalem in 326. A more historically reliable account dates the image back to the ninth century, and has it first appearing in Poland by the late 1300s. Most distinctive about this image are the two scars on Mary's right cheek caused by a Hussite invasion in 1430. An eyewitness reports how the Hussites' horses refused to pull the wagons now filled with the monastery's looted riches, and in frustration, one of the robbers scarred Mary's face with his dagger.

(*above*) Our Lady of Częstochowa, photo by Aw58, public domain via Wikimedia Commons

66 The Sistine Chapel is dedicated to the Immaculate Conception

The Council of Basel (1431–1439) affirmed the doctrine of the Immaculate Conception as a most "pious opinion" for the Christian faithful to hold. This devotion thereafter became more and more widespread, and one of the next popes, Pope Sixtus IV (1471–1484), not only robustly promoted the Immaculate Conception universally, he even dedicated the chapel named after him, the Sistine Chapel, to this developing doctrine.

(*above*) Sistine Chapel, photo by Burkhard Mücke, public domain via Wikimedia Commons

(*above*) Our Lady of Perpetual Help, Knokke-Heist, Belgium, Godong / Bridgeman Images

67 Our Lady of Perpetual Help comforts the Christ Child after he dreams of his Passion

In the Redemptorist Church of St. Alphonsus in Rome hangs a famous icon of Our Lady of Perpetual Help. This is a depiction of Mary's comforting the Christ child after he wakes from a dream about his passion (noted by the angels carrying the cross and the lance), running to her so fast he almost loses a sandal. This icon is traced back to the Keras Kardiotissas Monastery in Crete but has been in Rome since 1499. The Redemptorists are the only religious order who have been mandated by the pope, Pius IX in 1867, to enshrine and protect a Marian image.

Martin Luther had a strong devotion to Mary

While so much of what was intended by Christ for his Church was stripped away by the Protestant Reformers, his Mother Mary survived, at least for a while. Devotion to Our Lady obviously began to wane after 1517 and was soon outright rejected as "Mariolotry." But even someone like Martin Luther showed an early love of the Blessed Mother and encouraged his flock to dwell on her as well: "She became the Mother of God, in which work so many and such great good things are bestowed on her as pass man's understanding. . . . It needs to be pondered in the heart what it means to be the Mother of God" (*Luther's Works* 21.326).

(*above*) Martin Luther's dispute with the Swiss reformer Ulrich Zwingli, Christian Karl August Noack,1867, public domain via Wikimedia Commons

69 Marian art flourished during the Counter-Reformation

The years following the Protestant break anchored Mary's place in material culture. Eventually rejected by Lutherans and Calvinists, Mary and the scriptural scenes of her life were all the more celebrated in art, hymnody, and liturgical devotions. From the Marian frescoes commissioned for the papal palace on Rome's Quirinal Hill in 1573 to Caravaggio's Dormition of Mary in 1605 to Murillo's celebrated Immaculate Conception in the Escorial (1665), the Counter-Reformation cemented those basic Christian truths which were being chipped away, only expanding Marian aesthetics throughout Europe and the New World.

(*below*) The Immaculate Conception of Los Venerables, or of `Soult', c.1678 (oil on canvas), Murillo, Bartolome Esteban (1618-82) / Spanish, Bridgeman Images

(*above*) Mary among a Multitude of Animals, Albrecht Dürer, c. 1503, public domain via Wikimedia Commons

Butterflies and ladybugs have connections to Mary

70

Throughout the ages, certain Marian devotions became associated with some of God's creatures. For instance, the Spanish word for butterfly, *mariposa*, comes from the words, "Mary, descend and settle," supposedly named so after the praying hands of Our Lady. There is also an old Romanian legend that butterflies come from Mary's sorrowful tears. Finally, the ladybug ("Mary's Beetle" in German) is so named because its seven black dots represent Mary's seven sorrows as well as her seven joys.

71 St. Ignatius of Loyola taught that Jesus would've first appeared to his mother after his resurrection

Upon surrendering to Christ, Ignatius of Loyola first made a pilgrimage to the Shrine of Our Lady of Aranzau where he spent the night in vigil and offered his sword to the famed Black Madonna. Years later, as the Society of Jesus was forming, Ignatius chose the feast of the Assumption in 1534 for the first companions to profess their vows. In his *Spiritual Exercises*, Ignatius assumes anyone who understands the love of Jesus and Mary would know that the Resurrected Christ would go first to his mother, "and although this is not said in Scripture, we understand it when 'he appeared to many others,' because Scripture supposes that we have understanding, as it is written: 'Are you also without understanding?'"

(*above*) The risen Christ appears to the Virgin Mary, line engraving, R. Strange, 1773, public domain via WIkimedia Commons

Our Lady of Guadalupe appeared where a pagan temple to a mother goddess once stood

Between December 9–12, 1531, Mary appeared to a peasant named Juan Diego on the Tepeyac Hill outside Mexico City. The Blessed Mother desired that a place of pilgrimage be constructed here, and to authenticate this vision to the local bishop, Juan gathered flowers in his cloak, or *tilma*. The superhumanly indescribable imprint of Our Lady left in Juan's *tilma* convinced Bishop Juan de Zumárraga to build the chapel where a pagan temple to the Aztec mother of all the gods, Tonantzin, once stood. In 1921, anti-Catholic fanatics used dynamite to blow up the image but, although the marble and glass all around it were demolished, the *tilma* remained perfectly unscathed. Juan Diego was canonized on July 31, 2002.

(*below*) Guadalupe Basilica postcard. University of Dayton Libraries, 1923, public domain via Wikimedia Commons.

(*above*) The Battle of Lepanto, fresco, 1572-73, Giorgio Vasari, public domain via Wikimedia Commons

73 The Christian victory at the Battle of Lepanto was attributed to Mary's intercession

One of the great propulsions in the history of Marian devotion was the Battle of Lepanto on October 7, 1571, the largest naval battle up to that time. After the losses of the Reformation, this victory of the Catholic fleets over the Muslim marauders provided a renewed sense of identity and was wholly attributed to the Blessed Mother's intercession. Pope St. Pius V called upon all of Europe to pray the Rosary for victory. Likewise, a primary leader among the admirals of the Holy League was Juan of Austria, better known as Don Juan, led his men in a Rosary before the battle commenced and continued to call on Our Lady during that day-long conflict which surely kept Islam from spreading into Western Europe. A little-known fact is that among the wounded was Miguel de Cervantes, author of *Don Quixote*.

The Sacred Heart Devotion may have never come about without Mary's intercession

The lanced side of Jesus (Jn 19:34) and the pierced heart of Mary (Lk 2:34) have been long-standing objects of devotion, but their modern forms came about only after a series of visions by a young French nun. Bedridden for years with rheumatic fever, the teenaged Margaret Mary Alacoque vowed to the Blessed Mother that she would enter religious life if granted full health. Miraculously and immediately healed, Margaret Mary entered the Visitation Sisters at Paray-le-Monial in Burgundy where she enjoyed visions of the Lord's Sacred Heart, confirmed and given popular expression by her confessor and spiritual director, Claude Colombiere, SJ. Sister Margaret Mary died in 1690 and was canonized in 1920. Her feast is October 16.

(*below*) The basilica du Sacre Coeur in Paray-le-Monial, France, photo by DyziO/ Shutterstock

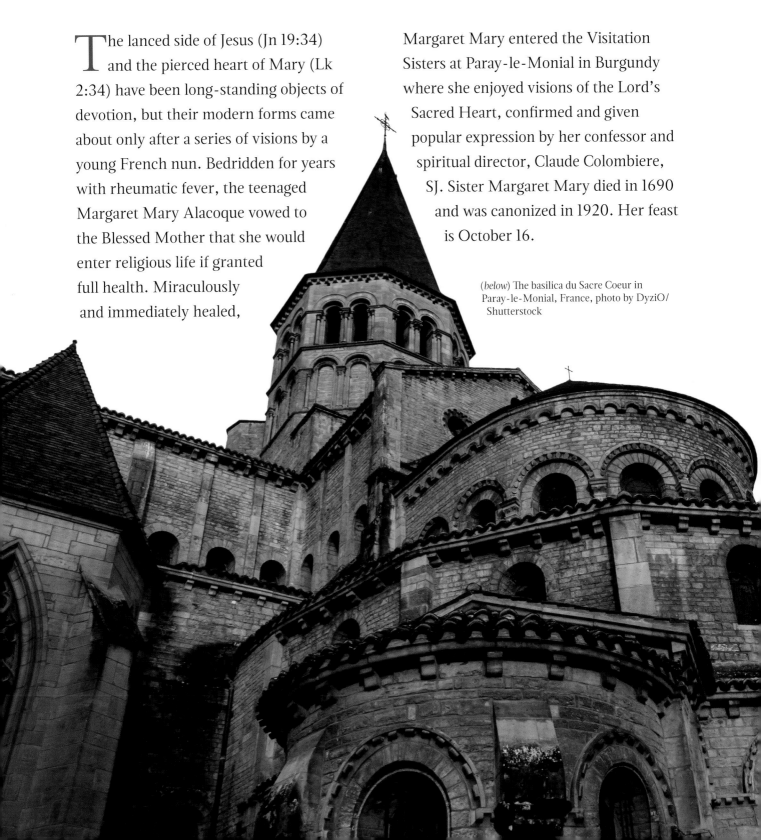

75

St. Louis de Montfort is one of the Church's greatest champions of the Blessed Mother

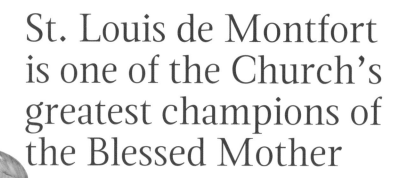

St. Louis-Marie Grignion de Montfort (d. 1716) was a diocesan priest blessed with a singular love of Mary. His personal motto—*Totus Tuus*—was adopted by St. John Paul II for the same reason, giving Mary all he was. After being educated by the Jesuits and Sulpicians, de Montfort spent most of his priesthood giving parish missions in France, emphasizing the need for daily communion, frequent confession, and zealous imitation of Mary's virtues. Louis de Montfort founded the Missionaries of the Company of Mary, and his *True Devotion to the Blessed Virgin Mary* has guided millions in their own consecration to the Blessed Mother.

(*left*) Statue de Saint Louis (Saint-Louis) Marie Grignion de Montfort (1673-1716) conservee a la basilique saint Pierre de Rome (Vatican) ©Frassinetti/AGF/Leemage/Bridgeman Images

(*above*) Portrait of Andrew Jackson, the seventh president of the United States, Ralph Eleaser Whiteside Earl (1785/88–1838), public domain via Wikimedia Commons

Andrew Jackson credited Our Lady of Prompt Succor for a U.S. military victory

76

In 1809, the New Orleans Ursulines were desperate for assistance. They sought "quick help" from Pope Pius VII who, although currently held captive by Napoleon, inexplicably received and granted more sisters. To honor this, a statue of Our Lady of Prompt Succor was commissioned. As the fire of 1812 threatened New Orleans, the nuns set this statue in their convent window, praying, "Our Lady of Prompt Succor, hasten to help us or we are lost." The winds quickly changed direction. Then, in the 1815 Battle of New Orleans, General Andrew Jackson defeated a significantly larger British battalion, swearing, "The divine providence of God through the intercession of Our Lady of Prompt Succor has shielded us and granted this stupendous miracle." After the battle, Jackson thanked the Ursuline sisters for their prayers and visited them each time he returned to the city.

(*above*) Miraculous medal by piosi/Shutterstock

77 Mary gave the model for the Miraculous Medal to St. Catherine Labouré

Along with the scapular, another tangible sacramental of Mary's maternal closeness is the Miraculous Medal, given to St. Catherine Labouré (d. 1876), a sister of the Daughters of St. Vincent de Paul in Paris. On November 27, 1830, Mary appeared to Catherine encircled in an oval medallion and perched on the globe, with light cascading from her hands, and below this vision were the words, "O Mary, conceived without sin, pray for us who have recourse to thee." A French goldsmith was immediately employed to imprint this appearance and make the Miraculous Medal available to the faithful. St. Catherine is laid to rest in the Chapel of Our Lady of the Miraculous Medal in Paris.

The American novelist Nathanial Hawthorne was enamored with Mary

Nathaniel Hawthorne (d. 1864) once implanted his jealousy of the Catholic love of Mary into a tender scene in one of his novels, *Blithedale Romance*: "I have always envied the Catholics that sweet, sacred, Virgin Mother who stands between them and the Deity, intercepting somewhat his awful splendor, but permitting his love to stream on the worshiper more intelligibly to human comprehension through the medium of a woman's tenderness." This work was written as Hawthorne had become disillusioned with Unitarianism, and perhaps expressively enough so that his youngest daughter converted to Catholicism and eventually founded the Dominican Sisters of Hawthorne on the Feast of the Immaculate Conception, December 8, 1900.

(*right*) Portrait of Nathaniel Hawthorne from The whole history of grandfather's chair; or, True stories from New England history, 1620-1803, 1896, public domain via Wikimedia Commons

79

The *Pietà* is the only piece Michelangelo ever signed

Arguably the most famous sculpture in the world, the *Pietà* (Italian for "duty" or "compassion") is housed near the entrance of St. Peter's Basilica in the Vatican. It presently sits behind protective glass after a madman attacked it in 1972, damaging it considerably with a geologist's hammer. One is struck by both how young Mary looks, despite this scene taking place at the end of Jesus's life, and how large she is in proportion to her deceased Son, emphasizing visually and spiritually how life is greater than death. In these two ways, Michelangelo set out to highlight Mary's purity and perseverance. The *Pietà* is the only piece the famous Italian artist ever signed.

(*below*) Pietà (Michelangelo), author's signature "MICHEL ANGELUS BONAROTUS FLORENT FACIBAT", photo by Nux, public domain via Wikimedia Commons

(*above*) Lourdes, France: pilgrims praying in front of the grotto and portrait of Bernadette Soubirous, wood engraving, Iconographic Collections, public domain via Wikimedia Commons

Over six million pilgrims visit Lourdes annually

80

On February 11, 1858, Mary appeared to Bernadette Soubirous in the famous apparition of Lourdes, visions that were approved by Pius IX as soon as 1862. Construction for a basilica began fifteen years later near the cave where Our Lady first appeared and where the miraculous healing waters flow from a spring. Lourdes became a place of universal pilgrimage and healing that today welcomes over six million pilgrims annually. Perhaps the most compelling part of the story of Lourdes is how Mary confirmed her immaculate conception, which had just been promulgated by Pius IX. Bernadette tells us, "I went every day for a fortnight, and each day I asked her who she was. This petition always made her smile. . . . With her arms down, she raised her eyes to heaven and then, folding her hands over her breast she said, 'I am the Immaculate Conception.'"

(*above*) Interior of Saint-Simon and Saint-Jude church in Pontmain, France, photo public domain via Wikimedia Commons

81 The visionaries at Pontmain said that Mary sang with them

Shortly after Lourdes, Pius IX approved the apparitions of Our Lady of Pontmain in France. On January 17, 1871, Mary appeared to several small children in the northwest of France who were losing hope under the strains of the Franco-Prussian war. "But pray, my children. God will hear you in time. My Son allows himself to be touched." That night, for no apparent reason, the Prussian forces turned back from Pontmain in Brittany, signaling an apparent end to the war (an armistice was reached in less than a week's time). Whenever Mary appeared, the children would intone a local tune, *Mère de l'espérance* ("Mother of Hope") and Our Lady of Hope would smile and sing along!

A vision of Mary consoled the Irish in the aftermath of the great potato famine

On a stormy evening in 1879, the local parish housekeeper and a young girl were running home trying to beat the late summer rains of County Mayo, Ireland. Taking shelter at the local church, they looked up and witnessed a brilliantly white Mary flanked by a bowing St. Joseph and the apostle John, vested and gesturing as a bishop. At the vision's center rested Christ the Lamb on the altar of sacrifice. The visionaries were soon joined by many townspeople. This vision bolstered the locals' faith and provided much-needed consolation following the great potato famine and years of paltry crops. To this day, millions of pilgrims visit the church annually, a recognized site of healing and miracles.

(*left*) Statue of Our Lady in the Apparition Chapel, Knock Shrine, photo by Michael McLaughlin Photography, public domain via Wikimedia Commons

83 The Little Flower had a strong devotion to the Blessed Mother

Before Thérèse of Lisieux (d. 1897) began her classic *The Story of a Soul*, she admitted, "Before I took pen in hand, I knelt down before the statue of the Blessed Virgin. . . . I begged her to guide my hand and not allow me to write a single line that might displease her" (*Autobiography*, 15). Having lost her mother early on, the Little Flower's devotion to Mary consoled her greatly: "I was chosen for this because I was left without my mother on earth. . . . In consecrating myself to the Virgin Mary, I asked her to watch over me, . . . and I saw her once again looking down and smiling on her petite fleur" (*Autobiography* 60).

(*above*) Altar in Chapel of Therese of Lisieux, Romanus Jacobs, 1923, public domain via Wikimedia Commons

84 Mary played a role in John Henry Newman's conversion

Among the Church's newest saints is the Anglican Divine turned Catholic cardinal John Henry Newman (d. 1890). A prodigious theologian and writer, Newman's growth in intellectual awareness was intertwined with his heart's development toward Mary, whom he called "the bulwark of our Lord's divinity. And it is that which heretics have ever opposed, for it is the great witness that the doctrine of God being man is true. . . . The truth is, the doctrine of our Lady keeps us from a dreaming, unreal way. If no mother, no history" (Sermon on October 14, 1849). Writing to his former mentor and colleague Edward Pusey in 1865, Newman challenged him to a Marian Christianity in which "devotion to her is a sine-qua-non of salvation."

Engraved portrait of John Henry Cardinal Newman, published in 1882,
The Century Magazine, public domain via Wikimedia Commons

85 The apparitions at Fatima greatly influenced the Church and the world

On May 13, 1917, Mary appeared to three children outside Fatima, Portugal, asking they return at the same time on the thirteenth of the next five months. During these visits, Our Lady showed them the peace that passes through her heart alone and asked them to make reparation for the world's sinfulness. Years later, in visions given to Lucia, Mary showed her the Immaculate Heart as we tend to envision it today: "Look, my daughter, at my Heart, surrounded with thorns with which ungrateful men pierce at every moment by their blasphemies and ingratitude." From these encounters arose the First Saturday Devotion, the Consecration of Russia, the Blue Army, and the Secrets of Fatima. Additionally, Fatima touched the historic life of Pope St. John Paul II, who was nearly killed by an assassin's bullet on May 13, 1981, sixty-four years after Mary's first appearance at Fatima. For these reasons, Fatima had a profound influence on the Church and the world in the twentieth century and beyond.

(*right*) Our Lady of Fatima, photo by Ronnachit Klumchantuek/Shutterstock

G. K. Chesterton used statues of Mary holding baby Jesus to make a deeper theological point

In his typical brilliant fashion, the English wit and writer G. K. Chesterton (d. 1936) defended the use of Marian statues by showing how they reflect the powerful reality of the relationship a mother shares with her child, and how important she is for the child's well-being. Speaking of statues that depict the Christ Child, Chesterton quipped, "You cannot suspend the new-born child in mid-air.... Similarly, you cannot suspend the idea of a newborn child in the void or think of him without thinking of his mother. You cannot visit the child without visiting the mother; you cannot in common human life approach the child except through the mother.... Those holy heads are too near together for the haloes not to mingle and cross" ("God in the Cave," *The Everlasting Man*).

(*below*) Portrait of Chesterton Sitting, c. 1914, public domain via Wikimedia Commons

(*above*) J. R. R. Tolkien and characters from Lord of the Rings. English School, (20th century) / English, © Look and Learn / Bridgeman Images

87 Mary played a key role in J. R. R. Tolkien's life and his writing of *Lord of the Rings*

J. R. R. Tolkien's *Lord of the Rings* was voted "the best book of the twentieth century." Reflecting on this masterpiece, Tolkien wrote to his priest friend Robert Murray, "I think I know exactly what you mean by the order of Grace; and of course by your references to Our Lady, upon which all my own small perception of beauty both in majesty and simplicity is founded. The *Lord of the Rings* is of course a fundamentally religious and Catholic work; unconsciously so at first, but consciously in the revision." What may remain "unconscious" to many contemporary readers is the climactic fact that the ring's final destruction took place on Ladyday, March 25, the day Mary's "yes" defeats all death.

Mary was a powerful influence in the life of saint and Holocaust martyr Maximilian Kolbe

Mother Mary visited little Raymund Kolbe when he was only twelve, and later as a Conventual Franciscan, Fr. Maximilian recalled, "She came to me holding two crowns, one white, the other red. She asked me if I was willing to accept either of these crowns. The white one meant that I should persevere in purity, and the red that I should become a martyr. I said that I would accept them both." St. Maximilian went on to found the *Militia Immaculata* which relied on Mary to fight social injustice and political tyranny in 1917. Years later, he went to his death in Auschwitz, asking to substitute himself in place of a man with a family.

(*right*) Maximilian Kolbe (colour litho), Fototeca Gilardi / Bridgeman Images

89

Mary plays a vital role in the Divine Mercy devotion

The most impactful devotion of the twentieth century is the Divine Mercy, stemming from the visions of a young nun of the Congregation of the Sisters of Our Lady of Mercy, Faustina Kowalska (d. 1938). She recorded her interactions with Jesus in her popular diary, titled *Divine Mercy in My Soul.*

Throughout these pages, the merciful Christ instructs St. Faustina (and all of us) to "Unite yourself in prayer with My Mother. Pray with all your heart in union with Mary" (Diary §32). Mary later tells St. Faustina, "I am not only the Queen of Heaven, but also the Mother of Mercy and your Mother" (Diary §330).

The Shrine of the Immaculate Conception is North America's largest Catholic Church

90

Taking its name from Mary's title of the Immaculate Conception, this pilgrimage site for Catholics rests in the nation's capital. It is the largest Catholic church in North America and stands as the tallest habitable building in Washington, DC. The basilica has over eighty chapels dedicated to Mary and has welcomed the last three popes. Its construction took nearly one hundred years.

(*below*) Basilica of the National Shrine of the Immaculate Conception, Washington, DC,

91

The Church holds four Marian dogmas

In 1854, the papal charism of infallibility was invoked once again to teach the world about Mary. In 1950, Pope Pius XII promulgated in *Munificentissimus Deus* the teaching that Mary has indeed been bodily assumed into heaven: "By an entirely unique privilege, completely overcame sin by her Immaculate Conception, and as a result she was not subject to the law of remaining in the corruption of the grave, and she did not have to wait until the end of time for the redemption of her body" (§5). The Marian dogmas of the Church are therefore (1) Our Lady's perpetual virginity, (2) her title as the Mother of God, (3) her immaculate conception, and (4) her bodily assumption into heaven.

The Mississippi River and the city of Los Angeles had names that were once tied to Our Lady

When the Jesuit explorer Jacques Marquette moved westward across New France, he wrote in his diary of 1673, "I placed our voyage under the protection of the Holy Virgin Immaculate, promising that if she granted us the favor of discovering the great river, I would give it the name of the Conception." Today, we call that river of the Immaculate Conception the Mississippi, but we do continue to honor other places with Mary's name: Asuncion, Paraguay, Mariefred in Sweden, the pilgrimage site of Mariazell in Austria, and most recently, Ave Maria in Florida. Yet how many remember that the full name of Los Angeles is officially Nuestra Senora la Reina de los Angeles, Our Lady Queen of the Angels?

(*below*) Our Lady Queen of Angels Catholic Church in Los Angeles - California, United States, photo by Leonid Andronov/Shutterstock

93

The concluding parts of the Second Vatican Council concerned Mary

Afraid that a separate document on Mary might appear too divisive, the fathers at Vatican II decided to treat Mary as a fitting conclusion to the Dogmatic Constitution on the Church *Lumen Gentium*. The final chapter is accordingly entitled "The Blessed Virgin Mary, Mother of God, in the Mystery of Christ and the Church" (§52-69) and teaches that Mary has been redeemed "in a more exalted fashion, by reason of the merits of her Son and united to him by a close and indissoluble tie," and so "far surpasses all creatures, both in heaven and on earth. But, being of the race of Adam, she is at the same time also united to all those who are to be saved."

(*below*) Second Vatican Council, Album / Oronoz / Mondadori Portfolio / Bridgeman Images

(*above*) Statue of the Blessed Virgin Mary holding a red rose while Saint James Church in Medjugorje

The Church has not yet ruled on the authenticity of the visions at Medjugorje

94

In the summer of 1981, Mother Mary is said to have appeared to a group of teens in the village town of Medjugorje in Bosnia and Herzegovina. Countless conversions have been reported from these messages, based on five Catholic mainstays (what the seers call "stones" or "weapons"): incessant prayer from the heart, regular fasting, praying with Scripture, daily Holy Communion, and at least monthly confession. Because these visions are relatively recent, the official position of the Church remains *non constat*, not approved, calling for ongoing studies. This did not prevent the Vatican from sponsoring its first pilgrimage to Medjugorje in the summer of 2019, drawing sixty thousand young people and seven hundred priests in celebration.

95 Mary gave a warning of the Rwandan genocide

Beginning in 1981, Our Lady of Kibeho in Rwanda appeared to three young girls at their school, warning of a bloody war to come. This devastation was confirmed with the outbreak of the great genocide, especially the slaughter of innocent Hutus that took place in 1995 at the Kibeho school itself. Today, the Shrine of Our Lady of Sorrows stands there as a sign to end to tribal hatred. In 2000, Mary appeared again as Our Lady of Assiut in Egypt, shining miraculously from the sky on many occasions. The Coptic Church has approved these apparitions, as well as those of Our Lady of Warraq in 2009, where Mary was seen appearing again as a bright light calling for peace.

96 Pope St. John Paul II credited Our Lady of Fatima with saving his life

Of all the modern popes, St. John Paul II's (d. 2005) reflections on Mary will prove most timeless. His encyclical *Mother of the Redeemer* is as illuminating as his "Theology of the Body" and his concept of the "feminine genius," teachings which will guide the Church for centuries. John Paul attributes the saving of his very life to Mary. On the feast of Our Lady of Fatima, May 13, 1981, a hired assassin came centimeters from killing this great pope in St. Peter's Square. John Paul later claimed, "One hand pulled the trigger, another guided the bullet," attributing his survival to the Blessed Mother's intercession on that otherwise fateful day.

(*opposite*) Pope John Paul II praying illustration, photo by Archiwiz/Shuttertock

97 The Church holds the name of Mary in strict reverence

Scripture tells us, "At the name of Jesus, every knee should bend" (Phil 2:10). By extension, the Church continues this teaching that "a bow of the head is made when the three Divine Persons are named together and at the names of Jesus, of the Blessed Virgin Mary, and of the Saint in whose honor Mass is being celebrated" (*General Instruction of the Roman Missal*

§275). Moreover, the *Catechism* officially instructs the faithful, "The second commandment forbids the abuse of God's name, i.e., every improper use of the names of God, Jesus Christ, but also of the Virgin Mary and all the saints" (CCC §2146).

(*below*) Chalice and ciborium on the altar during the traditional latin mass, photo by Thoom/Shutterstock

(*above*) Pope Benedict XVI, Vatican City, Vatican City State, 2012, Mondadori Portfolio/ Archivio Grzegorz Galazka/Grzegorz Galazka / Bridgeman Images

Pope Benedict XVI spoke lovingly of Mary and stressed her powerful intercessory role

98

As a leading biblical scholar, Pope Benedict XVI saw how, "as the word of God became flesh by the power of the Holy Spirit in the womb of the Virgin Mary, so sacred Scripture is born from the womb of the Church" (*Verbum Dei* §19). Yet, for Benedict, Mary is even amazingly greater than that: "Mary has such a big heart that all creation can enter it, as the votive offerings from all over the world demonstrate. Mary is near, she can listen, she can help, she is near to us all. God is near and Mary, as she is united to God, is very near and has a heart as big as God's" (Homily on August 15, 2012).

(*above*) Mary Untier of Knots, 1700 (oil on poplar), Schmittner (Schmidtner), Johann Georg Melchior (1625-1705) / German, Artothek / Bridgeman Images

99 The devotion of Mary, Undoer of Knots, points to her role of reversing the disobedient actions of Eve

While a Jesuit doctoral student in Germany, Pope Francis discovered the eighteenth-century painting by Georg Schmidtner titled Our Lady, Undoer of Knots, in the Bavarian Church of St. Peter am Perlach. Years later, as archbishop of Buenos Aires, he promoted this devotion by commissioning a copy of Mary, Undoer of Knots, for the San José del Talar Church in the Argentinian capital, and even had it engraved on a chalice which he presented to Pope Benedict XVI. The theology of this image states that Mary, having through her obedience untied the knot Eve bound through her disobedience, helps us sinners undo the knots of our lives caused by our own transgressions. A prayer accompanies the devotion that reads, in part, "Holy Mary, Mother of God and our Mother, to you who untie with a motherly heart the knots of our life."

The rich Marian spirit of the Church has flourished in the last several decades

100

On February 11, 2018, exactly 160 years after Mary's apparition at Lourdes, Pope Francis instituted a new obligatory Memorial Mass—Mary, Mother of the Church—to be celebrated on the Monday after Pentecost, the birth of the Church. Other new Pentecosts with Mary at the heart are also occurring everywhere in the Church today. Think, for example, of Mother Adela's founding of the *Servants of the Pierced Hearts of Jesus and Mary in Miami* in 1986, who had heard Jesus ask her, "Let me pierce your heart so others may have life," or the burgeoning *Sisters of Mary, Mother of the Eucharist*, founded in 1997 in Ann Arbor, Michigan, who live the Dominican charism in a uniquely Marian manner.

(*below*) Pentecost, Borgo San Lorenzo, photo by Sailko, public domain via Wikimedia Commons

(*above*) Vision of St. John on Patmos, by Anonymous artist, 16th century, oil on canvas, Mondadori Portfolio/Electa/Sergio Anelli / Bridgeman Images

101 The Church teaches that Mary is the "woman" from Revelation

As the story of eternal salvation comes to a close, an infinitely beautiful woman appears "clothed with the sun, with the moon under her feet, and on her head a crown of twelve stars" (Rv 12:1). About to give birth to her Savior Son, a malevolent dragon awaits below her, thus summarizing the entire Gospel drama.

Mary is thus how the Holy Spirit brings his Sacred Scripture to a victorious conclusion, depicted as watching her children make their way eternally homeward, interceding for our safe homecoming, and already overjoyed with the reunion of so many of her sons and daughters in Christ.

The Litany of Mary

Lord, have mercy on us.
Christ, have mercy on us.
Lord, have mercy on us.
Christ, hear us.
Christ, graciously hear us.
God the Father of Heaven,
Have mercy on us.
God the Son, Redeemer of the world,
Have mercy on us.
God the Holy Ghost,
Have mercy on us.
Holy Trinity, one God,
Have mercy on us.
Holy Mary, pray for us.
Holy Mother of God, pray for us.
Holy Virgin of virgins, pray for us.
Mother of Christ, pray for us.
Mother of divine grace, pray for us.
Mother most pure, pray for us.
Mother most chaste, pray for us.
Mother inviolate, pray for us.
Mother undefiled, pray for us.
Mother most amiable, pray for us.
Mother most admirable, pray for us.
Mother of good counsel, pray for us.
Mother of our Creator, pray for us.
Mother of our Savior, pray for us.
Virgin most prudent, pray for us.
Virgin most venerable, pray for us.
Virgin most renowned, pray for us.
Virgin most powerful, pray for us.
Virgin most merciful, pray for us.
Virgin most faithful, pray for us.
Mirror of justice, pray for us.
Seat of wisdom, pray for us.
Cause of our joy, pray for us.
Spiritual vessel, pray for us.
Vessel of honor, pray for us.
Singular vessel of devotion, pray for us.
Mystical rose, pray for us.
Tower of David, pray for us.

Tower of ivory, pray for us.
House of gold, pray for us.
Ark of the Covenant, pray for us.
Gate of Heaven, pray for us.
Morning star, pray for us.
Health of the sick, pray for us.
Refuge of sinners, pray for us.
Comforter of the afflicted, pray for us.
Help of Christians, pray for us.
Queen of angels, pray for us.
Queen of patriarchs, pray for us.
Queen of prophets, pray for us.
Queen of apostles, pray for us.
Queen of martyrs, pray for us.
Queen of confessors, pray for us.
Queen of virgins, pray for us.
Queen of all saints, pray for us.
Queen conceived without Original Sin, pray for us.
Queen assumed into heaven, pray for us.
Queen of the most holy Rosary, pray for us.
Queen of peace, pray for us.

Lamb of God, who takes away the sins of the world,
Spare us, O Lord.
Lamb of God, who takes away the sins of the world,
Graciously hear us, O Lord.
Lamb of God, who takes away the sins of the world,
Have mercy on us.

Pray for us, O Holy Mother of God,
That we may be made worthy of the promises of Christ.
Grant, we beseech Thee, O Lord God, that we Thy Servants may enjoy perpetual health of mind and body and by the glorious intercession of the Blessed Mary, ever Virgin, be delivered from present sorrow and enjoy eternal happiness. Through Christ Our Lord. Amen.

Approved by Pope Sixtus V in 1587

About the author

Fr. David Meconi, SJ. is a Jesuit priest and professor at Saint Louis University where he directs the Catholic Studies Centre. A specialist in the early Church, Fr. Meconi holds the Pontifical License in Patrology from the University of Innsbruck in Austria and the Doctorate of Ecclesiasicalt History from Oxford University. He is also the author of *101 Surprising Facts About Church History.*

Saint Benedict Press

Saint Benedict Press publishes books, Bibles, and multimedia that explore and defend the Catholic intellectual tradition. Our mission is to present the truths of the Catholic faith in an attractive and accessible manner.

Founded in 2006, our name pays homage to the guiding influence of the Rule of Saint Benedict and the Benedictine monks of Belmont Abbey, just a short distance from our headquarters in Charlotte, NC.

Saint Benedict Press publishes under several imprints. Our TAN Books imprint (TANBooks.com), publishes over 500 titles in theology, spirituality, devotions, Church doctrine, history, and the Lives of the Saints. Our Catholic Courses imprint (CatholicCourses.com) publishes audio and video lectures from the world's best professors in Theology, Philosophy, Scripture, Literature and more.

**For a free catalog, visit us online at
TANBooks.com**

**Or call us toll-free at
(800) 437-5876**

Domestic
Sex
Goddess

Domestic
Sex
Goddess

Kate Taylor

FIREFLY BOOKS

Contents

Having it all and having it off

Don't you just hate sex books? They sit there on the shelves in their pinky-purple packaging, smugly promising your relationship will be bed-breakingly passionate and fake-strokingly intimate if you'd just light a ylang-ylang candle, shove your kids away for the weekend, and learn to do something complicated and vaguely Eastern-sounding with a banana, a rubber sheet, and a length of inner tube.

You get enthused with the idea, and happily show the book to your partner. He gets enthused, too, and lies back waiting for you to fill his body with ecstasy. Afterward, he drifts off to sleep while you strip the banana-splatted sheets off the bed, pick up the kids from your parents' house, and book an appointment to get the inner tube surgically removed. Worst of all, none of the promised intimacy has appeared. Instead, you've just set yourself another chore on your never-ending to-do list: "Be incredible in bed every night."

To my shame, I have written three of those kinds of sex books in the past. In my time as sex columnist, I've invented a million different ways to do the deed. When I was a single sex writer, I couldn't understand why women would ever try to get out of having sex if it were available to them. I thought sex would be amazing if only we could concentrate on being more inventive and spontaneous, and use a few props.

And then I got married.

And then I had two kids.

Now I find the only way that most sex books could improve my nighttime pleasure is by barricading my five-year-old into his own room so he doesn't come into our bed every night. The bananas? Fed to my toddler. The rubber sheet? On my oldest son's bed. The inner tube? Used to repair the wading pool.

Sex books never make more than a passing reference to the problems faced by long-term couples, yet it's these couples who most need advice. New lovers have the advantage in bed, as a lot of sex's enjoyment comes from novelty and spontaneity. But when you've been together so long that you know every inch of your partner's body and all five of his Best Bedroom Moves, how can you get back that loving feeling or sense of blissful discovery? When you have to get up at 6 o'clock every morning to get the kids off to school, how can you face beginning a sexual technique that you know will take two hours to complete and use up all your tissues? And how can you look at baby oil as anything erotic, when you've actually started using it on your baby?

This is where this book comes in. It's a sex book for couples in long-term relationships, with or without children. It's for couples who adore each other, but have understandably felt the bloom go off their bedroom. It's for couples who would like new ideas to take to bed that bring back the initial excitement but don't require days of planning or other people, and who want real-life sex tips they can fit in around a busy day and eight hours of sleep at night.

It will help both of you, but I'm mainly writing for women, because it's women who can suffer more under the weight of a sex-free relationship, or one that's lacking in intimacy. When we have sex, we release a powerful hormone called oxytocin that can bond us to our partner. It's the same hormone we release when we have a baby. In long-term, settled love affairs, we need this oxytocin, and lots of it, to keep us attached to our mate.

Are you awash with it? Are you happily bonded to—and getting it on with—your man, or so unattached you're in danger of falling apart from him? To find out, take my quiz.

Are you a Domestic Sex Goddess?

1 Have you ever faked a headache?
a) No! If anything, I have a higher sex drive than my partner.
b) Once or twice, but only in dire—and exceptional—circumstances.
c) Put it this way, my man's urging me to go for a cranial MRI scan.

2 Do you feel on top of things both at home and in your relationship?
a) Very often, I am on top of my man.
b) I feel on top of the housework—but sex, not so much.
c) I feel I'm on top of a cliff, considering jumping.

3 How do you feel when you meet your man at the end of the day?
a) Excited and aroused.
b) Serene and calm.
c) Annoyed—he didn't get my note telling him not to bother coming back.

4 How often do the pair of you have sex?
a) Once or twice a week.
b) Once or twice a month.
c) Once or twice a year—birthdays and Christmas.

5 Does he buy you romantic presents?
a) He buys sexy underwear for me.
b) He buys me jewelry and flowers.
c) He buys me household gadgets, household appliances, and things he wants. So, in short, no.

Scores on the bedroom doors

Mostly A: *Sex Goddess*
You and your man have a passionate relationship, but might be lacking in intimacy. While he might be keen to get to grips with your naked body, the contents of your brain remain unravaged.
What you'll get from this book: Suggestions of ways you can get closer outside the bedroom.
Sex might be the glue that holds relationships together, but you'll want to be able to talk to him in the times you're not clutching his manhood. This book will help you do that.

Mostly B: *Cherished Goddess*
You are serene at home because you feel in control. You run the house well, but might be in danger of mothering your man. While it's good to run your home efficiently, keeping tabs on your guy might make him feel controlled and itch for some freedom.
What you'll get from this book: A way to maintain an air of lofty distance from your fella. If the thought of that frightens you, it's a sign you need to read on. The best long-term relationships aren't about living in each others' pockets.

Mostly C: *God Help You*
Oops. It's all gone belly-up—which is probably the position you lie in when you have your annual shag. Feelings of resentment have built up between you and your man, meaning that neither of you goes out of their way to please the other. Sexy? Nope. But don't worry, things can improve, and rapidly.
What you'll get from this book: A way to wipe the slate clean and start again. This book will change your attitude, giving you the tools to create a new relationship out of the wreckage of the old one. You'll find a million ways to enjoy lusty, thrilling sex with your man, and bring back your feelings of love.

Kitchen

Here we are, **in the heart** of your home. This is

the place where you'll make most of the domestic decisions

that greatly affect the everyday smooth-running of your house

and your **sex life.** It also contains

several implements that you can use to great sexual effect,

like rubber gloves, clothespins, and ice-cube trays, but

we'll get to those later. What I want you to look at first is how

the **boring daily chores** are shared between

you and your man. So get something soothing to drink—cocoa

is good, brandy is better—because nothing is likelier to make

you **start fuming** than this topic.

You have to get clean before you can get dirty

At first glance, cleaning and sex seem to have little in common bar the obvious—they both get you hot and sweaty, they both require you to get down on all fours, and they both can be done with a vacuum cleaner. But after that, what's the connection? The answer is … they both cause friction.

The sharing, or lack of sharing, of domestic duties is the number one cause of resentment between couples. And resentment is like cancer in relationships. It grows silently until one day you discover a lump—probably on your man's forehead after you smash it with the saucepan he "left to soak" five months ago. You can't expect to have a wonderful sex life in the bedroom if you're secretly harboring a million grudges about how he chooses to live in every other room in the house. More importantly, you can't expect to fancy him for very long if you keep finding his underwear stuck to the wall. So, here we're going to tackle the chores.

How can I get my man to do more around the house?
Whatever type of man you are with, there are ways to encourage him to contribute more to the running of the home than he already does.

Decide specifically what you need help with
If you've been festering under a pile of resentment bigger than your laundry basket for a while, it's easy to lose sight of what you actually would like your man to do around the house. "I just want him to do *more!*" you rage, scrubbing the toilet with his toothbrush and using his favorite CD to scrape the burnt bits off the stove top. But do you know *exactly* what you'd like him to do around the house?

Draw up a list of tasks
Men, being rational, respond well to lists. So sit down and draw up a list of all the tasks that need to be done to keep your house running. Not the lovely extras, like putting fresh flowers on the dining-room table every day or embroidering everyone's names on their duvet covers, but just the basics. Then divide this list between you and your partner fairly.

Note: Fairly does not necessarily mean 50/50. If you are at home more than your fella, because you are looking after the children or work fewer hours, it is fair for you to do more chores within the house. The goal here is not for you to become a pampered princess whose man runs around after work getting everything done, it's for you both to contribute to the maintenance of the home you share.

Ensure you've split the tasks logically
When you go through the list together, decide if you've split the list in the best way, bearing in mind what each person's likes and dislikes are. For example, one of you won't mind vacuuming but will have a strange aversion to ironing, so you can assign chores accordingly.

It seems fair for one person to cook and the other person to clean up but I don't think this is always wise, as it encourages the cook to go all TV chef and use every pan in the house, knowing that it'll magically get tidied up afterward. They might weigh the ingredients into tiny glass dishes, like on a cooking program. Instead, how about one person cooks and clears up the kitchen, but you take it in turns every night? You do three nights each, and on the seventh day you order takeout or go out to eat. If one of you really can't cook, give them another job, like being in sole charge of the laundry.

Give him manly jobs

The one phrase that will always appeal to any man, regardless of his domestic type, build, or interests, is "manly." So if there are certain jobs you really want him to take over forever, call them "manly jobs." You might balk against this, and that is completely up to you. I've heard women rage against this kind of thinking, demanding the right to be the one to lug heavy trash bags out, chop down trees, or re-tile the roof. I'm sure you could do these tasks equally well, but that's not really the point. Do you want to be the one who does them?

For example, I hate taking out the trash. If my husband were to sit back and watch my struggling to lift the trash bags, tie them up, and labor under the weight and smell of it all the way across the street to where our trash cans are, I'd feel furious, resentful, and ugly. I'd feel that he didn't cherish me at all. If he saw me as pretty and desirable, wouldn't he want to help—to stop the trash bag smearing muck all over my clothes, to take the weight out of my hands, to take the load off my back? So, I encourage him to do it. When he uses his special system of tying the ends of the plastic bags together, I stand there and coo appreciatively at his scientific mind. When he lifts up the bag, I sigh and wonder aloud at his muscles. And when he returns from depositing it into the trash can, I thank him warmly and tell him I'd be lost without him. Every time. This way, the trash gets taken out, I get to avoid the dirty job, and my husband gets to feel like a hero. However, my husband has a blind spot for the trash, so I have to be the one to initiate the process. Which brings me to the next tip ...

To spur him into action, look as if you're about to do the job yourself, badly

It doesn't do to create the aura of a wildly efficient super-woman if you ever want help around the place. There should be several areas where your incompetence is legendary. These areas, coincidentally, could be the ones you particularly detest. To get your man immediately started on a project, look as if you are just about to launch into

action and make a complete mess of the job. This will get him off the couch faster than stuffing the cushions with explosives.

Admiration, admiration, admiration

Your man has one motivation for doing anything, and that is to make you admire him. They are desperate for our admiration; even the ones who seem deliberately to court our contempt. So, admire the things he does around the house. Do you find that your man gives you a running commentary on every chore he has done? "I've just put a milk bottle out." "I've put my toothbrush back in the holder." "I've flushed." It's infuriating if you assume that he is constantly asking for thanks, but he's not—he's asking for *admiration*. He knows that household things are important to you, so when he has done something, however small, he tells you so he can receive his reward—your glowing eyes and happy smile. Really. I know that you do a billion things around the home every day that are never noticed, and that you realized years ago that housework is literally a thankless task, but your man is different. He tells you what he's done so you will admire him for doing it. That's his payment.

Bite your tongue. Next time he announces a job done, just smile at him. When he's done something bigger, admire him. Don't thank him—that implies he needn't have done it, that it was your job. Instead, seem amazed. "I just looked around this house for mugs to put in the dishwasher but couldn't find a single one! They're all already in there. Fabulous." You get the idea. Another way to admire him is to ...

Compliment him publicly

Boast about him. Always compliment him to other people. When you are on the phone to your friend and your man is in earshot, tell your friend something nice he has done. "Mike bought me the nicest flowers today, they're enormous!" If your man buys you jewelry and somebody compliments you on it, be sure to pass that along to him. "My boss told me that my new necklace was gorgeous. I boasted that you always buy me the best stuff."

Don't only praise him in private, make him feel you brag about him to everyone.

On the subject of public speaking, resist any urge to criticize him publicly. It's the equivalent of sitting your man at the head of the table and then announcing to your assorted guests that he has the tiniest penis in the world.

Relinquish control

After you have divided the chores and your man is doing his share, you might find that he is not doing them to your standards. What should you do about this? It depends. Is he doing things inexpertly, idiosyncratically, or deliberately wrong?

If he's doing them inexpertly, ignore it. It's to be expected at first, and he'll get better on his own. People only learn through their own experience and once he's had to wear pink shirts to the office every day for a month, he'll start remembering to check the bottom of the washing machine for stray socks before he loads a white wash. (Perhaps you shouldn't put your expensive handwash items in the laundry basket until he's got the hang of it.)

If he's doing things idiosyncratically, again, ignore. This is one of the reasons that women end up shouldering the domestic load: we are hideously "helpful" when we see our men doing things. Men don't like unsolicited advice. If you watch two men doing a task together, you'll notice that they don't tell each other what to do. They're not chiming in every five minutes with cries of, "Ooh, no, I know a much better way of doing that!" They hang back, and then laugh manically afterward instead when it all goes wrong. I know your man gives you unsolicited advice every minute of your life, but that's his way of showing love. Your way of showing love to your man should be to trust that he can do it by himself.

But what if he seems to be doing it wrong on purpose? The tactic of deliberate ineptitude has long been suspected, by women, as the males' passive-aggressive attempt to get out of having to do their share. You need to outwit him. This will be a game of bluff and double bluff at the beginning, but you are female, you can win this. Just treat him with the gentle, careful, ever-so-slightly patronizing understanding of an elementary school teacher. He'll soon knock it on the head.

Nags don't get laid

The main reason you're reading this book is to improve your sex life, so it's worth reminding you that women who constantly belittle, criticize, or "helpfully remind" their partner have far worse sex lives than those who don't. If you have noticed that your man has lost some of the initial lust he had for you, don't merely assume that it's down to familiarity, stress, or changes in your body (like your legs' inability to walk past a cookie jar without stopping). It could be that your nagging has neutered him. Think carefully: do you praise your partner as much as you could? Do you appreciate what he does, or simply complain about everything he doesn't? Have you adopted his ego and taken care of it lovingly, or is your attitude simply: "He should grow up and not expect to be complimented every minute of the day?" When you first got together, were you much more appreciative and complimentary than you are today? And was your sex life better? There's a link!

When men feel criticized by their women, they retreat sexually. They're not actively withholding sex as a punishment, they just don't feel as much desire for you. If your man has started to go to bed later than you, or has stopped making advances, it's worth considering whether your moaning has withered his manhood. To see if you have allowed yourself to fall into the habit of bitching, try this exercise: tomorrow, allow yourself to say only positive things to your partner. Not, "I'm positive you're a twit," but genuinely nice, lovely things. Do it all day. You'll soon realize how often your first response is critical. Try to keep up the exercise for as long as you can—days, weeks, or a lifetime. It gets a lot easier. The more you praise and appreciate your man, the more he will return the favor. And when you begin having more sex, you will both be a lot more affectionate and loving toward each other all the time.

Tidbits to boost your ardor

If your normal nookie sessions have the speed and satisfaction of a microwaved ready-meal, the reason probably lies in your kitchen cupboards. What you and your partner eat will have more of an effect on your sex drives than almost anything else in your lives, so it's important you start incorporating the right ingredients in your menus.

Once you know what the sexual superfoods are, you can enjoy slipping them in to your man's meals knowing that you'll both be reaping the rewards later on. It's the noughties version of your grandma telling you to eat your crusts "because they'll make your hair curl," except we'll be concentrating on the foods that will make your toes curl.

So, what to eat? Well, if you were going to do this thing properly, you'd take yourself and your man along to a nutritionist and have both your blood levels checked for vitamin deficiencies, because if either of you in lacking zinc, iron, or vitamin E, you'll be harder to start than a 1970s car. But because you're probably too busy, we'll just concentrate on the most general bang-boosters. These are the most important sources of nookie-nutrients.

Berries: The best-kept-secret source of love juice
Strawberries, raspberries, and blueberries make great *whores d'oeuvres* as their seeds are bursting with zinc, which boosts the sex drive. Keep a fruit bowl in the kitchen and nibble whenever you like.
Top tip: Take a bowl of strawberries to bed and take turns with your man to eat them as sensuously as possible. Watching him suck and nibble the fruit will give you clues to how he likes to be stimulated, so concentrate! Then he can insert a big strawberry into you and gently eat it out again. The sexiest way possible to get one of your daily food requirements.

Shellfish: Oysters aren't the only underwater aphrodisiac
Another wonderful source of zinc, which is probably how oysters got their reputation as the ultimate aphrodisiac. The act of eating oysters is erotic, too, as you slide the slippery saltiness onto your tongue. All shellfish is good, so go for what you like best.
Top tip: Shrimp are a good starter to a passionate evening in, especially fresh ones fried in garlic butter, served with watercress salad (full of iron) and wholewheat bread (a good source of vitamin E).

Asparagus: Finger food you can't keep your hands off
Not only is it shaped like a penis, it's good for penises, too. The vitamin E it contains is vital for the health of the reproductive system. Keep it whole to give your man a visual feast as you slide the long stems into your mouth, or chop them up small (don't let him watch) and use in soups and quiches.
Top tip: Pack a passion picnic and serve it up in the living room. Include spears of asparagus dipped into butter or hollandaise sauce, a glass of wine, and saucy cinnamon muffins (see page 16).

Ginger: Spice up your sex life
This ancient root is said to encourage bloodflow toward your southerly areas, so slip grated fresh ginger into your food whenever possible. Just the taste of it will cause your heart rate to rise slightly, and chewing on fresh ginger will plump your lips, making them look rosier and more Angelina Jolie-esque.
Top tip: Create a spicy massage oil by mixing a teaspoon of ground ginger with a small bottle of almond oil (from health food stores). Take turns to massage each other. Don't let it get inside anywhere, however, as it will sting.

Chocolate: Melt in his mouth, and his hand

Stimulating to body and mind, chocolate contains phenylethylamine, a chemical that tricks your brain into feeling like you're in love. Obviously a vital ingredient in every long-term couple's daily diet.

Top tip: Melted chocolate served at room temperature is especially sensuous, so invest in a fondue set for the bedroom. Everything can be dipped into gorgeous gloopy chocolate, including fruit, marshmallows, his weenie (but check the temperature first! A burn will make him swell impressively but the ER isn't the sexiest of venues), or a brush to paint chocolate messages on each other that can then be licked off.

Cinnamon: Smells like teen lust

Research by the Smell & Taste Institute has revealed that the smell of cinnamon has a dramatically positive effect on men's sex drives, so grab that innocent-looking jar off your spice rack and start baking immediately. Cinnamon muffins are an easy weekend breakfast that will start your day with a bang. But if you can't be bothered baking, remember it's the smell, not the taste, that has the effect, so add some cinnamon to unscented body lotion and rub yourself liberally.

Top tip: Make Fortune Muffins. Bake some cinnamon muffins and wait for them to cool, then write on a pink piece of paper exactly how much you want him to ravish you later. Fold the paper up and slide it inside the muffin. Make sure it's visible, or brush up on the Heimlich maneuver first. Serve them in bed or on a saucy picnic.

Alcohol: Just one tipple before you lick nipple

One or two units of alcohol can raise you and your man's testosterone levels slightly, making you more passionate and aggressive (grrr) in bed. So relax with ONE glass of wine before nookie-time. Three glasses of alcohol or more, however, will make his love-pasta seriously less than al dente, and turn you into a raging harpy who screams sweet nothings like, "Would it kill you to take out the trash?" So don't finish the bottle—take my word on that.

Top tip: In bed, open a bottle of sparkling wine and fill your mouth with fizz. Then slide your man's penis inside. The bubbles will stimulate him as you gently suck. He can do the same to you, letting the fizzy fluid gush over your clitoris.

Honey: I've shrunk the sex slump

Once a great luxury, honey is wonderfully healthy but deliciously sexy, too. It goes well with cinnamon, so you can mix them together and sensuously feed them to your man on a spoon or your finger, or use it as a lubricant in bed.

Top tip: Honey has a slightly granular texture, which means it increases friction between your bodies if you use it as a lubricant. Add it to the tip of his penis before he slides in, or have him put honey on his fingertips before he massages your Lady Garden. Note: Don't try this if you have a history of yeast infections, as the sugar can aggravate them. Instead, just apply the honey to your nipples.

Whores d'oeuvres

Amazing sex doesn't have to be a three-course affair requiring hours of preparation and a lot of clearing-up. Quick naughty "snacks" are delicious, too. The following tricks are brief tasters of great sex that will satisfy your hunger until you can sit down to a full meal. An *amuse* bush," if you will …

• When he's just started doing the dishes, reach around him and warm your hand in the water. Then dry it off and slide it down into his jeans. Tell him you'll pleasure him for as long as the dishes take. This is how I got my title of "Owner of the Shiniest Plates in the County."

• While you're there, lick and kiss the back of his neck. This is a very sensitive spot for him—especially on the bone right on the nape of his neck. Suck on that little bone like it's a tiny penis. (But not when he is handling your poshest glassware.)

• My last dishwashing loyalty scheme: pull up his shirt while he's at the sink, and press your naked breasts into his back. Tease him with the tips of your nipples, then rub oil onto your globes and sensuously slide them in big circles. Drop a kiss on the very base of his spine, and tell him you'll meet him upstairs—when he's finished.

• Bend over to load the dishwasher wearing just a short skirt and no underwear. Really stretch down to get those plates in. Is he coming to give you a hand? I thought so.

• When you're both in the kitchen getting food for guests or the family, cup his chin in your hand and pull him close for a deep, sensual kiss. The next time you meet him in there, massage his groin through his trousers. The next time, grope his rear and wrap one leg saucily around his hips. Try to keep his erection at simmering point through the whole meal, and reap the rewards later.

• Decide on code words you can use when you have company over. You can either use these as signals that you're desperate for sex, or challenge each other to use very obscure words in conversation, like "dodecahedron." The one who uses their word first—and isn't met with blank looks and "huh?"s—gets to have whatever treat they like in bed later.

• Get a refrigerator magnet that is your sign for "I'm in the mood." When either of you sticks it up, it signals that Thunder-Pants Are Go. If the other person removes it, don't bother brushing your teeth.

• Use refrigerator-magnet letters to write mucky messages to your partner, as long as you never let other people in your kitchen and you have all the letters you need. And you can spell … Actually, forget this.

• Instead, dig out a romantic, smoochy photo of the two of you and stick that to the fridge. One where you both look happy and passionate and thin. If you're anything like me, you'll be looking at that photo approximately 18,659 times every day.

• When you're baking, call to your partner to taste something for you. Then let him find you in the kitchen with cake mix spread over your nipples. His penis will be standing to attention.

• Don't encourage your children to read. Ever. Then you can make a habit of decorating family pies with filthy messages made from leftover dough.

• Bake cookies cut into letter shapes, then arrange a few on a plate so they spell out something obscene, like "BJ?" Give them to your man with a coffee. Or use squeezy ketchup on his meatloaf to announce your disgusting intentions.

Kitchen toys

Pull open your utensil drawer and start looking at all those kitchen gadgets with a lusty eye. Many of them can be used in various depraved ways. The only rule is: they must be squeaky clean first! Wash them in the dishwasher at a high temperature to sterilize them, and if they are going to be inserted, buy new ones that you use specifically for this purpose and cover them with a condom. Then it's easy-peasy, lemon squeezer…

Turkey baster
These have become so synonymous with sex, I'm surprised sex-toy stores don't sell a pink rubber version, with rotating beads in the shaft. Fill it up with massage oil or a self-heating lubricant and drizzle it all over his body. Even better if you've blindfolded him first. Then use your breasts to rub it in, and get back out to your lunch guests.

Spoons
Spoons can be very sexy. Forks—though more promisingly named—not so much. Choose a big, clean soupspoon or serving spoon and warm it with hot water in the sink so it's slightly above body temperature. Now you, or your partner, can use the back of it to massage your clitoris with it in firm, circular motions.

Olive oil
I'm basing this tip on a scene from Nicholson Baker's novel *Vox*. Remove the lid from a glass bottle of olive oil—extra-virgin if you insist, but you're not fooling anyone—and warm it in the microwave for 10 seconds. Replace the lid and shake it thoroughly. Stand your man in the bathtub, get his penis out, and hold the bottle over it. Tell him how sensual and warm and slippery it's going to feel. When his penis starts twitching with expectation, tilt the bottle and pour a glug straight down the length of it. Slowly massage in with your hands. Then repeat—again, leaving him twitching in anticipation before you pour. Soon he should be fully erect, and it's up to you what you do with him: finish him with your hands and breasts, clean off the oil and jump on for some action, or walk out of the room dominatrix-style and tell him to clean the bathtub.

Plastic wrap
This can be used to create a dental dam—a barrier over his (or your) anus to prevent germs and viruses passing into the mouth when you lick it. This is a lot sexier than it sounds, which wouldn't be difficult.

Ice cubes
Run an ice cube over your nipples or clitoris and let the water drip into your fella's mouth. Run an ice cube over his nipples, then use your tongue to catch the drips as sexily as you can. Make long thin ice cubes (you get the trays from Ikea) and use them to masturbate with while your bloke watches, make him lick up all the melted ice, then pull him into you to shag your ice-cold, tingley vagina.

Pastry brush
Bring a new, soft pastry brush into the bedroom and use it to paint anything runny and sexy onto each other's bodies—chocolate sauce, melted peanut butter, cream … Make it into a game where he paints words on your body and you have to guess what they are while he licks them off again. Let's hope they're not "Help, I have a nut allergy." You can also use the brush to paint warm liquid honey onto his penis before you hump him.

Rubber gloves
Rubber gloves give very good massages—with hands inside them, obviously—as the bumps on the fingertips feel great on the skin. Use plenty of lubricant and run your hands over your man's nether regions, resisting the urge to spray on some furniture polish.

Clothes pegs
Clothespins are—in real life, I'm not making this up—what S&M devotees on a budget use for economical nipple clamps. Fancy a go? It can't be more painful than hanging out washing, can it? Of course it can. There are so many nerves concentrated in the nipple area that it is exquisitely agonizing when they are clamped. And it's even more harrowing when the nipples are then tweaked or pulled. It finally becomes *tortuous* when heavy things are then hung from the clamps and your partner slithers off to answer the door to someone chatty. But do try it!

Oral sex

Kitchens are the perfect place to indulge in oral sex. I know I've just put you off ever eating *chez moi*, but it's true. It's the counters. Those innocent-looking worktops are positioned at just the right height for one of you to sit on them, stark naked, while the other licks, chomps, slurps, and munches for dear life. No, it's not hygienic, but what would you like your gravestone to read, "Her Food Never Tasted like Pussy" or "Boy, Did She Love Her Oral"? Actually, maybe neither of those would be great. Let's move on.

Him to you

Sit up the countertop, and hold your thighs tightly together. He will give you a puzzled look, then boldly spread your legs open, which will arouse both of you. With him between your legs—sitting on a chair if it means he'll be there longer—pull both your feet up flat onto the counter for maximum exposure, or just one. He should start by licking you up and down your inner thighs where the skin is especially sensitive, and gently breathing just above your clitoris. Then he can try any of the tips in the Bedroom chapter (see pages 106–108), including:

• Spreading your lips apart with his fingers, and using the flat back area of his tongue to lap upward and downward over the entire vaginal area. Running the point of his tongue in a wavy up-and-down motion from the left side of your clitoris to the right, and back again.

• Circling around your clitoris with the tip of his tongue, pushing in firmly. He can also use his fingertips to circle around your clit, from wide circles getting smaller and smaller until he's lightly tracing a spiral over the very tip of you.

• He can use one hand to push up on your pubic mound (that flat, fleshy, hairy area at the top of your Lady Garden), lifting it out of the way. With the skin pulled up like this, the area is much more sensitive.

• Meanwhile, hold onto his head and making lots of noise when he does something you love. When you feel yourself beginning to climax, push down with your PC muscles to intensify the sensations.

You to him

When he is sitting in front of you, legs spread in delighted anticipation, begin by running your hands up his thighs and tickling the soft skin between his legs with the very tips of your fingernails. Look him in the eye lustily, and comb through his pubic hair with your fingers—this will remove loose hairs and prevent you coughing up a fur ball later on. As before, use any of the tips in the Bedroom chapter (see page 104–105), especially:

• Hold his penis firmly at the base using one hand. If he's uncircumcized, this keeps his foreskin drawn back, exposing the ultra-sensitive tip of his glans.

• Find the little string that runs along the underneath of his penis—the side closest to you now. Lick that area. Swirl your tongue up and down it, and "gum" it, with your lips pulled over your teeth.

• Use one hand to press onto his perineum.

• Keep something moving at all times, whether it's your hand or your mouth. Don't stop, and only decrease the speed a couple of times. It's best to work up slowly but steadily—don't start off at breakneck speed, it will hurt him, just build up gradually.

• When you feel he is nearing his orgasm—his testicles will tighten and draw upward slightly, you'll taste some of his pre-cum, and he'll begin groaning like he's sitting on a bread knife—keep doing what you're doing. Don't change techniques now.

• Remember: immediately after he's climaxed is the perfect time to ask for a lie-in in the morning.

Positions for the kitchen

According to a survey, 40 percent of women prefer having sex in the kitchen to in the bedroom. It certainly worked for Glenn Close in *Fatal Attraction* (remember her in the sink?) and Demi Moore in *Indecent Proposal* (rolling round on the dirty laundry with Woody Harrelson). If you want to be a real Domestic Sex Goddess, then boffing in the heart of the home is the only true way.

Start by giving that kitchen the clean of its life. Nothing breaks the mood more than spotting a forgotten bit of bacon under the oven halfway through a romp, or getting up afterward with your tush looking like the toaster's crumb drawer. You could make cleaning the kitchen the foreplay, if you do it stark naked and let your partner stumble in on you. Many men fantasize about employing a naked maid … Oh, who am I kidding? You'll only spend the entire time holding your tummy in and festering with resentment that you have to be a sex goddess *and* a housekeeper. Get someone else in to clean, then try these positions.

Mind my onions

Stand facing the kitchen counter—that heaven of humping—and bend forward. Stick your bottom upward as far as you can. Don't let it drop, raise it up as much as possible. (Wearing high heels is a good way to do this.) The idea is to lift your rear out of the way, so when your man penetrates you, your vagina is close to being in a horizontal line. It worked? Yes! The penetration will be deeper as more of his penis will go inside you. While he is thrusting, use your hands to reach around and grasp the base of his penis, stimulate your clitoris, or just get on with the supper. For a sexy alternative, which is bad for the environment but fabulous for your sex life, try this position while you bend over the open door of the freezer. The cold air will sensitize your nipples, and because they're hanging down, your breasts will feel more responsive.

Good for: Giving you both hot, passionate penetration.

Bad for: Eye contact or kissing, but he will love the view as he watches your tush and you'll enjoy the G-spot stimulation.

Flash floor wipes

Lay your man down on the kitchen floor. If you're
feeling loving and caring toward him, you could lie a
towel down there first, but if he's annoying you, don't
bother. Squat over his penis, keeping your feet flat on
the floor, and lower yourself up and down on top of
him, with your hands on his chest for balance. Before
you get started, grasp his penis and use it like a dildo,
rubbing it over your clitoris and the very entrance of
your Lady Garden—dipping it in then whisking it away.
The sight of you using him purely for your own pleasure
will thrill him to his very core. As you squat over him,
try moving your hips in wide circles from side to side,
as if you're screwing him into you. This will hit all the
right places inside your vagina and, if he masturbates
you while you do it, should have you coming hard.
Yee-ha, cowgirl!

Good for: Very deep penetration, with you in control.

Bad for: Long sessions. This position is very, very
stimulating for him both physically and visually, so don't
expect him to last very long. If he looks like he's going
to finish before you're ready, change the position
slightly so you're kneeling on the floor instead, and
grind forward and backward with him deep inside.
This is great for hitting your G-spot (and giving your
thigh muscles a break) but not so stimulating to him,
so it'll give him a recovery period. Then move back to
squatting to finish him off.

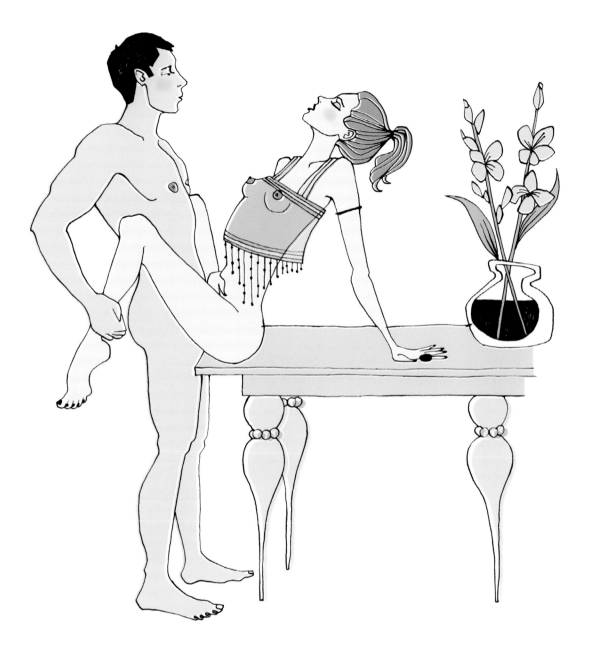

Elbows off the table

Sit on the edge of the kitchen table (although this position works well on any strong surface that is the same height as your partner's hipbones) with your legs hanging down. Open your legs lustily, so your man gets a spectacular view of your vagina. Always remember the power that this sight has over your man: to him, it's the sexiest view in the world, even if you privately think it looks like a burst sleeping bag. Let him lick and kiss you there for as long as possible, then slide his penis inside you. Bend your knees and open them wide until you're in a "frog" position, and let your man hold onto your ankles for leverage. This way, he'll be moving you backward and forward with every thrust, deepening the penetration and enabling you both to work up to a fast, furious rhythm.

Good for: Making frenzied, passionate love; and you'll have a hand free to massage yourself.

Bad for: Distracting the children from their homework.

Is that a front-loader?

This one is a good way for rewarding him for doing the laundry. Stand up against the washing machine—or, if that's too indiscrete, up against a similar-height chest of drawers in the bedroom, or just against a wall—and have him standing up in front of you. Raise one leg to allow penetration. He holds this leg as he thrusts into you, giving him something to work against, and taking the strain off your thighs. Because you're standing up, the penetration is fairly shallow but he can rub and lick your breasts while he thrusts, and you can raise your leg higher to improve the sensation.

Good for: Spontaneous, quickie sex.

Bad for: Deep penetration and clitoral stimulation.

To improve things, massage your clitoris as you make love, or grind your hips powerfully into his.

Living Room

The living room is a great venue for sex as more often than not it contains a comfy, bouncy couch—or even better, a sofa-bed—sexy little accoutrements like candles and maybe even a real log fire. Plump pillows and soft rugs both help to lessen the wear and tear on elbows and knees. There are also the electrical gadgets – TV, DVD player, computer—to use in all manner of filthy ways. Things I Wish I'd Remembered to Do #857: just don't forget to remove the DVD afterward.

How to date your own husband

For years after we got married, I resisted that age-old advice to go on regular dates with my husband. "God, how dull," I thought contemptuously. "That advice is just for bores that need everything in their life planned and organized. I'm a spontaneous, seat-of-my-pants type wife. I'll simply grab excitement whenever I find it!"

And so we didn't go out for four years.

If you want to go out on lovely dates with your husband or long-term partner—and for the sake of your sex life, you *do*—then it's going to be up to you to organize them, even if your man is usually the more romantic out of the two of you. Most of the male population seem to be content to stay in a lot. It's a harking back to their cavemen roots—they drag a pretty girl back to their cave and sit there with her, grunting. They can do this for years. Do not allow this to happen. Going out on regular dates with him will give you three things:

1 The chance to dress up

This isn't so much of an issue if you go to work every day. But if you work from home or are a full-time mom, it's astonishing how quickly you can let yourself go. No, don't look at me in horror and say you're as clothes-conscious now as you ever were, because I don't believe you. I know you've paused over ads for tracksuits and thought, "I never thought I'd say this, but that looks practical *and* comfy." I know you've heard the siren song of the slipper-sock. It's natural. So a regular standing date with your partner is a very good idea. For one thing, it'll remind him how lovely you look in your eveningwear. For another, wearing clothes that have zippers and buttons, and whose labels read "dry clean only" not "elasticated for comfort" will help you keep an eye on your weight. The severely overweight don't end up wearing jogging pants because they're the only things that'll fit—they start off wearing them. Remember that.

2 The opportunity to see each other with new eyes

It's easy to take each other for granted when you spend all your time together. He tells the same joke every day, you wear the same bra. You stop seeing your partner as the one special person you chose out of all the others; he simply becomes the annoying phantom who leaves his dirty plates on top of the dishwasher. But when you go out, you have the opportunity to see how other people react to your other half; if the waitress laughs at his boring old jokes, you remember that he's funny. If a man winks at you as you walk past, your man remembers that you're prettier than most girls.

3 Warning of an imminent sexual encounter

If you're the type of woman who likes a bit of notice before being ravished, you're normal. You can't forever keep yourself sex-ready—tottering around every day oiled, perfumed, and plucked, in matching underwear, on the off-chance that tonight will be *the night*. For some reason, it's when we are looking our worst that our partners are most often stricken with lust. My friend Julie's husband Nick seems to have a sixth sense about when she is wearing her old gray panties and hasn't shaved her armpits for a week, and that's when he always makes his move. Then Julie has to pretend to nip off to the bathroom to brush her teeth and fit in a two weeks' worth of grooming into three minutes before he falls asleep.

How often should you go out?

Once every two weeks is plenty. Every week sounds better, but quickly becomes forced and if you have to cancel it once, you'll stop doing it at all. Once a month is better than nothing. If your partner has really gotten out of the habit of socializing, lure him outside once a month for three months, then increase it to once every other week. The first few times you go out he'll stand blinking in the streetlights like a newborn foal, saying things like, "Who are all these people out at 7 o'clock on a Thursday evening?" But before long he'll be circling events in the local newspaper and booking tickets left, right, and center, especially if you've seemed thrilled by going out.

Babysitting

Many couples use the excuse of not having babysitters as a way of avoiding going on dates. Unless you live on your own private island and are wanted by Interpol, it's almost always a cop out. Salman Rushdie goes out regularly, for goodness sake, and he has spent 20 years living under a fatwa, so I think you can manage the occasional movie. If it's your first baby, you might feel uncomfortable leaving them with anyone except blood relatives until they are slightly older (like, 25). But when the next kids come along, you are usually happy to leave them with anyone, including that man in the park who always carries a camera. If you don't live close enough to the grandparents to use them, ask a local mom if she'd like to start a Babysitting Swap Shop with you, where every second week you sit for each other. Chances are she'll jump at the opportunity to go out more, and to have a peaceful evening at your place regularly with no responsibilities other than to watch TV and eat ice-cream.

No local mom friends? Search the Internet for babysitting circles in your area. Nothing? Local child-care facilities are a good contact: often the staff babysit in the evenings to subsidize their wages. You will have to pay, but they're not expensive and they are all trained in first aid.

Remember, you don't have to pay for an entire evening: just two hours would be enough for you to nip out and have a quick meal, and you could cover the babysitter's fee by skipping dessert. Come home all romantic, and wild sex on the couch can be the dessert. (Maybe wait till the babysitter's gone.)

9 1/2 dates

Just like monogamous sex, dates will get less exciting if you do the same thing every time. Going out for dinner is a safe choice, but as soon as money's tight you'll stop doing it, as eating is something you can do at home. Instead, try one of these ideas, which aim to provide the maximum of sexiness for the minimum cost.

1 Visit your local market together one Saturday, and recreate that scene from the film *9 1/2 Weeks*. No, not the one where they rut like pigs under the water spilling from a gutter in an alleyway—although, thinking about it, that is more exciting than my suggestion—but the one where they stroll around the market trying on hats and being suggestive with melons. Buy delicious, impractical food and cook it together, then serve it without cutlery so you have to feed one another.

2 Go to a comedy gig. Make a pact that the first person to laugh has to be the other's sex slave for the night.

3 Have a picnic using only the aphrodisiacs in the Kitchen chapter (see pages 14–16).

4 Evening picnics are even sexier than daytime ones—grab spicy takeout and eat it in the park. Bring along some edible nipple cream and serve your breasts as dessert.

5 Ice-skating is a very sexy date, especially if you hold onto your man with a terrified death-grip. In the winter, visit an open-air skating rink in the evening—they are floodlit and very romantic. Bring along a hip flask of mulled wine or whisky.

6 Go to a movie. Sit in the back row and make out like teenagers. Hide a sexy surprise in the popcorn—like a condom with a vibrating ring on it—and when he finds it, tell him that you want to use it before you go home …

7 Visit a casino with 30 dollars each to spend. The person who loses the most money can borrow more from the other in return for "favors"—the more money you borrow, the bigger the favor.

8 Go to a wine-tasting evening together at a winery. Take a taxi home, and neck passionately all the way back, as if you were out on a date. Because you are!

9 Loud music is very arousing. Go to a nightclub and dance until you're both dripping with sweat, or have a more sedate—but just as steamy—night at the opera. Wear nothing under your full-length dress, and take his hand and let him discover that fact for himself.

1/2 Going out for a meal is always seductive, but you don't have to go too far. Set up a dining table outdoors, complete with white tablecloth, candles, fancy glasses, and your wedding china. The change of scene will make even fish sticks sexier than before … And if your tablecloth is long enough, you can crawl underneath it and ravish your man for dessert.

Dates at home

If you can't get a babysitter—or if you can but would like to have regular at-home dates, too—you can still have memorable evenings at home. Try any of these. Ideally, you would have one night a week for at-home dates, but whatever suits you.

Game time

Sex-up any kind of game by making it a strip version. Strip poker, strip snap, strip monopoly … For the ultimate strip game, play strip twister. Once you're both naked, cover each other in massage oil then go through all the moves again. Tremble. Buy pairs of "love dice" which have sexual activities on one side—Kiss, Lick, Suck, Stroke, etc.—and body parts on the other. You take turns to roll them, and then roll around on each other performing the action. You could simply make your own by using normal dice and deciding in advance what sexual activity and body part the numbers correspond to. This will give you a thrilling little flashback when you next use the dice to play an innocent family game.

Spice up your TV

If you spend most evenings in front of the television, you can still improve your sex life. Make up naughty games and satisfy your crotch while you watch. For example …

Sexy TV bingo

Each of you writes down a five-word sexual command. "TAKE ME TO BED NOW," for example, or "KISS ALL OVER MY CHEST." Make sure you use different words from each other. Then watch the TV, and when your word is spoken, cross it off. The first person to cross off all their words wins, and gets to have their command fulfilled by the other.

Saucy subtitles

Turn the volume off on the TV, but keep watching. Now make up the dialogue yourselves, with one rule: the characters have to be talking filth. He speaks for the men, you speak for the women. Not immediately arousing, but hilarious, and laughter is a powerful aphrodisiac.

Lust lottery

With a lip-liner, write the numbers 1–24 all over his body; then he writes the numbers 25–49 all over yours. Watch a lottery show together and if your number is picked, the other person must do whatever you want to that part of your body. Concentrate, obviously, on erogenous zones: fondling his elbow isn't erotic for either of you. This sounds jokey, but is a good way to discover what you each like, as you get to tell your partner exactly what to do to each place.

Shag-along live

You've seen cook-along TV shows, now try the X-rated version. Watch a naughty movie together—it doesn't have to be pornographic, but it does have to have sex scenes. *Nine Songs*, *9 1/2 Weeks*, and *Betty Blue* are all good, or choose your favorite. Then, just as the title of the game suggests, you do what they do. A good way to inspire yourselves to try new things, as the point of the game is that you must copy their actions—no sliding into missionary if they're doing passionate doggy style, OK?

Arousing TV commercials

Watch TV normally, but during the commercials leap on each other and kiss, grope, and fondle passionately. Make it as lusty as possible. When the commercial finishes, you must, too—then sit there panting until the next one.

Seductive suppers

Just having dinner at home can be erotic, if you eat aphrodisiac foods or serve them in a sexy way. The main rule is not to serve too much food: a big meal will tire you both out, and you'll feel bloated. Other than that, anything goes! See if any of these ideas whet your appetite.

Bangfest in bed
Create a tray of sensual foods, like fruits, whipped cream, chocolate sauce, and sparkling wine. Take the tray and your partner up to the candlelit bedroom, and feed each other lustily, perhaps while a sexy film plays on the TV.

What's your pleasure, sir?
Dress up like a geisha girl, by wearing a silky robe wrapped tightly around your naked body and little slippers, and put your hair up. Wear black eyeliner flicking up at the edges, whiten your face with powder, and paint on a little red mouth. You will feel incredibly silly, but the more you throw yourself into the role, the sexier this will become. Tell your man you are his own private geisha for the evening. Serve him tea on a starched cloth spread out on the floor, then offer him a foot massage. Be incredibly respectful and bow a lot. Ask if he would like you to do anything else. He'll say, "What did you have in mind?" Reply flirtily, "Anything master wants."

Blind man's buffet
Tie a blindfold around your partner's eyes, then lay down on the bed. Place a treasure hunt of food all over your body—a blob of chocolate sauce on your nipple, some cream between your breasts, a dab of sweet chili sauce on your ear lobe, pieces of chocolate leading up your thighs, and a strawberry on top of your clitoris. Break all the health and hygiene laws imaginable. Then tell him that dinner is served. He has to find all the food before he can ravish you, and he can only use his tongue.

Wait for it
Serve him dinner while you wear nothing but an apron and high heels. Bend over a lot—to reach over the table for the salt and pepper, to pick up a napkin from the floor, to pick up imaginary specks of dirt. Ask him if he'd like to try the wine, then pour a little bit of it over your breast and let him lick it off. If—oh, who am I kidding—when he tries to fondle your bottom, leap away and make him chase you around the house.

Foreplay takeout
Order takeout food from somewhere with a speedy delivery service and challenge your man to see if he can make you come twice before the food does. If he manages it, you pay for the meal. Swap next time; your challenge could be to perform oral sex on him while he telephones in the food order—if you can make him groan out loud during the call or forget the names of anything, he pays for the meal.

Titillating desserts
Prepare a lavish, romantic dessert and lay it on the table. The game here is that you have to feed one another using only your hands. And if you "accidentally" spill any food on yourself, your partner has to lick it off. Funny how manners fly out of the window when couples play this.

The secret's in the sauce
Challenge your partner to guess what's in your meal, before he's eaten it or knows what it is. Every time he guesses an ingredient incorrectly, he has to remove an item of clothing. Every time he guesses correctly, you have to remove an item of clothing.

That old black magic

Gypsy Passion Recipe: This is an ancient recipe used by Romany women when they wanted to increase their partner's lust for them. Get some rye and pimento—buy new, don't use any you have in the cupboard—and while you prepare dinner, stir them into the food while reciting the following spell: "Rye of earth, pimento of fire, eaten surely fuels desire. Serve to he whose love I crave, and his heart I will enslave." Then serve the dinner, but don't mention the spell. (If you mention it, so folklore states, it will reverse the spell and he'll fall out of love with you. Probably because he thinks you've gone bonkers.)

Squeeze me, please me

Get a squeezy bottle and fill it with chocolate sauce, then pipe obscene messages around the edge of his plate when you serve dessert.

Rumpy pumpy

Bake him a pumpkin pie and serve it to him for dinner. While he's eating it, tell him this interesting fact: the smell of pumpkin pie is men's sexiest-ever aroma, according to the Smell and Taste Institute. Most men find it incredibly erotic and arousing. Ask him if he agrees.

Lusty laptops

If you and your man often zone-out in front of your computers in the evening, at least show willing by switching off the parental controls and searching for some filth. There are millions of things you can look at, but as a starting point, think along these lines:

• Search for erotic fiction, and read them together. Many sites feature very good naughty stories, often written by women, ranging from gentle and romantic to hardcore. Erotic fan fiction is more amusing than arousing—it's where people create their own scripts for well-known TV shows like *Star Trek* and *CSI*, using the original characters, and then quickly turn it into one big sex-fest.

• Find free downloadable erotic audio. Yes! You can get erotic stories read to you now if you're too lazy to do it yourself, complete with sound effects and panting. Most of the stories are read by actresses rather than actors. Why? Because it was discovered that men are put off by the sound of another man's voice.

• Sex blogs are revealing, intimate, sexy, and sometimes poignant. The ones written by male gigolos are especially enlightening. Others offer advice, ideas, and new positions.

• If you enjoy reading sex blogs, you could create one of your own. Why not? Because your man would hate it. But would he? You could ask him. Or, better still, you could create a sex blog together, where you both list your thoughts and feelings about sex, describe what you did, and tell the world what you're going to do next time.

• Thinking of re-vamping your décor? Search for sex furniture. Lots of online shops offer merchandise that will having you sitting come-fortably. Some is just wrong—think black vinyl couches with massive rubber dildoes sitting proudly on top—but several companies now offer discrete tasteful pieces. I'm saving up for one of the ottomans that double-up as a vibrating sex-box.

• Homemade porn. Not for the faint-hearted, there are one or two sites (maybe more, I'm too scared to look) where people can upload their own homemade X-rated videos. Some are a con, asking for credit card details, but there are several free ones.

• Sex tips and positions. Interested in trying tantric sex? Check out page 121 of the Bedroom chapter for an easy, starter position, but search online, too. Millions of people out in cyberspace want to show you how to insert his lingam into your yoni to boost your spiritual connection. Log on and let them. Need step-by-step instructions to perform that complicated backflip-double-slipknot sex position you heard about in the bar? Search for it. *Cosmopolitan* magazine has a very good sex-position archive, but there are many other sites, too.

• Sex advice. From looking up that scary warty thing you found in your bikini line this morning (relax, it's probably a Rice Krispie thrown around by your toddler), to finding details of different contraceptives, the Internet is a goldmine for sexual health advice.

• Sex toys. These are covered in more detail in the Bedroom chapter, but without doubt the best place to buy toys is online. Stick to a well-known retailer and you know your purchase is safe, secure, and soon to arrive. Many sites offer user reviews, and advice on which toy might suit you. Browse online together and see what tickles your fancy. It's also a great way of bringing up a topic you've been too scared to broach; instead of having to say, "if you don't spank me soon I'll divorce you" in a big frustrated rush, just casually search for handcuffs and paddles and check out your man's reaction.

Foreplay

Novelty is very sexy, but it's the first thing to vanish in a long-term relationship. Don't give in—there are countless ways you can inject some flirty surprises into your love life. Try these as starting points; simple sexy ways to tell your man you're in the mood …

• While your man is zoning out in front of the TV, sit next to him and slip your hand into his jeans. Don't catch his eye, just watch the TV while you stroke and fondle him. Then, when he is bursting out of his boxers, slide between his legs, lick him and then climb aboard.

• Sneak into bed wearing your sexiest underwear. Use your cell phone to video yourself masturbating, then text it to your man. He'll be in within seconds!

• Or, video yourself performing a sexy striptease, and copy it onto a DVD. Then one evening, mention that there's a good movie on and settle down to watch it together.

• Set a sexy treasure hunt around the house. Put up clues—written on pink sticky notes—around the house, leading him upstairs to where you're waiting, naked, tied to the bed. Only try this when you know he's on his way home.

• Just before your man gets home, remove your clothes and leave them in a trail leading toward the bathroom.

• Hang your sexy warm panties over the bathroom doorknob, and be waiting in a bubble bath.

• While he watches TV, lean over and run your tongue over his ear. Nibble gently on his ear lobe (this is a very sexy spot for most males), then swirl it inside. Place your mouth over his ear and inhale gently, then move down to kissing his neck, shoulders, and chest, undressing him as you go. Warning: Do not try this while he is engrossed in the final episode of his favorite show.

• Buy some luminous body paint. One evening, get naked then paint the words "Fuck Me" on your chest. Shine a flashlight on the words so they start to glow, pull on a silky dressing gown and a sexy thong, and run downstairs to where your partner is, inevitably, sitting on the couch. In silence, turn off all the lights in the room then slip off your gown in front of him.

• Change his home computer screen to a sexy picture of you.

• Then change it back again before your young child uses the computer. (Things I Wish I'd Remembered To Do #858.)

• Record an audio clip of yourself telling him exactly what you'd like him to do to you, making it very lusty and graphic. Send it to his cell phone while you're entertaining guests, and let him wait impatiently for them to go home so he can make it come true.

• Text a filthy message to him in the middle of a dinner party.

Oral pleasures

Yelling, "Hi honey, I'm horny!" is one way of using your tongue to tell your partner you're in the mood. Thankfully there are other, more subtle, ways, too. The following techniques focus on using oral sex as a sexy surprise for your lover; either as a way to begin a full sex session, or just to seduce your man then and there.

Kiss it better
From the kitchen, drop a pan loudly so it makes a noise. Stagger into the living room and sit down as if you're in agony. Say you've hurt yourself and need him to kiss it better. When he asks where, pull up your skirt to reveal your naked Lady Garden.

Digital quality
Slip one of your own fingers inside yourself and run it over his mouth.

Scent of a woman
One evening, dab your innermost juices behind your ears, on your throat and on your wrists. The French call this your "cassoulet" and it's a way of sending out your pheromones. Once he's smelt it, he won't be able to keep his hands off you but he won't know why.

Please replace the handset
When he's on the phone, pull down his trousers and start giving him a slow, lusty blow job. This is a sexy tip, and a thrifty one, as he'll end that call in record time.

Taste the difference
In your kitchen, you probably have some flavor essences in the cupboard, like vanilla or peppermint. Sneak off and dab some over your clitoris and labia (not inside, because the sugar could spark a yeast infection) then find your man and challenge him to a game of "Guess that Flavor." Then vice versa—let him anoint himself and you guess.

Homes and hard-ons
Look up from your magazine and pretend you've been reading an article about oral sex. Say that 90 percent of women say that if their man suddenly surprised them with oral sex in the middle of a boring evening, they would feel so passionately turned-on that they would immediately want to jump on him and give him the best sex of his life, doing … (insert his very favorite sex act here).

Positions for the living room

If you worry the neighbors might be catching an eyeful, invest in heavy curtains or a black-out blind to hang behind your usual drapes. Don't forget any French doors or glass internal doors, too. Secondly, check the noise: in mid-summer with the windows wide open, you might accidentally be giving everyone in your road a live performance. Thirdly, if you've got kids, you might worry they'll burst in and witness behavior that will take years of therapy to forget. Just fit a lock in the door and hide the key, or put a bolt on it, high enough up so young kids can't use it to barricade themselves inside for a TV marathon.

Don't mention it's there—chances are no one will notice.

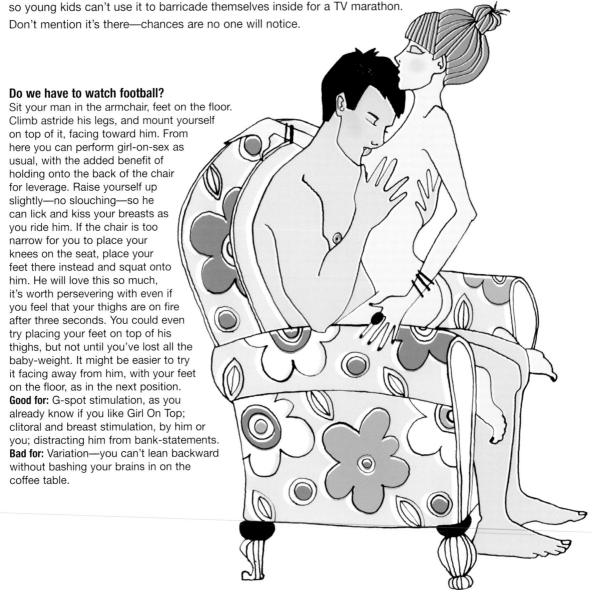

Do we have to watch football?

Sit your man in the armchair, feet on the floor. Climb astride his legs, and mount yourself on top of it, facing toward him. From here you can perform girl-on-sex as usual, with the added benefit of holding onto the back of the chair for leverage. Raise yourself up slightly—no slouching—so he can lick and kiss your breasts as you ride him. If the chair is too narrow for you to place your knees on the seat, place your feet there instead and squat onto him. He will love this so much, it's worth persevering with even if you feel that your thighs are on fire after three seconds. You could even try placing your feet on top of his thighs, but not until you've lost all the baby-weight. It might be easier to try it facing away from him, with your feet on the floor, as in the next position.

Good for: G-spot stimulation, as you already know if you like Girl On Top; clitoral and breast stimulation, by him or you; distracting him from bank-statements.

Bad for: Variation—you can't lean backward without bashing your brains in on the coffee table.

He'll never notice it's *Beaches* again

With him sitting in the armchair as before, you climb on top of him, but facing away, so you're the one watching TV, not him. Keep your feet flat on the floor and sit on his lap, leaning forward to increase the depth of the penetration. He can reach around and grab your breasts or the remote-control.

Good for: Deep thrusting. Lean forward and support yourself on something low, like the coffee table or a footstool, for even more depth. You can also reach down and stimulate your clitoris or fondle his testicles.
Bad for: Kissing, or gazing into his eyes as he comes. But you could position a mirror in front of you to improve the view—and he can watch you riding him.

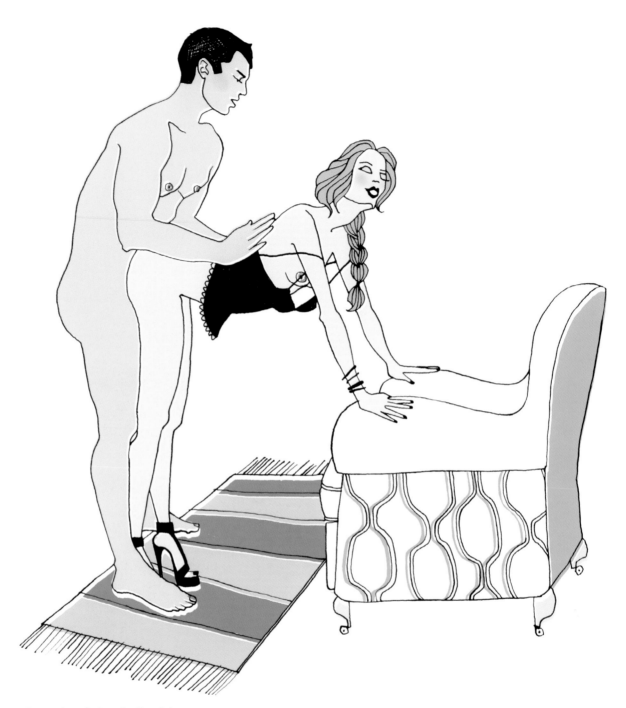

Go on then, but make it quick

Stand up and lean forward, holding onto the arm of the chair, while he takes you, doggy style, from behind. You might find this position more comfortable if you wear high heels, as you'll probably end up on tiptoes. This position is great for both of you—he gets the depth and view of doggy style, you get the G-spot stimulation and the freedom to use your hands. He can also be as rough as he likes, as you

can use the chair for support. By the end of this you might find yourself head-first in the chair, but you'll be happy. Also try this position with your thighs pressed tightly together, and his legs outside yours. Even more stimulating.

Good for: Everything! This is lounge-lovin' at its hottest.
Bad for: Slow, sensual, face-strokey romance, if you're not long past that nonsense already.

Ooh, I think I found a quarter

Sit on the armchair with your legs wide open, resting them on the arms of the chair (or on his shoulders). Your man kneels between your legs and slides in. From here it's very easy for you to massage your clitoris or hold your lips open so he can enjoy the wide-open view of you. Or you can place your hands right next to your vagina and press in on either side of your opening. He'll feel the extra pressure on his penis as he thrusts into you. You can stroke and fondle your breasts as he watches (a good move to save for when your favorite TV soap opera starts and you want him to finish), and he can take turns to shag you, then pull out and give you oral sex. Nice!

Good for: Comfort (it's bliss for you) and being completely opened-up.

Bad for: His knees—get him to use your gardening kneel-pad.

They'll never believe this at your reading group

Stand on the couch. That's right. Stand on it—like you tell your kids never to do—while your man stands on the floor in front of you. Now bend or straighten your legs until you're at the right height so he can enter you. It's not comfortable, it's not safe, and it's not good for your couch-covers, but by God, will it feel new and risky. Grab onto his bottom if you feel you're losing your balance, and keep your legs well apart.

Good for: Rough and ready, thrill-seeking sex like you haven't had since you bought the mobile home. It's not the most stimulating position for either of you if I'm honest, but it corrects the height difference that can stop some couples humping upright.
Bad for: The springs.

If you're sleeping on the couch, I'm coming with you

If your couch is deep enough for you both to lie on, side-by-side, it's good for the spoons position. You know the drill: you both lie on your sides and he enters you from behind, while you raise up your top leg to make access easier. This is better on the couch than in bed in some ways, as he can brace his feet against the arm of the couch to help him do more interesting up-and-down moves (as opposed to the vintage in-and-out), and you can casually leaf through a magazine or watch TV. Reach down and rub your clitoris, caress your breasts, reach back and fondle the base of his penis—it's all good.

Good for: Slow, leisurely nookie, lots of G-spot action for you—and it's classic pregnancy position.

Bad for: Deep penetration, but you can always stay in this one until you climax, then move into a rear-entry position to help him finish.

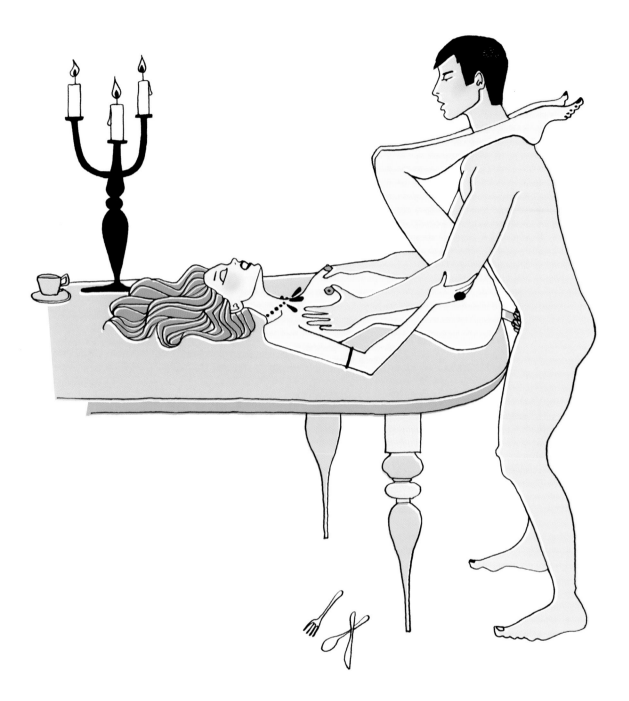

Mind the napkins

Does your dining table reach your man's naughty bits? If so, it's perfect for this position, which is very stimulating for both of you and a great way of subtly telling dinner-party guests it's time to go. Lie back on the table and open your legs. Let your man enter you, place one leg, or both, on his shoulders, then he just thrusts away. From here he can rub your clitoris, stroke your breasts, or clear away the plates, whichever you prefer.

Good for: All-over body stimulation for you, and he gets a lovely view of your lust-stricken body as you writhe by the condiments.

Bad for: Your ego if the table collapses, as it did for a friend of mine. (Turned out it had wood-rot, but she is scarred forever mentally.)

Thank heavens I vacuumed

Lie on your stomach on the floor, ideally a carpeted floor—not just for comfort, but for stimulation. We'll get to that in a minute. Now raise your bottom slightly and let your man enter you, supporting his weight on his hands as if he was doing push-ups. While he thrusts, push your clitoris into the floor— or any small soft toys that happen to be abandoned there—and circle it around to stimulate it as much as possible.

Good for: Giving him the rear-entry he loves while making it more satisfying for you.

Bad for: Kissing, watching each other, the carpet.

Bathroom

Show me the state of your bathroom and I can instantly tell the **state of your sex life.** Really. I know that's a bold statement, and one that means I'll never be welcome to have a pee at your house ever again, but it's true. The bathroom reveals how the woman of the house feels about her sensuality. It tells me whether you're feeling **fiesty and feminine,** or frazzled and frumpy. It shows me how much time and effort you're spending on yourself, and whether or not you've allowed your **inner vixen** to become buried under the strain of running the home. It also shows how good an aim the men of the house have, but I'm not so concerned with that, to be honest …

Scrub up before you get down

So, let's explore your bathroom. If you have more than one, head to the bathroom that you usually use. And let's start our inspection for signs of a healthy Inner Sex Goddess …

Candles

An indication of how often you set time aside to wallow in a deep, luxurious bath, many candles burned right down means you either take lots of pampering time or you have more than your fair share of outages. If you don't see candles in there, put them on your shopping list as you'll need them later. Not a candle fan? Then order some bathtub lights—small, colored lights that you can stick on the sides of the bathtub to glow prettily under the water.

Bath oils

Not bubble bath, and especially not bubble bath that comes in a novelty bottle shaped like a pirate, but sensuous bath *oil*. It slips into the water and turns bathtime into a deep, sensuous love-fest. If you need to get some, choose some in sexy scents like ylang-ylang (said to rev up the sex drive), cinnamon, eucalyptus, or lavender (men love it).

Beauty treatments

Lots of them. They show you feel worth pampering and prettifying. Face packs, deep-conditioning hair treatments, moisture masks, and body lotions are all wonderful for looking after your Inner Minx. Really. They also show that you're not suffering from depression (unless the packets and tubs are hidden under layers of cobwebs); when a woman suffers from depression, research has shown that she stops looking after her health and hygiene. So the more beauty treatments you do, the better you'll feel inside. Tuck them away in a pretty basket. Anything with labels like, "Shampoo for Thin, Greasy, Lifeless, Really Quite Horrible Hair" and "Facial Hair Remover for Girls Who could Work in Circuses" should not be in full view of your man when he brushes his teeth. It will remove your mystery instantly. Keep your beauty treatments and sanitary protection out of view.

Erotic art

Many artists have painted female bathers, and prints of these look fabulous in a bathroom. One very sexy friend of mine commissioned an artist to paint a portrait of her draped in a towel, poised to climb into the bath. It looks wonderful in the bathroom, but she complains that male guests go in there to wash their hands and don't come out for hours.

Music

Very posh readers may have speakers in their bathrooms that play music from the main stereo in the house. The rest of us can rely on a shower radio. Both are good for playing sexy, soft music while you bathe alone or with your lover.

Toys

Neatly store away toys in boxes between bathtimes—this is something that few moms bother to do, but it's worth it. If your bathroom is constantly littered with garish plastic toys, foam letters stuck all over the tiles, and pieces of plastic building blocks waiting to spear your rear when you sink down into the bath, it will not feel like a sensuous space. Get an attractive box and make putting toys away part of the bathtime routine. I would suggest that you keep the foam letters up on the tiles and use them to spell out sexy messages to your partner, but remember to remove them or you'll either get questions from the kids such as, "What does 'schlong' mean?" or sly smiles from the plumber who knows all too well.

Coming clean

Get an attractive box (besides your own) to put a collection of bathtime toys in. These are such a great, fun aid to your sex life that I'd go full-out and recommend you buy a separate, lockable medicine cabinet solely to store your underwater gadgets. Most sex toys now come in waterproof versions, and there are enough to make any bathtime steamy. (Boring Note: Remember to use only waterproof toys in the bath or shower.) You could also keep some erotic fiction in that medicine cabinet to read in the bath. Pour a glass of wine, play some sensuous music, relax in a deep, oily bath, and relax. Or you could listen to some audio erotica.

I rub my ducky

If you want to buy a specific toy, I'd suggest one of the naughty rubber ducks that contain a powerful vibrator. They say it's discreet enough to sit on the edge of the bath without declaring, "The woman of the house likes to rub herself off in the shower!" but I'd still tuck it away. If your kids find it, the younger ones will just play with it for hours until the batteries run out, and the teenage ones will stop using the bathroom completely. The vibrating section is in the beak—shaped to give clitoral satisfaction—so you can hold it against your clitoris or, on lower speeds, against the tip of your man's penis. Not so discreet is the newly launched I Rub My Bondage Ducky.

Waterproof vibrator

A normal vibrator, but safe to use in the shower or bath. If you've never tried this, I'd encourage you— either slip into your man's early-morning shower (men's testosterone is at its highest level in the morning) and hold it against his perineum while you give him a sensual hand job, or keep it to yourself and give yourself a naughty treat during the day.

Waterproof vibrator with suction base

Quite an advanced toy, but delicious. It's a vibrator that you can stick onto the base or side of your bathtub—or onto the bathroom tiles—and ride passionately. Absolutely intense, but make sure you have a nonslip mat underneath you! You don't have to keep this in the bathroom either—it sticks very well to any smooth surface. Pretty noisy, so use it while the shower's running if you have elderly relatives staying, or a jealous partner.

Clitoral massage pad

A gentler version of bathtime bliss comes from this clitoral massager. It's just a little pad covered with plastic beads that you can use to masturbate with under water. A good way to get yourself in the mood during a pre-sex bath, or a soothing way to relax.

Glass dildo

Most major sex shops now sell glass dildos and sex toys, which make perfect bathing companions. The glass adjusts its temperature to that of the bath water, gently warming you up from the inside. Also they're silent, so nobody will know what you're up to.

Power showerhead

The best investment you can make in your bathroom sex life is a power shower. Many women have found they can orgasm really easily by holding a showerhead against their clitoris for just a few minutes. Don't spray the water inside your vagina, but allow the stream to pound against your love-button instead. Keep it a sexy secret, or invite your man into the bathroom to watch your good, clean fun.

Look sexy on the outside

Apart from playing with waterproof toys and reading erotic fiction, you can use the bathroom to get clean as well. Who knew?! You can also use it to make yourself look your absolute sexiest every day. That's what we're going to discuss now. How to look sexy—not pretty, but sexy, there's a difference—and how to maintain your body so it's delectable and sex-ready all the time, even when you don't have hours to spare. There is a big difference between looking pretty and sexy. Sexiness lasts longer, so that's what we're going to concentrate on here. You probably already know how to make the most of your appearance prettiness-wise, but do you know how to smoulder like a siren, radiating sex appeal while you do your shopping at the supermarket?

Long hair

This is the easiest way to change your appearance from "sensible" to "siren." Long hair has traditionally been used by women to tempt men, so wear your mane with pride. If you don't have a mane of hair, slap yourself and start growing one. Now.

Don't fall into the trap of getting a sensible bob once you have children. There will come a point when you want to, but resist. Long hair is no harder to look after than short hair, in many ways its easier as you can go longer between trims and won't spend as long styling it. You can wear it up during the day to avoid low-flying jars of yogurt, then release it at night to look sexy for your man. It's one thing to look sensible and practical at the school gates, but do you want to look sensible and practical in bed?

Don't, either, feel you have to cut your hair on the stroke of your 40th birthday. A mane of hair is flattering to everybody, long after you'd expect. Look at Madonna, Twiggy, Goldie Hawn. After the menopause, a woman's hormone level drops and hair might become dryer, but regular moisturizing treatments and specialty hair products can keep it looking lovely, so ask your hairdresser for advice.

Long hair is very sensual in bed—let it trail over your man's skin as you work down his body before performing oral sex. Coil it around his penis. Let him bury his hands in your hair as you kiss him. Wear it up in a French bun, then let him watch as you remove the clip and it spills over your shoulders.

Sexy make-up

Don't complain that you haven't time to wear make-up every day. The following look takes five minutes and concentrates on making your face look the sexiest that it can.

Light-reflecting tinted moisturizer: A dewy glow is the sexiest look for skin, so start with this. If you buy one with sun-screen, you don't need to apply separate sun-screen lotion. Use it all over your face. Don't use powder unless you have to, and then just keep it to your T-Zone. Shiny skin is sexier.

Blusher: Rosy cheeks are very sexy; when aroused, blood rushes to your face. Recreate that effect with a liquid blush tint applied right over your foundation. Apply some to your earlobes and your neck, too, as these naturally grow flushed when we're turned on.

Lip gloss: Shiny lips are very sexy, because they look poutier and more like you're drooling with lust. They also look fuller, which will make men imagine kissing you and, um, other things. Don't use clear gloss unless your lips are naturally rosy—colored glosses give your lips the look of arousal, so choose a warm red tone. Liquid cheek-tints can be used on your lips, too.

Eye shadow, liner, and mascara: Don't spend hours over these, use just enough to open up your eyes and give you the confidence to gaze at people instead of the floor. Brush your eyebrows into shape with a special comb (a baby toothbrush works well), then finish with eye drops—a good way to give you the sparkly eyes of a woman who's just enjoyed a vigorous porking. And you're done! That wasn't so hard, was it?

Sexy skin

Men love the feel of women's soft skin. When he touches your hands and find them meltingly soft, he imagines those dainty, delicate digits gently unzipping his trousers and performing obscene acts to his undercarriage. So slap on hand cream every day. But—and forgive me for asking such a personal question—how smooth is your bottom? Go on, have feel around in your panties now and tell me. Is the skin on your cheeks soft and silky, or as rough as sandpaper?

According to Sydney Biddle Barrows, who ran a highly successful brothel and wrote about it in her book of sex tips, *Secrets of a Mayflower Madam*, most women in long-term relationships neglect the skin on their bottoms. A smooth rear, she says, is the mark of a high-class call girl, and she imposed a blistering regime on her girls' cheeks, sandblasting them and dipping them in acid. Or something. Anyway, make sure yours is silky: use a body-scrub on it every day, or make your own by mixing sea-salt crystals with olive oil, scrubbing your bottom furiously, then washing it off in the shower.

Sexy tan

A healthy glow will make you look and feel instantly sexier. It can also be the difference between having the lights on or off during sex. However, going to bed smothered in fake-tan lotion is a real passion killer; it gets all over the sheets and, if your man accidentally touches you in the night, he wakes up looking like a piebald pony. Use the body lotions that contain just a hint of fake tan and gradually build up color over a few days. Rub it in every morning after your shower.

Sexy feet

Providing you take care of them, your feet can be one of the sexiest parts of your body. Even though

he might not actually come out and say, "Sweet Jesus, are you growing those talons for Halloween?" he won't fantasize about giving you toe-jobs either. So treat yourself to a pedicure, and have your toenails painted in an impractical but delectable fuck-me red. Make sure you keep your feet hair-free, too: one of my male friends actually uses a mental image of a woman's hairy toes to stop himself coming too soon! Nice.

Once you've prettified your feet, perform a sexy surprise on your man. Next time you're sitting opposite him at a dinner, slip off your shoes and use your feet to massage his penis through his trousers. When he's naked, you can also cover the soles of your feet with massage oil, place his manhood between them, and stroke him sensually up and down.

Feel sexy on the inside

Of course, all the nail-polishing and bottom-scrubbing in the world won't make you look like a sexy woman, if really, you're not that bothered about having sex. Sex appeal shines from inside—it's said that Marilyn Monroe radiated sexiness because she thought about sex all the time. She'd imagine what it would be like with every man she met, and visualized them in bed. Do you do this? Are your regular, daily thoughts along the lines of, "I wonder how he would feel inside my pussy" or more like, "Did I remember to feed the cat?" If you're not interested in nookie, you might think it's worse if you go leaping around the house all groomed and glamorous, only to turn your perfectly tanned shoulder on your partner in bed. So let's discuss the reasons behind a lowered libido. These could be affecting you or your partner.

Prescription medicines

As we're in the bathroom, we'll start with your medicine cabinet (the one with medicines in, not the filthy one) to see if either you or your man are taking any medications that might be affecting your libido. The following are known to interfere with it:
• Birth control pills
• Hormone replacement therapy
• Anticonvulsion medication (used to treat Epilepsy)
• Antidepressants

Long-term solution: If you are on any of the above medications, make an appointment with your doctor to discuss whether there are other options available, preferably a drug that won't interfere with your sex drive. It's hard enough to stay sexually aroused when you live together, so you don't need any chemicals inhibiting your sex drive even more. If you are taking antidepressants, ask your doctor if you could be moved onto a variety that doesn't affect libido. In fact some treatments have been shown in studies to boost sex drives.

Stress

One of the most common causes of disinterest in sex but, thankfully, among the easiest to solve. Basically, when our minds are buzzing with to-do lists and reminders, the brain runs out of the space in which to fantasize or think about sex. For him,

receiving a sexy text in the middle of his work day will be an unwelcome distraction; for you, sex will be one more chore on your list at the end of the day.

Short-term fix: The least-stressed half of the couple should make life easier for the more stressed. This means no more demands for sex, but an offer of a relaxing massage would be good, as would running a warm bath filled with bubbles. Don't feel annoyed if the massage or bath lead to your partner instantly falling asleep—it will relax them and so they're much more likely to be up for a romp the following night.

Long-term solution: If stress goes on for more than six months, you'll have to look at rearranging your life to get rid of it. It's one thing to undergo intense periods of stress in search of a goal, for example moving to a new area or pushing for a massive work promotion, but if stress becomes your life as you strive for a vague "better future," you'll lose more than go gain. Consider sitting down with your partner to see if they can lighten the load, or if you can alter your lifestyle completely.

Becoming a parent

It's not only mothers who suffer after a baby joins the family, dads do, too. The identity and self-image of both partners change forever, and it can feel like your time at home together is engaged in a constant game of "who's the most tired." It's also tough as you are both under such different pressures—mom has to recover from the birth, adjust to her body's new shape (see "I'm unattractive" on page 66), cope with breastfeeding and maybe even battle post-natal depression. New dads feel extra responsibility to provide for the family, share the weight of baby care, navigate his partner's often confusing mood swings as her hormones stabilize, and adjust to being a third-wheel in the family for a while. Whew! No wonder it takes new parents an average of six months to get back in the saddle sexually.

Short-term fix: Talk, talk, talk. Nothing will keep you together during this point in your life better than opening up to each other about how you feel. Admit it's a shock and exhausting, confess to feeling you're a hopeless parent, come clean that you often don't have a clue what the baby wants when it's crying—everything is OK. It's a relief to hear your other half confess their bewilderment, so let it all out! Then praise each other's efforts, share the load as much as possible, and mourn the loss of your freedom together, while you celebrate the new arrival. Often talking is cathartic and can lead to a sexy encounter; if not, realize that most couples regain their pre-pregnancy level of sexual activity within one year, so hang in there.

Long-term solution: A babysitting circle—set one up yourselves with friends with children, or look for details of a local one on community or school websites. Going out as a couple regularly will help you see each other as sexual beings again, not just Mom and Dad. Also, work at getting the baby into a routine as early as you feel is right—once you reclaim your evenings as child-free zones, you'll have more time to snuggle on the couch again.

Illness

Recovering from a major illness can have a huge effect on the sex drives of both halves of a couple; the one recovering and the one supporting. Some drugs affect the sex drive, and adjusting to the aftermath of surgery can be difficult.

Short-term fix: Take sex off the menu for a while, and use the sensate-focus-massage technique to readjust to each other without sex. It's a form of massage, where you and your partner stroke and caress each other without intercourse—first in nonsexual areas, gradually building up to sexual touching. You don't have to be naked to do it, and most couples report it is an excellent way of rebuilding intimacy in their relationship without having sex. The most common reaction to a sensate focus massage is to burst into tears—which will either put you off the idea completely, or make you even keener to try it.

Long-term solution: Join a support group for people recovering from, or living with, illnesses, and their carers. Ask for details from your local healthgroup, or sign up for counseling.

Emotional problems

Good sex is an emotional activity, so it's perfectly understandable that emotional problems may interfere with your desire to make love, or the pleasure you receive from it. Recovering from bereavement, infidelity, or sexual abuse can all cause shockwaves in a couple's sex life, as can the simple strain of going through a bit of a shouty patch.

Short-term fix: Sorry boys, it's talking again! Communication will get you through most emotional problems and out the other side, and it doesn't have to be talking to each other, although, of course, that can help your partner know what you're going through. Widening the number of people you talk to can be a good way of avoiding feeling like a big, blubbering burden to one person.

Long-term solution: Counseling is the only really effective way to work through deep-seated emotional problems, and it can be used in conjunction with antidepressive medication or antianxiety pills to get you through a period of real trauma. Do be aware that these can cause you to lose your sex drive even more, though, so ask for one of the newer types that don't interfere with sexual function.

I'm unattractive

Feeling unattractive can severely dampen your libido, and it's something that women and men can suffer from. A change within your body, from gaining weight to having a baby through to major surgery (see Illness above), may spark it off, but some people simply grow up feeling they're unattractive. Traditionally women have been plagued with looks-based self-esteem issues, but counselors are seeing more and more men suffering from the problem, as well as increasing numbers of males developing associated eating disorders. As well as causing low libido, feeling you're not good enough for your partner can damage your relationship, causing jealousy, paranoia, and general doormat behavior. The good news is that this will lower their libido, too, so at least you'll be in synch … The bad news is, it will ruin any chance of a healthy future together.

Short-term fix: I hate to be brutal but—have you considered that maybe you're not honestly looking your best? If you've gained weight and stopped exercising, you won't be in tiptop shape and your insecurity might be perfectly justified. No, your partner won't leave you if you gain 10 pounds or only go to the gym to buy lunch, but they will notice how you're constantly putting yourself down. It gets draining being a cheerleader to someone who's unhappy for a reason, so stop demanding reassurance and start moving your butt! You'll feel better as soon as you start tackling the problem. However, if your appearance hasn't changed but your perception of it has, take a look at your relationship. Does your partner put you down, or withhold compliments as a way to keep you guessing? Do you feel controlled by them, do they order for you in restaurants ("She'll have a salad, without dressing") and stop you seeing your friends? If so, run! Leave this relationship before your confidence is destroyed forever. This is a very real form of emotional abuse. If your insecurity comes from seeing your body in a different way—perhaps after having a baby—you can try the love-your-body exercise on page 69.

Long-term solution: Once you've tackled any physical body issues and reached a healthy target weight, and lost the 180 pounds of unsightly weight (your ex) that was putting you down, any remaining insecurity is most likely to be down to emotional issues. Therapy is a very effective tool here—ask your primary care physician for a referral to a cognitive behavioral therapist who'll teach you ways to sidestep any negative thought-patterns you've acquired. And start looking outside yourself for other interests: volunteering is an excellent way to help in your community while building up your confidence. Volunteers regularly score lower than the rest of the population for depression and anxiety.

Love your body

Do you feel you have a sexy body? Do you enjoy pampering and beautifying it, smothering it with sensual creams and potions as often as possible? Or do you prefer not to think about it? Here's an exercise to do right now—or as soon as you can grab 10 minutes of complete privacy—which will help to see your body as desirable and beautiful as possible.

Love-your-body exercise

Find 10 minutes when you can be alone in your bedroom, grab your hand mirror, strip naked, and lie down on the bed. Relax. Now, holding the mirror, use it to look at specific parts of your body. Don't start with any Points of Paranoia you have (danger zones that you don't like looking at); start with neutral places like your face, neck, shoulders, and arms. When you lie down, see how your neck joins your chest—look at the little hollows there. If you were a man, wouldn't you like to kiss that skin and trace your tongue over your neck? Look at your arms and the soft skin of your hands—how lovely must it feel when you run those hands over your partner's body and wrap your arms around him?

Look at your legs. The soft skin, and how it gets softer as it goes into your inner thighs. Imagine running your hands along those legs—they must feel very soft and smooth in contrast to your man's hard, hairy legs. Imagine how he must feel when those legs go around his waist when you're having sex with him.

Now look at your breasts. Don't think about their size or shape—just look at your nipples. Run your hand over them and feel how they instantly respond. Imagine your partner sucking on them gently, feeling them stiffen in his mouth. Hot! Run your hand over the smooth curves of your breasts. Imagine his mouth is caressing every inch of them.

Look at your tummy. Feel how soft it is. You may feel differently toward your tummy after pregnancy, especially if you have had a cesarean, but even if it's not as flat as you'd like, it still feels smooth and feminine. Look down and see how the skin changes as we approach your pubic bone—see how the hair starts growing there. Look at the way your legs open, and how your lips are exposed. Slide a finger inside you and feel how hot you are. Put yourself in your lover's mind—how warm and welcoming must it be when he runs his hand over your vagina and feels how deep and slippery you are. Imagine his hard penis, and how it must feel for him when he slides himself inside you …

Look at every area of your body. From your soft, wet mouth down to the curving arches of your feet. You bring all this to the bed when you have sex with your partner. You are smooth and warm, soft and tempting, wet and luscious. He is lucky to have you! This is how your partner feels when he reaches over to you in bed next to him. He's not thinking, "She's got cellulite on his bottom and I think I saw a varicose vein earlier." He's thinking, "Mmm, curves. Mmm, bits that stiffen when I lick them. Mmm, softness." You are a contrast to him in every possible way, and that's why men's minds are absolutely fixated on having sex with us. When you walk around in your everyday life, banish negative thoughts about yourself and your body. Remember how you look now. That's how you should think of yourself every day: that warm, smooth body with all its mysteries and temptations. If you can keep those thoughts in your head, you will exude sex appeal, as your movements will be slower and more fluid. You won't have the jerky, head-down walk of a woman who feels unattractive—you will saunter a bit more, swing your hips a little bit more, and pull your shoulders back naturally because it shows off your boobs.

Hot and cold running lust

When your man is having a shower or a bath—whether that's a daily or annual event—there are several ways you can give him a very sensuous and passionate surprise. These are some of my favorites. Note: If you have kids, start seeing your bathroom as a venue for sex, making the most of the lock on the door and its discretely frosted windows. To make it a sexier space, paint it a soothing color—pink and pale blue are meant to increase the libido—and add a few pictures of women bathing. You can also buy a separate, lockable, medicine cabinet and fill it with sensuous supplies like waterproof sex toys, flavored condoms, and massage oils, to keep the passion alive but even the keenest-eyed teenager blissfully unaware.

Wet 'n' wild

When your partner heads off for his shower, follow him into the bathroom and undress him. Most men fantasise about having a woman pleasure them in silence, so don't say anything, just start to remove his clothes. Run your hands sensuously over him as the garments fall to the floor. Then help him into the shower and use a fruit-scented shower gel to soap him down. Make sure you wash every inch of him, and then shampoo his hair. Give him a head massage, using your thumbs to press into the nape of his neck, and gently squeeze his earlobes with your fingers, as they contain acupuncture pressure points and are very sensitive. Then have him step out of the shower. Dry him by licking the water off with your tongue, then either lay him on the floor on several towels and straddle him, or wrap him in a warm towel and take him upstairs.

Warm water dip

When a man's testicles are surrounded by warm water, he feels ejaculation very strongly, so the bath is a good place to give him a hand job. Start by running your hands all over his stomach, then let them slide down so they are both surrounding his penis. Use one hand to hold the base of his penis so it gently pulls his foreskin back (if he has one). Keep that hand in place all the time, and use the other to grip the shaft gently, and slide it up and down. When it comes to pressure, the best way I heard to describe the right amount was "the same force with which you'd hold a can of coke." Stroke up and down, and occasionally twist your hand around in a helter-skelter motion. Keep your pressure steady, and slowly increase the speed. When he seems to be approaching orgasm, don't slow down or stop. But also don't go too fast and furious—too fast will tire your arm and you'll find yourself muttering, "Oh for God's sake, can we move this along?" and too furious will be painful for him. When he starts to orgasm, keep masturbating him very gently with one hand and use the fingertips of the other to push gently on his perineum (the area between his balls and anus). This will feel like you are milking every last drop out of him, which men love. Stop touching him when he's finished, as any touching after his orgasm can feel unpleasant to him. Then kiss him sensuously, and don't mention that it's his turn to clean the bathtub.

Naughty rubber ducks

Raise the temperature of your love-making from luke-warm to scalding by using sex toys in the bathroom. You can now buy several different toys for bathtime bliss (see page 60) or you can make any existing toy waterproof by slipping it inside a condom and tightly tying the end in a knot. If you want to buy a specific toy, I'd suggest one of the naughty rubber ducks. They look like normal, innocent rubber ducks and so can live on the edge of the bath without giving any visitors heart failure.

Shower power

For fast, furious frolics, you can't beat the shower. The heady combination of pounding water, billowing steam, and upright position makes it a passion hot spot. So the next time you're feeling grubby, grab your man, jump in, and perform one of the treats described below.

• While your man is in the shower, write a sexy message in the steam on the mirror telling him what you want him to do to you that night. Make it explicit!

• If you have a shower with a glass door, press your boobs up against the glass when you're showering, so your man can see them on the other side. Men love the sight of your breasts squashed against the glass, and he'll get in to help you wash.

• Take the showerhead off the wall, and press it against your clitoris with the water coming out at full strength. Many women can orgasm this way. If your man is around, ask him to massage your breasts while you pleasure yourself. Afterward, return the favor: let him hold the shower so the water is drumming against his testicles or perineum, while you relieve him with your hand.

• Get into the shower with your partner and wash his hair under the water, then lick and caress the back of his neck. This is a very sexy spot for men—everything you do to his neck, he'll feel in his penis!

• When you are both alone in the house, get into the shower and start masturbating noisily. Squeal with delight, and let him come upstairs to investigate and "discover" what you're doing to yourself.

• If you are embarrassed about your body, get into the shower with your man wearing a thin T-shirt or blouse—the water will quickly turn the material transparent and look devastatingly sexy, but will hide any parts you don't like.

• Turn off the bathroom lights and place votive candles around the room—or buy the bathtub lights I mentioned earlier, and turn them on. Run the shower to make the room steamy, and if possible scent the air with eucalyptus. It will feel like you're in the middle of a rainforest in a tropical storm as you lead your man in there and make passionate love to him in the shower, or up against the door.

• Get into the shower together, and apply a fruit-scented shower gel to each other. Then wash—but one rule: you're not allowed to use your hands. See how clean (or how dirty) you can get each other just by slipping and sliding your bodies together.

• Screw a mirror into the wall of your shower, or swap the normal tiles for mirrored tiles. This will transform all your positions, as you can still look into each other's eyes during sex, even if you're doing it doggy style. If that's a bit drastic, open the bathroom cabinet so you can see each other in the mirror on the door.

Bathtime bliss

Don't just use the bathroom as your private retreat. While it's blissful to lock yourself in there and soak in a tub, or masturbate fervently with a battery-operated duck, it's not much fun for the man who's left outside. Men adore pampering, so next time you want to treat him, turn your bathroom into his private sexy spa.

Dress in a long, floaty outfit, tie your hair back with a long scarf, and get into character as a demure, submissive servant. If you need to go into the garden and let loose a Tourette's-syndrome-style stream of nags and commands before you can fully embrace this role, go for it.

Next prepare the bathroom: light it with candles, make sure it's nice and warm, and use an oil burner to scent it with lavender or ylang-ylang. Have stacks of fluffy towels waiting on the radiator, and flowers—sexy ones like arum lilies, or a sensual orchid—in a vase.

Find your man, bow when you see him, and tell him it is time for his "water ritual." Then demurely follow him into the bathroom and perform either of the following:

Salon selectives

Undress him and wrap a warm towel around his waist. Let him kneel on a towel in front of the bath, then bend his head forward, and wash his hair as reverently as you can. Let him feel your breasts pushing against his back "by accident" as you lean over him. Apply conditioner and massage his head while it sinks in, then rinse it off.

Wrap a towel around his head and use your tongue to capture any drops of water around his neck and ears—both very sensual places on your man. Then lead him upstairs, where he'll find a glass of wine or his favorite drink, and a copy of an erotic book on his pillow. Ask him to call you if he requires anything else, then demurely retreat and await further orders …

"Aroma" therapy

Run a very hot bath and sprinkle rose petals or herbs on the surface. Undress your man and, making sure he is warm enough, slather olive oil onto his body—concentrate on his buttocks, kneading and massaging them with firm, seductive strokes—then give him a salt scrub by rubbing handfuls of salt crystals (granulated sugar works fine, too) over his thighs and buttocks. Use long, firm strokes.

Then have him stand in the bath while you gently soap him down. (Whatever you do, don't let the soap get inside his penis—it stings.)

Let him relax in the water, lying down with his head on a folded towel, and hand him a drink. Then gently wash him by pouring bath water slowly over his chest and neck. Ask if he feels clean or if he needs further washing. One hundred dollars says he will feel that his genitals are still grubby, so gently run your hands up and down until he gets hard.

Lastly, help him out of the bath, wrap him in a warmed bathrobe, and take him upstairs to lick and suck him until he comes. Tuck him into bed and kiss his forehead.

Positions for the bathroom

Wet and wild! That's you and your man, skidding and slipping your way to orgasmic overload in your tub. Once you've experienced lovemaking underwater, you'll never want to get back onto dry land. So grab your oil-based lubricant, a nonslip bathmat, and your trusty cabin boy and set sail for unexplored shores, me hearties …

Pull my plug

The easiest position for bathtime humping is always doggy style. But there are a million variations. You can bend over in the shower, lean over the bathtub, or try this seated position. With your man lying down in the tub, lower yourself on top of him, facing away. Your legs should be inside his legs—it's more of a squeeze but it keeps you feeling tighter inside. Squat down onto his lusty lifebelt. You won't be able to move very much aside from raising and lowering yourself, but he can grab your hips and thrust himself into you.

Good for: Giving him a delicious view of your bottom rising and falling through the bubbles.
Bad for: Ease of movement; if you want to alter positions in any way, you're going to have to climb off first.
Variations: You can straighten your back and let him grab your boobs while you hump, or reach down with a hand and massage the base of his penis as he thrusts.

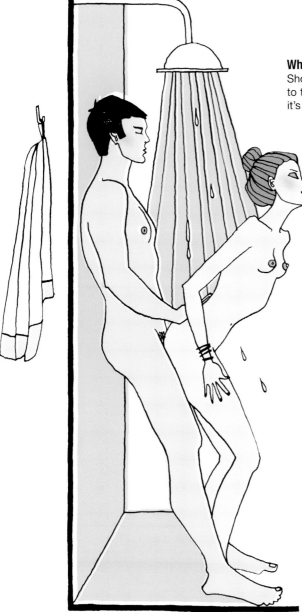

Who's got the loofah?

Shower-sex for the slightly lazy. This is a lovely position to try at the end of a hard day. First, run the shower so it's hot. Lead your man into the shower (or bathtub, if your shower hangs above it) and lean him against the wall. Then spin around and bend over in front of him. How deep you bend is up to you—very deep, so your hands are on the floor, will give you maximum penetration but a shorter shag (as it'll all get too much for him quite quickly); very shallow and you won't get the same intense penetration but it will be easier on your thigh muscles. Then let him thrust into you as the hot water cascades over your bodies.

Good for: Getting you deep-down clean.

Bad for: Any of that lovey-dovey, face-strokey, intimate business.

Variations: You can disengage, then spin around and face him, bracing one foot against the shower door or edge of the bathtub for leverage.

Slippery when wet

If your man is relatively snake-hipped, or you have one of those big, swanky tubs, this is the position for you. It gives you a feeling of weightlessness, so you can glide toward and away from him while he hangs onto your hips. (This is also a good position to try out when you're in a swimming pool, preferably one with forgiving lifeguards.) While your man kneels down in the bathtub, climb in with your back to him and place your legs either side of his hips. Then rest your hands on the tub and float your way back onto him.

Good for: That weightless feeling—very sexy.
Bad for: Clitoral stimulation, as you'll both have your hands busy.
Variations: Bend forward and rest on your forearms, raising your legs so they hook back up and over his shoulders.

While the tub fills, fill me

Most tubs are at an excellent height for naughtiness. Place one foot on the edge of the bathtub and suddenly you are opened wide for easy access from his tongue, fingers, a toy, or a throbbing shaft. Ditto for him, except you can suck and lick his throbbing tadge while he stands proud. And of course, you can make love in this position. Just stand facing each other and let him enter you, then wrap your leg around his hip. He then places a foot on the edge of the tub for support. You can then stand on tiptoe if he's taller than you, or bend your standing-leg if he's shorter.

Good for: Leaving your hands free to roam all over his (and your) body.

Bad for: Deep penetration, without a lot of gymnastics.

Variations: You can drop your raised foot and rest it on the edge of the bathtub (like him) for extra support.

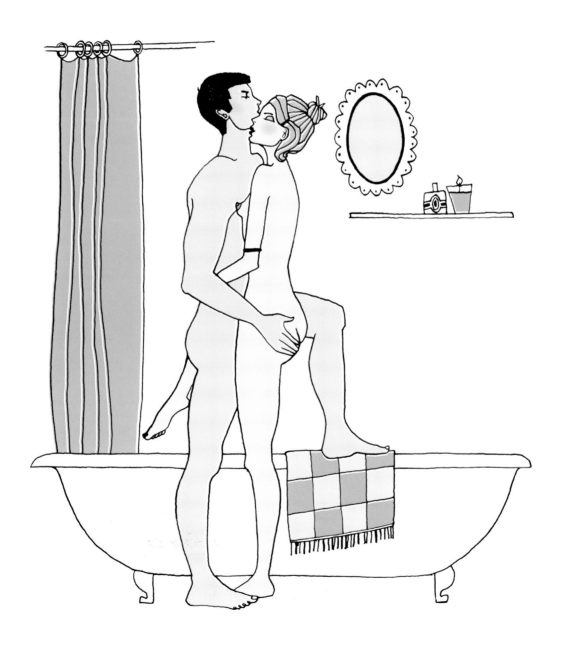

Back me up

Not a position for full sex (unless your man's penis is miles long), but one for lots of intimacy. After sex, relax in a bathtub together and sit in front of him. Let his hands glide all over you, concentrating on your exciting places like boobs, clitoris, and bottom. Let him gently soap you all over, while you lean back and let his penis nestle between your bottom-cheeks. He can kiss the back of your neck, and lick along your shoulders.

Good for: Working yourselves gently back up for another session. You might also find that you can clench your bottom-cheeks around his penis to give him gentle masturbation.
Bad for: Penetration, unless he is a medical marvel.
Variation: When you both are aroused again, just raise yourself up until you are sitting on top of his penis. Then, as you were.

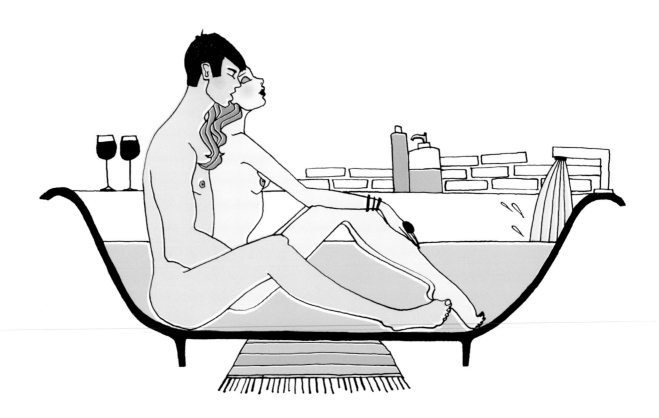

Party piece de resistence

No evening away from home would be worth attending unless you can break away from the pack and screw your man in private. The bathroom is the obvious place, so slip away with your fella and try this quick knee-trembler. Find anything you can rest a foot on—toilet seat, bathtub, bidet, passed-out guest—and brace yourselves while you enjoy a vertical knee-trembler. Make it lusty, passionate, and quick. Let him grab your rear with both hands to intensify the sensations and move you to his motion. Afterward, return to the party all blasé. If they guess, they'll just be jealous.

Good for: Making you feel you're 15 again.

Bad for: Everything else, but still worth a try.

Variations: Hang onto his tush and grind yourself into him feverishly. Rub your clitoris against his hips as you thrust. Grab a toilet brush and spank him madly ... (I'm kidding.)

Bedroom

Here we are then. We're here, in the one room of the home that's **synonymous with sex.** In this chapter we're going to explore everything about nookie—how to spice it up, how to cool it down, how to act out one another's **secret fantasies,** and how to do everything so perfectly that you'll get the top score for both technical expression and **artistic merit.** We'll even cover what to do when your only bedtime fantasy is a **cup of cocoa** and an early night, alone. But first, do you mind if I have quick nose around the décor?

Creating a sexy space

In my job, I've met many couples who are having a problem in their sex life and need help spicing things up. One of the first things I do is ask to see their bedroom. This initially scares them, because they think I might be one of those dubious "sex counselors" who insist on sleeping with couples to "find out where they're going wrong," but once I calm their nerves and we all troop upstairs, what do I usually find? Sweetly candlelit grottos of beauty? Well, what do you think? (Clue: No.) The average bedroom has very little in it that says "sex" or "desire." Instead, it has lots of things in it that say "I can't be bothered to hang my clothes up," and "I like to empty the change out of my pockets at night and leave it right here," and "I keep missing the laundry basket."

Very, very few of us bother to create a sexy bedroom in our house. And then we wonder why we never feel sexy. I know this feels like nagging, but think: what is so sexy about shagging in a fancy hotel? It's that fantastic bedroom. There are mirrors everywhere. Flowers stand on a little table, next to a discreet lamp. The closets hold all your clothes, and the dressing table has drawers inside so you can hide away your make-up and DNA-encrusted hairbrushes. There's also a basket of fruit, a Bible, and a pile of leaflets of Things to Do in the Local Area. These aren't so helpful though, forget these. But in general, we can turn your bedroom into a sex den in very few moves. Let's get started.

How to create a sex den

Stand in the doorway of the bedroom and look around critically. Pretend you're a CSI investigator. What do you see? Does it say "come hither" or "please go away"? Feng shui experts believe that a bedroom should contain only a bed. Unless you live in a 19-bedroomed mansion with separate dressing and laundry rooms, that's never going to be possible, but you can hide things away so it nearly looks like that. These are crucial:

A laundry basket with a lid

Clothes strewn everywhere are the biggest Sex-Den No-No. Hide them in a lidded basket. If your partner seems incapable of using one, you do it. Yes, you! Stuff dirty laundry in there whenever you see it. It will take you about 30 seconds. If you're dying for something to nag him about, ask him if he's called his mother recently. Hang clean clothes up right away, don't leave them to fester in piles.

A closet big enough to hold all your clothes

If it's not big enough, throw clothes away until it is, or do "seasonal storage" where you store winter clothes away in the summer (or vice versa) in a lidded box under the bed. If your partner has too many clothes, secretly put all the stuff he never wears into a big box and hide it in the attic. After a year, if he hasn't asked where any of it is, you can safely throw it away. Don't go through his clothes together, as he will refuse to ditch anything, claiming it's all his favorite. Also, find somewhere to store your shoes so they're out of sight. You can buy inexpensive shoe cabinets that tuck them all away.

A big dressing table, or other "beauty storage"

All your make-up, lotions and hair products (including styling tools and brushes) need to be out of sight. I use stacking baskets for mine. One of my friends is an interior designer and she always buys small, attractive suitcases from charity stores and uses those. Whatever you use, make sure it's packed away.

Buy a cabinet to hide any computer equipment

You might need to have your "home office" in the bedroom, but we really don't want to see it. Chain furniture stores sell inexpensive cabinets that keep it all out of sight. The last thing either of you want to do in bed is catch sight of your laptop and leap up, screaming, "My deadline!"

Get bedside cabinets with storage inside

You're going to need these (she hinted, enigmatically).

Once this is done, all you see in your bedroom should be the bed and furniture. Perfect! Now we can add the sexy touches. The following are good:

Bring back hanging

On the walls I want to see lots of pictures and things that celebrate you as a couple. Not as a family, as a *couple*. On the walls you should have big photos of the two of you looking blissful. Also, Valentine's cards you've sent each other, dried flowers from your wedding bouquet, train tickets from your first date, movie tickets … All these things can be collected together and made into a vomit-inducing but rather charming collage to put in your bedroom. Use a deep frame, and plenty of clear glue to keep it secure. If you've traveled a lot together, frame maps of the places you've been, with notes or tiny photos attached. Lovely.

Candles

Candlelight is flattering and romantic, so make sure you have a good selection of candles in here at all times. Or you could use Christmas-tree lights, night-lights, or put a pink, low-wattage light bulb in the overhead light to cast a sexy glow.

A footstool or big floor cushion

Both of these can be slipped underneath your bottom to raise you up during sex, making him more likely to reach the places other men can't reach, and you can place them underneath your rear before your man has oral sex with you, which makes the whole thing much easier on his neck and shoulders and means he'll go on twice as long. (Whimper.) You can buy foam wedges for just this purpose from online sex stores. But if you ever bought one of those pregnancy pillows that supports your body, they work well, too, and you'll soon get over any misplaced feelings of uneasy guilt you might have using it for such a naughty purpose.

An appropriate headboard

If you want to explore the thrilling side of gentle BDSM (bondage and sado-masochism) and tie each other up—either before sex, or just when your guy is really getting on your nerves—then you're going to need a slatted headboard and, preferably, footboard on your bed. The old-fashioned bed frames are good, with bars across them to which you can attach silky scarves or ties. (Don't use ropes—they take so long to untie, you'll never make it back to the school before the afternoon pickup.) You could also clip sexy handcuffs to them. If you don't fancy any of that, consider investing in *some* kind of headboard for your bed. Because you can hold onto them and support yourself, they make it much easier to get into a lot of sexual positions—for instance, where you squat over your man, or doggy style without you having to lean over completely.

Mirrors

You need a mirror that is near the bed, or that can be moved near the bed, so you can watch yourselves romping. Feng shui experts, however, say this is unlucky if it's there all the time—you are visually increasing the number of people in your bed and, therefore, inviting infidelity. Hmm. Another superstition is never to hang a mirror on the inside of your bedroom door, as it's also very unlucky. (You might be dubious but, if you notice, you'll never see this in hotels.) If you believe any of this, a simple solution is to bolt a full-length mirror onto the inside of a closet door that, when the door is open, reflects the bed, but can be hidden away easily just by closing the door.

Mismatched libido

Mismatched sex drives are the most common problem faced by long-term couples, and one of the biggest sources of unhappiness. If you'd known, right from the start, that your partner would end up fancying sex only by the light of Halley's Comet, you would have asked yourself if you could handle that long-term and, if you couldn't, you would have ended the relationship. Similarly, if your man had known you would have a T-shirt printed with, "If you point that at me, I'm cutting it off," he might not have called you for a second date. But it never starts like that, does it? It's accidentally deceptive. Early in relationships, the excitement and novelty of one another boosts even the lowest sex drive, so you roll around happily for entire weekends, thinking you've found your ideal mate. This excitement factor is enough to bring both of you into perfect sync—the lower-sexed partner experiences a rise in libido because of the excitement of the new relationship; the higher-sexed mate thinks, "At last! I've found someone who can keep up with me!" But then, after a few years, the first flush of Eros-based, romantic love turns into a second, longer, calmer stage that behavioral scientists call "apathy."

From my many letters from both men and women, I can tell you that you are by no means alone if you've gone off even the thought of sex with your partner. Women especially seem prey to the problem —although, it has been suggested that the number of male suffers is rising. I've listed what I believe to be the most helpful ways to improve the situation.

When he's gone off sex
It's not just women who start having interminable headaches. Men go off sex, too—and without fail it makes their partners feel frumpy, unattractive, and low. It can happen for many different reasons. Pressures of work, emotional worries, infidelity, performance anxiety, hernias … You won't find out what his reason is until you ask him and even then he won't always be forthcoming.

It's a difficult subject for him to talk about. If you've ever gone off sex, you'll know how unsexy and pressurizing it is to be asked why. You don't hear: "Why have you gone off sex?" You hear: "I'm really horny, so you should be, too." Or, "How long is this going to go on for?" Or, "I'm unhappy and it's your fault." Or, "I demand sex from you, for my pleasure, not yours." For men, it's a difficult subject because it

embarrasses them. Lots of men pride themselves on their sexuality and feel that they shrink when their libido does. If his sex drive has vanished completely, he will be worried about it too, and privately concerned that it will never return. As soon as you talk to him about it, he will hear your dissatisfaction with him, and be forced to face the problem. His reactions might vary from anger to sulkiness to denial. He might have started secretly blaming you for the problem, because it's easier to think that you're in the wrong somehow than to face the possibility that his "manhood" is failing. He will also become miserable at the thought that he is making you miserable—most men derive great pleasure from satisfying their women (in bed and out) and feel crushed when they fail.

There isn't a way of asking him about this subject without it sounding like you're concerned, so my advice is: don't question him directly at the start. Follow the suggestions I've given below for at least a month before you raise the subject verbally. Many times, the problem will have solved itself before then.

Space—the first frontier
The best way to deal with this problem at the beginning is to retreat sexually. Not for any negative

reasons at all, just to give him some space from the problem. If his lowered libido is caused by stress or work pressures, those problems could resolve themselves in four weeks, so the problem will pass naturally. In the meantime, a lack of pressure from you will be a great relief for him. Apply some reverse psychology—waft around as if you're content. Seem happy with the way things are. Don't fear that this will mean you settle forever into a sexless relationship! It's not forever, just thirty days. Whenever you feel lusty, masturbate instead. (On your own—not on his desk at work with a Meaningful Look.)

Give him lots of nonsexual touching

Maintain physical contact between you, but ensure it has a nonsexual air. He needs your touch to keep up the feelings of affection and oxytocin bonds, but anything racy will put him under pressure. So keep it friendly and light. Give him a hug and kiss, then leave and get busy with something else. Slap him on his rear in a friendly way, but don't then look at him hopefully, asking, "Anything else you'd like?" It's good to compliment him in a way that shows you think he is attractive, and not like a brother or roommate, so keep calling him "handsome," "sexy," "gorgeous."

Touch is a wonderful stress-reliever, so keep it going. Offer him a massage, but subtly show that you're not demanding extras—don't perform the massage in just a liquorice G-string and a lusty smile, for example, but instead choose something pretty but low-key—like a silky camisole and some pretty boy-shorts. Hold his hand when you're out together, stroke his hair in the car, touch his arm lightly when you talk to him. If he grabs you after one of these innocent overtures, wonderful. But otherwise, wait.

Make him feel virile in other ways

If his ego isfeeling diminished because of his lowered drive, you can boost it back up by ensuring he feels needed, respected, and admired in other ways. It's not enough for your partner to feel that you love him in bed but are dissatisfied with him everywhere else; he needs to feel that you respect him all the time, even if (or perhaps, especially when) you disagree with him.

So, listen to how you talk to him. Do you put him down, blatantly or otherwise? Are you critical? Do you offer unsolicited advice to him, especially in areas where he knows more than you (for example, in his job)? I'm not calling you a nag, but women can show their love by "over-caring." You think you're being helpful, he interprets your advice/criticism as proof that you don't trust him.

If you think you've fallen into the over-caring trap, try this exercise: for one day, vow that you will give no help, advice, or criticism to your partner at all. Bite your lip—don't use mime or finger gestures instead— either say something positive or nothing at all. It's only for one day. Even the most hopeless of men couldn't manage to lose his job, all your cash, and the children in one day, so it's not dangerous. (Note: The more frightened you are about this exercise, the more you need to do it.) This will greatly help you realize how you really speak to your partner, and if it's negative, change. You can henpeck a man into impotence!

Would you feel sexy toward your partner if he showed you no affection during the day at all? If he never kissed, cuddled, or complimented you? No, of course not. But men and women have different needs. We crave affection, but men crave admiration. By trusting him to make his own decisions, you are giving him the manly equivalent of a foot massage, Tiffany sparkler, and *Sex and the City* DVD box-set all in one.

Talk to him

If nothing has changed after a month, it's time to raise the subject. Start gently. Ask if there's anything on his mind. He might initially say no, but if you feel there's something there, gently press him. Have an open posture and make the atmosphere loving and relaxed. Tell yourself that whatever he says, you're going to accept it, lovingly. He'll feel this and be much more likely to open up. Listen thoughtfully and don't interrupt, let him get everything out. You could bring the conversation around to sex while you're still feeling close to one another, and ask him if there's anything new he'd like to try. At this point he'll usually explain the recent sex-slump and either *do it* immediately or tell you what's up—or rather, what's not.

When you've gone off sex

If you're the one who can't face sex, take steps toward getting your ardor back. Many women wonder if they could simply give up on nookie. In extreme cases, they idly fantasize about letting their husband get a lover. No, no, no. I don't mean to add to your guilt, but sex is an *essential* part of your relationship that you shouldn't give up on without a fight. Every time you have sex with your partner, you release oxytocin—a powerful bonding hormone. It keeps you feeling very close to your man, and he releases it, too, so it helps him bond with you. The more you do have sex with him or—at the very minimum—touch him affectionately, the closer you'll feel. Here's what to do.

Work out if you've gone off sex completely, or just with him

There's a big difference between the two. One points to a physical issue, and the other to an emotional one. If the thought of all sex—even frenzied elevator sex with Brad Pitt and a tub of marshmallow fluff—leaves you icy cold, then you might be suffering from a physical problem. To help discover what that might be, turn to pages 64–65 for a list of the most common turn-offs, from medication to hormonal issues. To cure them, look at the suggestions within those pages but also consider the following:

Shake your lil' booty

Research has shown that women who exercise regularly report higher levels of satisfaction with their sex lives than women who don't. If you're sedentary, you won't be at your physical peak and you won't look as good as you could. You don't have to join the gym—walking, swimming, a team sport, and dancing are great ways to boost your exercise level.

Aromatherapy

You can get discreet scented patches that you stick on the inside of your wrist and sniff throughout the day. The aroma they release mimics the effects of dopamine, the brain's natural feel-good chemical, which has been proven to raise the libido. I was as dubious as you are, but I tried them for a day and went from nunlike to nympho.

Feel the revulsion and do it anyway

If you feel just the faintest flicker of lust, the smallest tiny glimmer of a particle of arousal, grab it and make the most of it—preferably by boffing your man. Every woman I know who's reluctantly had sex with their partner from a cold start reports back, "I had to force myself into it, but by the end, I remembered what all the fuss was about!" If you can't face full-blown screwing, take your itsy-bitsy speck of horniness and masturbate instead. The more orgasms you have, the lustier you'll start to feel all the time. You could try boosting your enjoyment with a sex toy.

If you've just gone off sex with your man, it's a different issue. It's an emotional issue. Ignoring the possibility that you are madly in love with someone else, we'll need to help you recover those loving feelings again. Try the following:

Write a list of everything you love about him

Initially this will seem impossible, or if you do make a list, it'll be full of wishy-washy nonsense like "puts up with me" or "is gentle and tolerant." Those aren't the qualities that are going to fire you up, so think further. What swoon-worthy qualities does he have? Is he brave, strong, determined? Is he calm in a crisis, generous, and not afraid to tell you off in a rather knee-tremblingly masterful when you've got out of line? Does he drive sexily, make you laugh, pick you up when you're struggling through the snow in high heels? Those are the qualities that will make you fancy him again, so write them down. Next, list his physical attributes. Strong chest, deep voice, powerful thighs … You get the idea. Really get carried away, as if he were a romantic hero in a bodice ripper. You'll feel nuts at first, but do it.

Forget everything to detest about him

You need to reach a state of acceptance with your partner. If you really can't face the thought of being intimate with him, it's probably because you are boiling with resentment about certain things he's said, done, or refused to do. If you're thinking, "If he'd only change X, Y, and Z, we'd be happy," you've got resentments. What can you do about these? Honestly? Very little. If you've told him a billion times but he still won't listen, you're going to have to let them go. I know it's hideous, but you can't change him and the more he feels you trying to change him, the more he'll stubbornly persist in doing whatever it is that madly annoys you. Often, men aren't that bothered about doing these irritating things; they just want to be allowed to do them. As soon as you can learn to accept his bad points—not ignore, accept —he'll usually stop doing them on his own. Try it.

Remember the best sex you've ever had with him

Find a place where you won't be disturbed for 10 minutes and think back to the last great sex you had with your man. Relive every second. Try to recall how everything felt, sounded, looked like. Visualize it. Try to think about it long enough for your heart to start pounding again, and your legs to go a bit wobbly. If you can, go and masturbate feverishly while imagining your partner ravishing you. Start associating his body with great sex.

Arouse yourself before you see him

Before he comes home, or before you go home, start thinking really rude thoughts about him and all the things you could do to him. Be specific. Turn yourself on. It's effective to spend five minutes an hour thinking these thoughts over the course of the day. Then when you see him, grab him and kiss him deeply. Tell him that you'd like to seduce him, and he must not say a word but allow you to do whatever you like to him. Then make love to him in the way you like best.

When you've both gone off sex

If you've both gone off sex and are living together like vaguely irritated roommates, you're in a rut. This is common in long-term couples, especially those who had very passionate sex right back in the beginning. What often happens with lusty couples is that they get into an efficient, satisfying sexual routine. They find a string of moves that takes both partners from "Aah" to "Bliss" in the

shortest time, and keep repeating it, because it's guaranteed to please. But soon you can predict with psychic-like accuracy exactly when he'll kiss from your nipples down to your inner thighs, he knows to the nearest millisecond exactly how long you'll swirl your tongue around on him in a circular motion, and you're both absolutely bored to tears.

Lots of couples in long-term relationships become teeth-grindingly bored with their sex lives. I'm afraid it really is just a question of laziness if it's happened to you. No, you'll never get the thrill of experiencing a whole new body, but you both will feel the benefit of a warm, familiar, safe partner on whom you can practice brand-new skills and live out your dirtiest fantasies without worrying that they're going to run, clutching the duvet cover to their terrified chest, off into the hills.

Think back to when you were single and used to read those sex features in *Cosmopolitan* and sigh longingly for someone to practice them on? You have someone now, ready and waiting!

Sex games

Turn your bedroom encounters from grim orgasm-driven marathons into lighthearted, fun sessions by introducing some naughty games. Anything that mixes humping with pleasure would work—here are some ideas to get you started.

• Place a pretty bowl in the bedroom and make it your "Fantasy Wish List." Both of you are in charge of placing folded-up notes in there which explicitly describe something naughty you'd love to do. You write yours on pink paper, he writes his on blue. Every week, or two, take it in turns to draw an idea out of the bowl and make it come true. No balking!

• Steal some money from the children's Monopoly set and hand it to your man, along with a price list of sexy services you offer. Give him just enough to cover one or two, and tell him he can earn more money by either performing services on you—or, to be boring but practical—doing chores around the house.

• Set aside some time to have fun. For example, make Monday "man day" and Wednesday "woman day," and decree that on your specified day you're allowed to request a sexy treat from your partner. Whether that's 10 minutes of oral sex, 20 minutes of tantric missionary, or 30 minutes of playing on the Wii while he gives you a foot massage is up to you.

• Put satin sheets on the bed to send yourselves down the slippery slope to Happy Land. They're wonderfully sensuous to shag on, but hideously slippery to sleep on, so follow sexpert Pam Spurr's sage advice: Make your bed as normal, but put the satin sheets on over the top. Then after you've had your wicked way on them, pull them off and go to sleep on your normal comfy polycotton.

• When you were young and first moved in with each other, I'm sure you made a point of christening every room in the house. Well, guess what? Time to do it again! Vow that you'll do it in every room again in the next couple of months, and set to it.

• Role-play is always recommended in sex books, but do you ever actually bother? If you've never done it, make a real promise that you'll try it soon. God, it's sexy. Don't start too ambitiously at first, just pretend to be something simple like "the bored housewife and the saucy plumber," or "Steven Hawking and his naughty nurse." Once you get past the initial giggly stage, there's a whole new world waiting for you.

• Set a timer for 15 minutes and leap on each other—the goal is for you both to orgasm within that time. If you do, next time take one minute off. And so on …

• During the day when you're both at home, begin writing a sexy script and passing it between each other, each adding bits as you go. For example, you start with: "Tonight I'd like to lay you on the bed and massage your cock through your trousers, and then you'll …" Pass the note to him for him to add the next sexy installment. Then later on, act it all out.

• Start a sexy "Book at Bedtime" by reading aloud a chapter from an erotic novel every night. Take it in turns to read. When it's your turn, really ramp up the acting: do sexy accents, gasp, and moan during the filthy scenes, and writhe around as you read, stroking yourself. A clever little publishing company called U Star Novels now offers personalized sexy novels, where you and your partner play the starring roles. They include your names and enough personal details to make you feel you're really the hero and heroine.

• Whatever you usually do in bed, do it backward. No, not physically backward, but in the opposite order. If you usually have 10 minutes of oral followed by 5 minutes in the missionary position, ending up with doggy style, reverse it.

Sex toys

According to research by a well-known sex-toy store, more and more women now own a sex toy. The figures are growing every year, and it's soon estimated that more vibrators will be sold than washing machines. Which means that we won't have to perch on ours as it goes through its hot super-top spin anymore.

You can get toys for every kind of nookie imaginable—standard sex, anal, oral, masturbation, S&M … Most sex stores sell versions of the same things, so I've described generic tools here. You'll find these on all the major websites, including my favorites.

Remember to look after your sex toys. Clean them after each use (you can buy special cleaner from any sex-toy store) to prevent giving yourself or your partner an infection, always clean them after they have been inside an anus, and never switch them between anus and vagina. And don't give them to your baby as a teether.

Vibrators

If you don't own a vibrator at the moment, or just have your trusted, rusted one from years ago knocking around your panty drawer, it's time to invest. You can use them for different reasons. They're lovely to have just to give yourself a fast, furious orgasm at any time of day or night—when your partner's away, at work, or not in the mood. They're also recommended by sex counselors if you've never had an orgasm; vibrators give such strong stimulation that they are practically guaranteed to induce a climax, and once you've experienced that feeling, it's easier to recreate it during sex.

Don't worry about becoming addicted to your toy (like Charlotte in *Sex and the City*), that's rare. But what I would caution against is using one every time you masturbate, as that can lead to your eventually finding it harder to orgasm through the gentler stimulation of fingers or tongues.

If you want to use these on your partner, it's worth noting that men seem to find vibrators too intense against their penis, but you could massage his perineum with one of these and he'd probably thank you. Or, you can wrap it in a piece of material to soften the vibrations and apply it to the little "banjo string" on the underneath of his glans.

Basic vibe

A good starting point is a small, basic vibrator, often called a "Pocket Rocket" or a "bullet." They're purse-sized (some have a key-ring attached!) and quiet, so you can use them anywhere, and they're small enough to make your partner feel huge in comparison. Most have different speed settings, and waterproof versions are available, too. Hold the tip against your clitoris and the vibrations do the hard work for you. Swirl them around, rub them up and down, or just hold them in one place—anything goes. Try them against your nipples if you're sensitive there. But don't use them near your anus as they're small enough to slip inside and get lost! Battery operated.

Rabbits

These best-selling toys use a two-pronged approach, literally. The toy is usually made of hard plastic or very soft, rubbery plastic which feels warm to the touch, and consists of a main shaft with a tiny rabbit clinging to the side of it, with long vibrating ears. You insert the shaft inside your vagina, and the rabbit stays outside you, its ears buzzing away against your clitoris. Inside your vagina it's all go—usually the shaft is filled with little beads that jiggle around as it

rotates, stimulating your G-spot. The toy comes with different speed settings for both parts, and you can use them independently, for example just the rabbit, just the shaft, or both.
Battery operated.

Professional vibrators

I say "professional" because these babies really do the job. Some plug right into a socket which is brilliant, as they're super-duper powerful and don't start fading away at the wrong moment; others contain rechargeable batteries, so you just plug them in like your cell phone. You can get them for different purposes—some are molded to hit your G-spot, others are normal clitoral vibrators, others are meant to feel like oral sex, and some come with different attachments to do everything except bring you a cigarette afterward. Famous names are the Hitachi Magic Wand, the Durex Play range, and Tracey Cox's Supersex range. My favorite is the Eroscillator, which plugs in and has millions of attachments. I loved mine when I was single, so much so that I burnt out the motor. (Blush.) The only drawback of these is that they're expensive. However, you will save money on batteries and they'll probably last longer than cheaper toys, though not if you overdo it like I did.
Plug-in or rechargeable.

Butterflies

These are clitoral-stimulators which have elasticated straps attached. You slip them on and they sit on top of your clitoris, buzzing away, leaving your hands free to do other things (handling heavy machinery not recommended). They're powerful and quite comfortable, and devotees say that they get the job done every time. You can wear them during sex, too, for the ultimate effects.
Battery operated.

Dildos

These are lifelike vibrators. That is, they look exactly like a penis, right down to veins, skin color (black and white) and, often, testicles. They're a good choice if you like the feeling of—how can I put this?—being entered by a big, fat cock. Most are made of plastic but you can now get them in "cyber skin," which is an almost terrifyingly realistic skin-textured material. You can buy ones which have been cast from molds of famous porn-stars' penises, so if you've always dreamed of going to bed with Ron Jeremy, this is your big chance. They vibrate, and have different speed settings. Warning: men find these threatening. If your partner is the owner of an average or below-sized penis, don't buy an 18-inch Black Mambo dildo and expect him to be anything but hurt. Mind you, you'll probably be slightly bruised yourself.
Battery operated.

Strap-on dildos

As above, but with straps attached so you can wear them and give your partner anal sex. Includes a clitoral stimulator inside, so you get off, too. Talk to your partner about this—many men would run a mile, but some actually fantasize about being boffed by their woman. They are exciting to wear, as you finally get to experience that feeling of thrusting, and they have die-hard devotees.

Designer vibrators

About five years ago, a sex-toy store released a jewel-encrusted (ouch!) vibrator that cost one and a half million dollars, and since then the market's gone insane. Every sex-toy company now has to have a "designer" vibrator in its range, and the prices are high. They always hint that celebrities use them, as if that's going to make us shell out; personally, the only thing I want that's been up Victoria Beckham is David. But it's your choice. Several of them are good, for example "The Cone" which is a sleek, black pyramid, or Tom Dixon's infamous "Bone" vibrator, that launched straight into a six-month waiting list. At the 2008 Erotica exhibition in London, a gold-plated vibrator was on sale for 3,000 dollars. Yes, you could imagine that one ending up in Madge's vadge, but does that make it worth the money? Search for "designer" in any of the online sex-toy sites and make your own decision.
Battery operated.

Other toys

Love eggs

Balls. That's what I call these as they've never done a thing for me. The idea is that you insert these two weighted balls, attached together with a cord, inside your vagina and enjoy multiple orgasms all day as you go around your daily business. "Imagine the excitement of supermarket shopping!" they claim. Yes, just imagine it—you clanking your way down the aisles, holding your knees together so the eggs don't drop out and go rolling under the freezer cabinet. Some women really like them, but I've never gotten it. However, they are meant to be good for exercising your pelvic-floor muscles.

Cock rings

Cock rings come in different forms, but they all do the same job. Your partner inserts his penis and his testicles through the ring and wears it during sex. They stop the blood flowing back out of his penis, meaning his erection stays harder for longer and develops an impressively veiny appearance. Good for men who find it hard to keep erect for very long. Some include little vibrators to give him a buzz. What's in it for you? Quite a lot, actually. Many cock rings have clitoral stimulators attached which rub or vibrate against you with every grind of his hips. Plus he won't lose his erection and might feel bigger. They come in every material: metal, leather, string, rubber, cyber skin … They're available in different sizes (you know the drill, the smallest size is called "Massive" and they go up to "Freak-Show Enormo"). You can also buy inexpensive, disposable cock rings in most drugstores, which provide around 30 minutes' vibration before the battery dies. Save your money. They're not strong enough to give you anything but the feeling that a fly's landed on your extremities.
Battery operated or unpowered.

Butt plugs

As you can guess, these are anal toys. Usually they're a small, conical-shaped, unpowered "plug" with a good-sized handle on the end (to stop them disappearing up there forever), designed to be inserted up the bottom. He can do it to you, you can do it to him. Wash it in-between. Very good for giving you an idea what anal sex will feel like, and great for giving you the feeling of double-penetration when worn during sex. They come in different sizes. My advice: start small, and don't forget the lubrication. You can also buy vibrating butt plugs.
Battery operated or unpowered.

Anal beads

A small, often curved, string of plastic beads that you slowly insert into the anus (yours or his) during sex. At the point of orgasm, pull them out with a flourish. The feeling is indescribably good. Especially effective on him, as his G-spot (the prostate gland) lives inside his bottom and is stimulated by every little nodule of these beads.
Unpowered.

Masterstrokes

Do you know how to bring one another to orgasm using only your hands? If not, read on. If yes, I'm sure you've already discovered what a wonderfully *handy* skill it is to have for all those times when you want quick, discreet relief—like during family camping holidays when you're all in one tent, when you have a teenager sleeping the other side of a paper-thin wall, or just when either of you is tired, ill, or newly plastered in fake tan. All the moves I describe below can be used by themselves, or as part of oral sex.

Men love hand jobs. Learn to masturbate him as well as he can himself and you'll make yourself indispensable—truly his Right-Hand Woman. Here are my tips to give him the Perfect Hand Job:

Show and tell

Because he's been playing with his penis since he first discovered it inside his diaper, he'll have built up quite a fondness for a few certain moves that he regularly uses. The first thing is to learn those—just ask him to masturbate for you, while you watch. Then put your hand on top of his as he does it, noting the speed and pressure he uses (most men complain that women hold their penis too gently or too firmly), and what he does with the other hand.

Start slowly

The secret of a good hand job is a gentle start. The worst thing you can do is go in there are 80 mph, then quickly realize, as your biceps explode in pain, that you can't maintain that pace, and have to slow down again. Start in first gear and gradually build up speed. Aim not to slow down, unless you want to tease him or delay his orgasm.

Born slippy

Lubrication is the key to pleasuring him with your hand. Without lubrication, it will feel like you're using his penis to get your Boy Scouts fire-starting badge. Any lubrication is suitable, but stick to oil-free if he'll be wearing a condom later.

His sensitive side

The underneath of a man's penis is the most sensitive side, so try to stimulate this side as much as possible. If you're sitting next to your man, you can grip his penis normally. If you're in front of him, you'll have to adjust your hand: hold your palm out facing him, then turn it upside down so your thumb is pointing toward the floor. Now grasp his shaft. This way, your palm will be against the underneath side of him.

Run your thumb up and down the long vein

Grasp him with your hand and move it up and down. Alternate your strokes with each hand: move one up his shaft while the other hand grasps him at the base. When your first hand reaches the top, remove it and bring the second hand up his shaft. Keep both hands moving this way in a sensuous rhythm.

Where the magic happens

The head of his penis (the glans) is the most sensitive spot of all, especially if he's uncircumcized and it doesn't get bashed around in his jeans all day. Don't just rub it senseless, stimulate it at the end of a long up-stroke on his shaft.
- Swirl the palm over the top of it.
- Massage the little hole with your thumb.
- Form your index and thumb into a circle and roll his foreskin up and down over the glans.
- Give it a lusty lick with your tongue.

Don't forget the little guys

Keep an eye (and a hand) on his testicles as you play with his penis. Not only are they very sensitive and often sorely neglected, they will give you clues as to how aroused he is. When they swell in size and are pulled up very tightly toward his body, he is close to orgasm—you can either tease him now, bringing him close to orgasm then stopping, or deliver your masterstrokes and finish the job.
• Stroke his testicles with your hand.
• Roll them GENTLY between your thumb and index finger.
• Cup their weight in your palm and massage them softly.

Finish the job

When he's nearing his orgasm, gradually keep increasing the speed with which you move your hand up and down. Use the other hand to fondle his testicles, or press three fingers onto his perineum— the area between his testicles and his anus. This will give him gentle G-spot stimulation. If you want to give him added excitement, press one well-lubricated finger onto his anus and, if he responds by groaning happily, slip it inside him. You could also use a small butt plug.
• Keep up the pace—if you slow down, he'll lose his orgasm.
• As soon as he starts coming, stop moving. He will become very, very sensitive as soon as he ejaculates and any movements after that will irritate him.

Fellas—here's how to give her the Perfect Hand Job

Ladies, would you give me a minute to talk dirty to your man? Thanks! Women love to be stimulated directly, either with your mouth or your tongue— ideally both—because of the hopeless design of our bits for sex. If the clitoris were inside the vagina we could orgasm by intercourse alone, but as it isn't, we need you to literally "think outside the box."

Her must-see hot spots

You know where her clitoris is, I'm sure (if she hasn't shown you yet, bring her here so I can slap her), it's the little bud at the top of her labia. It's similar to your penis in that it is covered by a tiny foreskin (called "the clitoral hood"), and it swells with blood when she's aroused. If you think of it like a little tiny penis, it will help you get an idea of what it likes best. But remember, it's a *tiny* penis so you have to be gentle. No bullying it like the smallest kid in the playground.

Her other must-visit destination down there is her G-spot. Scientists are still grappling with this, as I hope you are, as it has still not been decided conclusively whether it's a myth or reality. My personal opinion is that it's real, but that the sensations it arouses in women are varied: some women love the sensation, some don't. With direct pressure it can feel very similar to the urge to urinate. G-spot stimulation sometimes causes ejaculation in women, where she squirts out a colorless, odorless liquid. The chances are if your partner loves doggy-style sex, woman on top with her leaning backward, or your stimulating the inside front (top) wall of her vagina, she likes it.

Are you sitting comfortably?

The first step to pleasuring a woman is to get yourself comfy, because she might take a while. Even if you feel it's not spontaneous, take a moment to grab a pillow or something else to kneel on before you begin, so you can stick with her for the long haul. She won't mind if you wander off to get these things; in fact it will quickly form a Pavlovian association in her, where she associates soft furnishings with slow, lengthy sessions. She won't be able to visit the department store pillow section, but who cares?

Sit next to your woman on the bed, and rest your arm on her tummy. This will take the pressure off your wrist and fingers and let you masturbate her for longer.

Another good position for masturbating her is to lie down and rest your head on her thigh. Make sure your fingernails are trimmed! And grab a bottle of lubricant. Use a water-based one without glycerine. Glycerin-based lubes taste better, but the sugar in them can cause yeast infections. Oil-based lubricants aren't suitable to use on her Lady Garden, as they can stay inside the vagina and encourage bacteria to breed. (Are you in the mood yet?)

Do you like to watch?

The quickest, easiest and most pleasant way for you to discover how she likes to be stimulated, is for her to masturbate while you watch. Ask her. Some women will be happy to help, others might feel embarrassed. If she doesn't want to, then a more gentle way is to—as I've suggested above—place your hand over hers while she does it. This way you'll find how she likes to use her hands, or even if she uses her hands at all. Some women skip the manual labor altogether and simply grind their clitoris against pillows, vibrators, the edges of furniture, small dogs ... Just like you, women learn to masturbate when they're very young, and often keep the same technique for life.

You could instigate a mutual masturbation session where you sit facing each other and touch yourselves to orgasm. If you're sure you'll be able to concentrate. And no turning it into a race, either.

Tease ready

As women take longer to orgasm than men, invest plenty of time before you even start directly fiddling. This will be much, much sexier for her, and ease the strain on your hands and tongue. The longer you spend massaging, kissing (especially long, slow, deep kisses), sucking her nipples and stroking her breasts, the quicker she'll climax when you start your Killer Moves. Also, remember a woman needs to feel "safe" before she can climax, so make sure you give her plenty of affection all the time.

• Stroke her on the underside of her breasts, often the most sensitive area.
• Massage her slowly, and press gently on her lower vertebrae. Masseurs say that pressure in this area can be deeply arousing.
• Don't press her panties into her vagina—this just soaks up lubrication and leaves her dry. Instead, kiss and lick all along the edge of her panties before pulling them off with your teeth.
• If she grinds and gyrates, rubs her crotch against you and raises her hips, she is desperate for more attention. Don't give it to her! Tease her for another couple of minutes so when you finally get down to business, it's unforgettable.

Fingerbobs

When you've teased her into next week, it's time to lay down your moves. Don't start by directly rubbing on her clitoris, especially not underneath the hood. Many women find this too sensitive. You can stimulate it indirectly, at least to start with, by moving the skin around the clitoris, or rubbing on each side of her clitoris, just inside the inner lips. The clitoris is more like an octopus than a cockle— it has long arms that extend down either side of her vagina.
• Place your index and middle finger either side of her labia majora (the outer lips), press them together to close her lips then press down. Now move them in a circular motion. This will push down on top of her clitoris, and pull gently on the skin that surrounds it.
• Use those same two fingers to gently press on either side of her clitoris, and move them in a circular motion. This is how many women masturbate.
• Gently pinch the clitoris between your thumb and index finger and roll it like a marble.
• You can tap lightly on top of the clitoris, or gently but insistently rub it on the very tip.
• Keep watching her body language—if she goes silent or stops moving, she's either passed out from pleasure or she's not enjoying it. If it's the latter, move on to something else, or let her take your hand and show you what to do.

Positive G

You can use your other hand to provide some G-spot action. Like I said, it can induce feelings of "I really need a pee!" in some women, so she might feel more comfortable if she goes to the toilet before you start. It can also make her ejaculate, so bring goggles. The G-spot is located about two inches inside her vagina, on the top wall (the one nearest her tummy). Insert a finger and "beckon" with it, until you feel a patch that is slightly raised, and more textured than other areas. It swells during arousal, which is why it's a good idea to turn her on before you begin. Now you know here it is, you can:

• Keep rubbing it in that beckoning motion with one finger, or preferably two. Use the flat pads of your fingertips rather than the tips. Press slowly and firmly—the G-spot can take more pressure than her clitoris.

• Push on the G-spot and press down on her tummy at the same time, for added intensity.

• Massage her G-spot and press on her anus simultaneously. The pleasure of one will detract from the mild embarrassment of the other.

• Flip her over into the doggy position, and massage her G-spot while you gently lick her anus and keep rubbing her clitoris.

Don't stop, oh please, oh please, don't stop

It's very off-putting for women if you keep changing your pace or technique. When you start performing an action that has her thrashing around like the little girl in *The Exorcist*, for God's sake keep doing it.

Don't worry that she'll get bored with you—we'd rather have half an hour of something predictably amazing than a whole day of on-and-off pleasure. Also, remember that you might need to do it for a while—if five minutes have passed and she's still bucking lustily but hasn't come, *do not stop*. Maybe increase the pace or pressure to help her get there, but don't swap to a completely different move, or she's perfectly entitled to give you a Ninja kick in the nuts.

• Licking or kissing her can help her to orgasm. Some women love to be kissed on the mouth during masturbation, but it puts others off. Don't ask her! Just feel your way.

• It can help to talk to her—women are very aroused by words. Tell her how sexy she looks, how much she's turning you on.

• Suck on her nipples—many girls can come from this alone.

Here she comes

When she orgasms, don't stop what you're doing. In fact, if you carry on doing the same thing throughout her orgasm, it can sometimes prompt her to have another one. And another one. And another one. Jealous much? Women's arousal doesn't include a refactory period—the time needed to recover after a climax—like yours does. Some women will feel agonizingly sensitive during or just after their orgasm, in which case stop or turn the volume down to level one. But if she loves it, keep on trucking.

Best-ever fellatio

Girls, all the hand-job moves I've just described on pages 99–100 can be incorporated into a perfect blowjob. In fact, using your hands is the secret of giving perfect head: simply putting his penis inside your mouth and bobbing up and down is not going to do much for him. Yes, it's sexy, yes he loves watching you do it, but no, it's not going to give him much stimulation, and certainly not enough to climax. Note: Always, always go last when it comes to giving oral sex. Don't believe any man's lie about "No, of course I'll be up for doing you after." Women are much better post-orgasmically than men are; we don't get the rise in hormones that they do, which cause sleepiness, and our multiclimax capacity means that we find things sexy long after we've come. Men, in contrast, can actually get squeamish after they've lost their wad.

Assume the position

There's a whole "worship" idea going on when you take his manhood into your mouth, and that might explain why most men's favorite position for oral sex is him standing up, you kneeling before him. There are benefits aside from the egotism—men's testicles are more sensitive when they're hanging down, and some men say their orgasm feels more intense when they're standing up. So do it this way for extra brownie points. Otherwise, kneel between his legs while he sits or lies down.

• Tie your hair back—he loves to see himself sliding in and out of your mouth, so don't block the view.

• Give him eye contact—he will love it if you watch him while you work. If you feel silly, you don't have to gaze at him the whole time, but a few long, sexy looks into his eye will be appreciated.

Crave it

As you know from when your man goes down on you, unless he looks like he's happy to be there and willing to stay as long as necessary, it's no fun. Same for your man—he has to feel that you're enjoying yourself. Any yawning, eye-rolling, or watch-checking is forbidden. As soon as you throw yourself into the job, you'll both enjoy it more, and you'll be better at picking up on what he likes best.

Empty your mind and start watching his enjoyment signals, they'll help you pleasure him best.

• Gaze at his penis with delight. If he's dressed, unwrap him like he's a birthday present.

• Moan with pleasure.

• If he's sitting or lying down, sit astride his leg and rub yourself on him, like you're so aroused you can't help yourself.

Tease him

Don't simply ram him into your mouth; build up to that happy moment. The longer you make him wait, the stronger the sensations will be when you finally pounce. But equally, don't drop him like a stone when you hear the distant strains of the theme tune of your favorite TV soap opera.

• Kiss and lick him everywhere except his penis.

• Run your tongue up one of his thighs, lick briefly over his testicles, then lick down the other thigh.

• Open your mouth wide and just breathe around his penis, not letting it touch your mouth.

• Brush his penis ever so gently with delicate butterfly kisses.

Get a grip

Before you begin licking and sucking on him, grasp his penis, just under the tip, with your hand. Keep it there—it will heighten his pleasure, and make him feel like even more of him is going inside your mouth than actually is. It's the manual version of deep-throating. Use the other hand to explore his body, or massage your own.

Who's picking a banjo here?

You see the little string on the underside of his glans? That's called the frenulum and it's dynamite. It's sooo sensitive, and responds very well to your tongue and lips. In fact, to be even more amazing, as you grasp him with your hand, use your thumb to gently press on the frenulum the whole time.
• Lick your tongue rapidly over the little string.
• Cover your teeth with your lips, and dumbly nibble on it, and up and down his shaft.

I suck at this

Once you've slid him, with a delicious plunge, into your mouth, then what should you do? Well, you use your mouth to create the sexiest pretend-vagina possible. Suck on him ever so gently, press the sides of your mouth together inside for more pressure, swirl your tongue around.

Keep your hand just under the base and keep your head moving, catch his eye occasionally, fondle his testicles and honey—he won't care what you do.
• Keep concentrating—don't, as it were, take your eye off the ball.
• Keep up the pace and pressure.

Someday my prince will come…

And when he does, what do you want to do with it? You might like to swallow it, in which case, perfect. If you're dubious, my advice would be to make sure he is very deep inside your mouth when he climaxes, as then it will just slip down your throat and you won't taste anything. If you really don't want to, that's absolutely fine, but plan what you do want to do. Any of the following are popular with males:
• Aim him toward your breasts, preferably (but not essentially) rubbing it into your skin afterward.
• Cup the end of his penis inside your hand and let him pump into that.
• Point him up into the air and let him fire at will.
• Let him come into a soft handkerchief.

Best-ever cunnilingus

Fellas, if you only knew how easy it is to keep us happy forever. So happy that we'd never nag you ever again. So happy that we'd let you do whatever you wanted, whenever. The secret? Read on. It's all about giving us the Lap of Luxury.

Positions

It's most relaxing for a woman to receive oral sex when she's lying on her back with you between her legs. However, this may be your very least-favorite way of giving it. Try the pillows tip from the last section, or one of the alternatives below. Don't make her stay in a position that doesn't work for her, though—it will put her off so much that your tongue will actually fall off before she orgasms.

• Kneel on the floor while she sits on the edge of the bed, a chair, a table, or even a kitchen countertop in front of you (see page 23 in the Kitchen chapter).

• Get her to lie on her side with her legs apart, and poke your head up between them.

• Move her into the doggy-style position and lap her from behind. Some women love this position as it leaves them free to fantasize (only about you, darling), some don't as they feel body conscious. Try it and see.

• Lie on the bed while she sits astride your face and holds onto that headboard. This way she can control the pressure, and even move herself around your mouth to control where your tongue goes. Do keep your hands free to push her up off your face if you begin to be smothered.

Tips for your tongue

Remember I said to think of the clitoris as a tiny penis? Well, with that in mind, think of the kind of licks you enjoy best when you're receiving a blowjob. Do you prefer short, jabby thrusts of just the tip of the tongue? Or long, slow movements using the whole of the tongue? It's the same for us. When we get a tongue battering away at our clitoris like a tiny pink pneumatic drill, it does very little to make us say, "Ooh." So, forget the tip of your tongue. Concentrate on the wide, flat expanse of it. And don't forget the underneath either.

• Use your flattened tongue to start by giving her slow, long laps all the way from the bottom of her vagina, right up to her clitoris. Repeat a good few times. When you get to her vaginal opening, slip your tongue inside occasionally.

• Place your lips around her clitoris, suck on it gently, and roll your tongue over it.

• Trace out letters over the whole of her genitals, or concentrate them on her clitoris. Spell out the alphabet or a message to her. Like, "After this you owe me big time."

• Pretend her clitoris is Paris and your tongue is a taxi. Take a trip around the Périphérique, getting lost en route occasionally.

• Move your tongue in a wavy W shape over the top of her clitoris.

Open wide

When she's really turned on, she'll love the feeling of being spread open, so place your hands either side of her vagina and pull them apart. Then dive straight down into her with your tongue.

• Pretend your tongue is a tiny penis, and use it to penetrate her.

• Plunge your thumbs inside while you lap, up and down, along her vagina.

She'll be coming like a fountain when she comes

When your tongue muscles are going into spasm and you've definitely swallowed more than the recommended daily eight glasses of fluid, you'll probably be very keen to bring her to her orgasm. As we've already discussed, the best way to do this is to carry on with all the moves she obviously really enjoys. If you've chopped and changed too much, go back to doing whatever it was that was getting the best results, and this time carry on. Increasing the pressure and speed of well-loved moves works well, as does using your hands as well as your tongue.

You have two hands and one tongue, so aim to be working on three main passion-points: clitoris and G-spot definitely, then—depending on what she likes best—her nipples, perineum (the flat area between her vagina and her anus), or her anus. Stroking her perineum is good at this late stage, as you'll be able to feel her orgasm building up: when you feel perineal contractions, she's almost there, so go for the big finish!

Stuck for ideas? Then gently apply a sex toy to her clitoris while you lick her Lady Garden, or use a G-spot toy inside her as you lick her clitoris. Still nothing? Encourage her to use her hands to masturbate to orgasm, while you lick her fingers. Nope? As a final measure, just this once, I'll let you have sex with her. Since you've been so good. Yes, shag her the way she likes best until she explodes in joyful bliss. Aaah. Well done. Down, boy.

Bottom love

There's no easy way to title this topic, so I went with my first instinct. Anyway, anal sex is a very good way to introduce some spicy … Hold on a minute. You! Yes, you there! The woman who just screamed and dropped the book in terror. Come back here! I'm not going to force you to do anything you don't want to do, OK? I promise. No, you don't have to do this at all, but hear me out before you decide. Even if you don't fancy it now, another few years into your relationship and you could well be so bored in bed that you'll be happy to try anything, and at least if you've read this you'll know what to do.

Like I was saying, anal sex is a very good way to introduce some spicy, more adventurous, moves into your sex repertoire. It's one of the easiest ways to get back the feeling of having dirty or illicit sex within a long-term relationship. It's really The Last Taboo. Both of you can try it, too, especially if your man is open-minded and responsive.

For you to have anal sex, you won't need anything except lubrication and condoms. The skin inside the anus is delicate and prone to tearing, making infections easily spread, so always use a condom for anal sex, preferably one of the tougher ones designed for this purpose.

If you're going to give anal sex to your man, you'll need a butt plug or a strap-on dildo (see pages 94–97), or just your fingers. But don't, don't, don't use a normal vibrator, dildo, deodorant roll-on, hamster, carrot, banana, candle, bicycle pump, Action Man, or anything which doesn't come with a wide-handle attached. If you do, chances are high that you'll soon be driving to the ER with very red faces, asking to have it removed. It's massive inside a bottom, and any toy, especially one that's slippery with lube, could easily get sucked up there and disappear.

Will there be poop?
No, there's not likely to be poop. Feces is stored quite a long way back, in the colon, at least 10 inches away from the anus, and only enters the "launch tunnel" just before you actually have a dump. If you're nervous about splodges, empty your bowels before you begin. If you're really nervous, that will happen naturally. Then wash and make sure you're confident that it's fresh down there, so you can relax and enjoy yourself. Keep baby-wipes nearby for an on-the-go freshen-up.

I have hemmorhoids!
Then try this later, when they've gone. There's your Get Out of Anal Free card.

Will it make me incontinent?
No. Your backdoor will slam shut afterward, just like normal. There might be a slightly "stretched" feeling for 24 hours afterward, but not enough to release anything messy, and it will go away. If you have repeated anal sex with a very large penis or toy, you do risk losing some of your tightness.

Will it hurt?
OK. You know the feeling of doing a really big dump? The kind of king-pin mega-poop that takes 45 minutes and the entire Sunday papers to get through? When a penis or sex toy goes inside you, it'll feel like that, in reverse. At first it will feel strange, but after a little while—especially if you also stimulate your vagina with a toy or your hands—it will feel simply feel a little odd, and then you might discover that it soon feels good. Start

slowly using just fingers, and remember the secret: LUBRICATION. Choose water-based or silicone varieties, as oil will rot the condom's latex.

If we decide we hate it halfway through, can we just go into a normal shag?

Not before he's removed the condom, and had a very thorough wash. Also remember that he mustn't touch your vagina with a finger, penis, or toy that's been inside your anus until he's scrubbed it.

Does he just aim straight ahead?

No, the anus is a gentle, S-shaped curve. Once inside, aim the penis or sex toy toward the receiver's backbone. Girls, if you want to hit your man's G-spot—his prostate gland, to give it its fancy name—then insert a finger and aim upward, pointed toward his belly button. About 3 inches inside you should feel a lump, that grows bigger with arousal. That's his G-spot and it likes gentle rubbing.

How to do it

For simplicity's sake, I've written these instructions as him giving you anal sex. If you want to give anal sex to him—and remember, we fought for equality—then just swap the instructions so he's taking your position, and changing "penis" for whatever implement you're using.

Relax

To start with, have a glass of wine, and then bring the bottle into the bedroom. Don't panic, nobody's going to insert it. But just have it nearby for a second glass if you're feeling tense. Don't get drunk however, as it'll make you more likely to be reckless and less likely to notice if it hurts.

Foreplay

You should be as aroused as possible before you try anal sex, as it will greatly improve your pleasure and you'll be more likely to orgasm. Start with him licking and tonguing your anus. Then he should apply lots of lubrication to his index and middle fingers, and slowly circle them around on top of your anal hole, gradually applying more pressure.

When you're ready, he can then slip his well-lubed index finger inside you. Don't rush things—leave it like that for a few minutes, him gently working his finger in and out, until you've got used to it. Then he should slip his middle finger in too, so he has two fingers inside you. Again, give yourself time to adjust to the sensation, then he can keep those fingers inside you and actually pour lubrication down them, so it goes just inside your anus.

Position

The easiest position for first-time bottom love is spoons. Later on we'll discuss other options, but for now spoons is best. Why? Because it's gentle, you can reach around and hold his penis, and he's less likely to get all carried away and thrusty in this position.

Set a rule: he doesn't thrust, you do. You push back against him, at least until you're used to the sensation, at which point he can take over if you want him to.

In the spoons position, he pushes just the tip of his penis against your anus. Push back against him until it slips inside, then push back more and more, taking it very slowly and giving yourself time to adjust every time more goes inside. He holds on top your hips for leverage, or uses a clean toy inside your vagina. And that's it! You're doing it! From this point, do whatever comes naturally, from leaping up off the bed screaming, "Never again!", or shagging your way to Happy Land.

Other positions

Once you've tried it in the spoons position, you could try missionary style, where everything's like normal missionary but he just aims lower. Or doggy style, except don't push your bottom high up into the air or he might go deeper than is comfy.

Positions for the bedroom

Most couples use only two or three sexual positions *ever*. Never torture yourself that every other couple you know gyrate like gymnasts all night. In fact, if you have four moves you use regularly, you're almost *freakishly* imaginative. But don't stick with these old faithfuls—try the Sex Position Swap Shop. Over the next few pages I'll describe the basic positions and next to each one, I'll give you a sexed-up and spicier version you can swap it for next time. I'm pimping your rides. Literally.

Missionary position

The most popular sexual position in the world. It has developed a reputation as being Sex for Dummies, but don't feel ashamed if it's your favorite.
How to do it: The woman lies on her back, the man lies on top of her. That's all, folks.
Best bits: Its Indian name would be "bringer of orgasms." This position is one of the safest bets for intimacy, kissing, and satisfaction, as he gets the thrusting he loves, while you get clitoral stimulation by grinding your pelvis against his, which tugs at the skin around your love-button and stimulates it. You can vary the

sensations of this position by raising or lowering your legs. The higher you bring them, the deeper he thrusts.
Variations: Raise up your bottom with pillows or the foam wedge mentioned earlier. The higher your bottom, the deeper the penetration. If you lower both your legs and clench them together, you get much more clitoral stimulation. To get G-spot orgasms, have your man kneel on the bed and pull your hips upward toward his. This way, his penis will be rubbing directly on the front wall of your sparklekitty.
Swap missionary position for: Coital alignment technique.

Coital alignment technique

Anyone who tells you that CAT is just the same as Missionary sex hasn't ever done it. You start off in the same position—woman on the bottom, man on top, his legs inside hers—but after that you veer off into completely new territory. Thrusting is banned (warn him first). This technique is all about the long, slow, daily grind. (The following instructions were greatly helped by sexperts Em and Lo.)

How to do it: Like I said, start missionary style. Then assume the CAT position. The man withdraws his penis so only the very tip of it is inside you. Then he pulls himself forward, up and along your body, until his hip bones are directly above yours. You should now feel his shaft of his penis rubbing directly against your clitoris—

and that's why we love this position so very, very much. To keep himself in this position most comfortably, get your man to brace his feet against yours (or the wall, or the headboard—told you it'd come in handy), and tuck his arms under your armpits so he's hugging you. Now begin the movement. It's not thrusting. Instead, you start by rolling your hips down toward the bed so he almost falls out of you. This will push his penis against your clitoris. Then he responds by gently moving his penis back up inside you, while you roll your hips upward to help him inside. Then you roll your hips down, he almost pops out, he moves back in, you roll your hips up. Up, down, up, down. Get the idea? If you're struggling, just remember that this position is all about maintaining direct pressure on your clitoris, so keep that part of yourself glued to his body. He will be very tempted to speed things up and get back to his beloved banging, but don't let him. Practiced properly, this is the most satisfying position you can experience.

Best bits: It's a long, slow comfortable screw. Lots of intimacy, as your bodies are welded together and you both have to concentrate on the job. Plus his face will be close to yours so you can kiss, and you can lick and bite his neck and ear.

Variations: None.

Spoons

The best position for sex during pregnancy, after you've stuffed yourself on a big Sunday lunch, or when you're so angry with him that you can't look him in the eye but still fancy sex. This is the classic side-by-side shag and it's equally good on a bed, the floor, or the couch (see page 53 of the Living Room chapter). What it lacks in depth of penetration it makes up for in comfort, ease, and having-both-hands-free-to-grope-each-other-ness.

How to do it: You and your man lie on your sides, him behind you, so his penis is nestled near your bottom. You move your upper leg forward until he spots an opening and dives in.

Best bits: It's relaxing and comfy. Also, it's only gentle stimulating, so is there less chance of his reaching the finishing line before you've even tied your sneakers.

Variations: You curl yourself up into the foetal position to give him extra depth. You roll onto your back, raise your upper leg and hook it over his body, so he is underneath you. This leaves you wide open to play with yourself, or let him play with you. He reaches around with a vibrator and applies it to your clitoris; you reach around and grasp the base of his penis to give him more sensation.

Swap Spoons for: The cross.

The cross

You've done this a million times before, I bet, but you never bothered to ask its name. Anyway, this is more complicated to get into than Spoons, but equally lazy-but-lovely once you're there.

How to do it: You lie flat on your back, facing North-South. Your man lies on his side, facing East-West, his legs underneath yours. Now you open your legs wide, and your man slides his upper leg between them, pulling you close until he can penetrate you. (Is this like trying to interpret bad furniture-assembly instructions? Trust me,

it'll make sense once you test it.) You can then place your right foot on the bed, behind his waist. If you look up at your mirrored ceiling, you'll see that your bodies are making the sign of the cross. This is apt, because now you can start Moving in a Mysterious Way.

Best bits: Your hands are free to roam over yourself or him. It's restful, and he will probably last a long time.

Variations: Use both hands to pull your lips wide open, and let him rub your clitoris with his thumb. Raise yourself up on your elbows to increase the sensation.

Doggy style

This rear-entry position is beloved by men, because of its unrivaled deep penetration, lovely view, it leaves their hands free to wander and their brain free to fantasize. Women love it because it feels animalistic and primal—oh, and they can fantasize merrily, too.

How to do it: You are on all fours while your man kneels behind you, holding onto your hips for leverage.

Best bits: If you've had a baby vaginally this is a great position. As you are ever so slightly roomier down below, your man's penis is more likely to rub against your G-spot as he thrusts. If you haven't, it's still good because you can vary it to alter your pleasure (see right).

Variations: He can place a well-lubricated finger or butt-plug inside your anus while he boffs you. This will give both of you electrifying sensations—him on his penis, you inside your vagina and bottom.You can reach back between your legs and tickle his seedpods; make a V-sign with your index and middle fingers and press them either side of your vaginal opening; hold the base of his penis and squeeze gently when he's getting close. Kneel on the edge of the bed, while your man stands on the floor behind you. He can now alternate between standing with his feet flat (which gives deeper penetration), and standing on tiptoe (shallower penetration but much more G-spot stimulation for you). From all fours on the bed, you can drop your upper body down onto the mattress. He can lie on his back, and you lie on top of him, facing upward. This gives you both very shallow penetration but is good way to slow things down for a while if he's getting near the top.

Swap doggy style for: Crouching tiger, hidden hard-on.

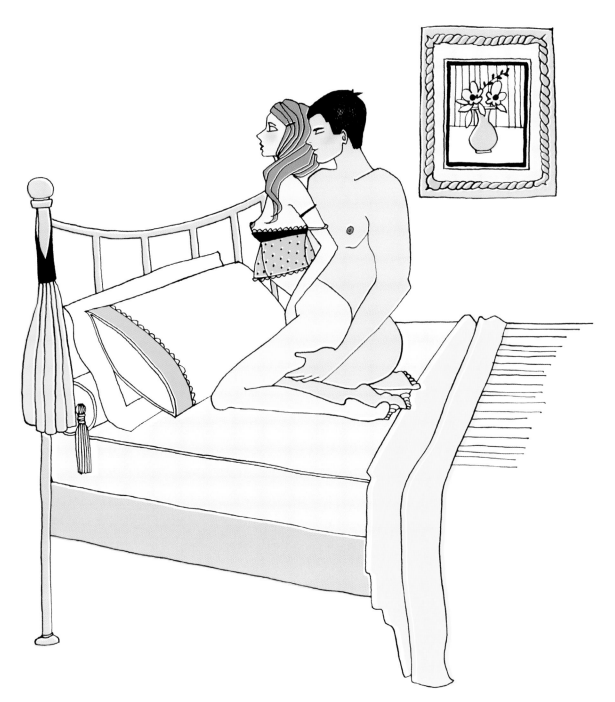

Crouching tiger, hidden hard-on

In this rear-entry position, you are on top of your man so he is thrusting upward. This gives you maximum clitoral stimulation.

How to do it: Your man kneels on the bed, floor, supermarket aisle, wherever, and sits back on his knees. Then you back toward him, and lower yourself down so you're sitting on his penis, one leg either side of his thighs. He can hold your hips to keep his balance; you can grip that trusty headboard.

Best bits: When he thrusts only shallowly—that's how your clitoris will get the most stimulation.

Variations: Collapse forward so you are supporting yourself on your hands for greater control.

Woman on top

All together now, in the style of Glen Campbell: "Like a rhinestone cowgirl, riding out on the cock of a spunk-spangled gigolo …" This is the position that the suffragettes fought for. You get to be in charge of everything, from whether you get G-spot or clitoral action, how long you're up there for and when he can climax. In return he gets to gaze fondly upon your bouncy boobs. It's a fair deal.

How to do it: He lies or sits on the bed, you climb on top of him, facing him. There are endless variations (see below).

Best bits: Total control, baby. You call the shots. He can fondle you all over; you can reach down and fondle yourself or caress him.

Variations: He can bend his knees and place his feet flat on the mattress. You can lean backward against his thighs, which increases the pressure on your G-spot.

More of a clitoral girl? Then simply lean forward as much as you like, and swap an up/down thrust for a forward/backward grind. You can stretch full-length so you are in the missionary position but with the roles reversed. His orgasm-face makes you giggle involuntarily? Then face toward his feet. This gives you maximum G-spot force, both of you new, thrilling feelings and he can massage or penetrate your anus with his fingers. In return, you can rub his seedpods. Try it on a chair (see page 49 of the Living Room chapter), with both your feet on the floor for bouncy leverage. Squat over him with both feet on the mattress. Go for the burn (in your thighs—not your vagina). He can prop himself up on his elbows, or a large pile of pillows. This way he can lick and kiss your boobs.

Swap woman on top for: Yab yum.

Yab yum

Despite sounding like something you'd order from a Japanese restaurant, yab yum is a classic tantric sex position. Its name means "father and mother," and it is meant to show a woman sitting lovingly on the knees of her husband. It's a very simple introduction into tantric sex. If you like this, I'd recommend exploring more about the subject as it's an excellent way to encourage emotional closeness in your relationship. You don't need to book one of the workshops offered by couples with ponytails—tantric sex is not difficult to master and you could find out everything you need from *Sexual Ecstasy* by Margot Anand or a website.

How to do it: If you're very likely to get a fit of giggles doing this naked, try it with your clothes on first. That's an easy to get the feel of the move without any pressure. If you like it, rip your clothes off! Tantric sex focuses on preparation before nookie, you don't just leap right in. Start with this simple exercise. Sit cross-legged in front of each other, look into each other's eyes, and "harmonize your breathing." This just means that you both breathe in and out at the same rate. After a few minutes, when you feel connected to each other, climb on top of your man. He stays cross-legged or, if he's very lithe, in the lotus position. Insert his lingam

into your yoni. (You can translate that one.) Wrap your feet around his waist and place their soles together. Hug each other and move up and down slowly, keeping your spines straight. Rock gently and sensuously. Build the sensations gradually. Don't rush toward orgasm—let the feelings grow.

Best bits: Rewards are huge: heightened intimacy, tender, loving sex, and yes, ultimately, orgasms that go on longer than a weekend with his parents.

Variations: You can begin with your feet flat on the bed, either side of your man's hips, if that's easier. He might like to place a pillow on his lap, to help support you. To help build the sexual energy between you, stroke each other's spines in an upward direction. For greater intimacy, create a sexual charge. Stop moving, then place a hand over each other's heart. Change your breathing so you are exhaling while he is inhaling. Let your man imagine that his sexual energy is passing from his lingam into your yoni. You then draw that energy up through your body into your heart, then breathe that energy back out into him as you exhale. Let him inhale your breath and take the energy back down into his lingam, until the circle starts again. When you feel you've built up a sexual charge, begin moving again until you orgasm.

Fetishes and fantasies

Should you go along with your partner's fantasies or fetishes? Unless it's something that makes you feel demeaned, frightened, or disgusted, I think you should try to be accommodating to his passions, and equally, he should be accommodating to yours. In a long-term relationship, you are (ideally) each other's only sexual outlet, and you have a responsibility to make each other's sex lives satisfying and enjoyable. So, as long as you don't feel in danger or revolted by something your partner suggests—and vice versa—keep an open mind and be willing to try it, at least once.

Fetishes

You'll probably find you can reach a satisfying compromise on what you're both willing to experiment with. Say, for example, he's desperate to try BDSM but the idea leaves you colder than Santa's sleigh bells—you don't have to refuse and tell him he's a pervert, but neither must you go along with it to keep him happy.

Instead, ask him what it is that particularly appeals to him about the idea, and bring in a little of that into your routine. Is it a sound? A sight? A smell? Are their particular words that turn him on, a certain material (rubber), or a situation? Similarly if you're the one with a special weakness for something, you could find a way to incorporate it in bite-sized portions.

Fantasies

Everyone has sexual fantasies. Everyone. You, your partner, your parents (eek!), everyone. They're one of the most enthralling parts of our sexual world because they're guaranteed to please. Unlike real-life sex which can all too often end in frustration, tears, or the ER, fantasies, and your fantasy lovers, are always there waiting to be absolutely perfect and fulfilling.

Because I've been so wonderfully accommodating to the fetish idea, you're now expecting me to demand that you live out your and your partner's fantasies, aren't you? Well—

I'm not. So there! Aah, the blissful unpredictability of women. No, it's a sad fact that, rather being the amazing-sex guarantee that you'd expect, most fantasies wither and die when they're exposed to daylight. You don't really want to be shagged senseless by Superman, you want what Superman represents—a strong, dominating force that takes all your guilt away from craving sex and literally makes resistance futile.

Also, fantasies are so incredibly private that revealing them makes us feel raw with vulnerability. I would bet millions on the fact that most people never reveal their number-one top sexual fantasy. We'll confess to numbers five, four, or three, even two at a push, but that favorite one … Ooh, no thanks, unless the thrill of actually experiencing it far outweighs the pain of humiliation or alienation that might ensue once your life partner discovers you want to do it with a house plant.

Male fantasy vs female fantasy

Men and women view fantasies very differently. Women see them as dreams—wild, improbable flights of fancy that will never come true—but men see them more as to-do lists, things they'd love to do one day, preferably tonight.

You'll notice this if you look at the eight most popular male fantasies compared to the favorite female fantasies, as compiled by Relate psychosexual therapist Paula Cole:

Top male fantasies

- Sex with an existing partner
- Giving and receiving oral sex
- Threesomes or group sex
- Being dominant
- Being passive and submissive
- Reliving a previous experience
- Watching others make love
- Trying new sexual positions

Top female fantasies

- Sex with an existing partner
- Giving and receiving oral sex
- Having sex with a new partner
- Romantic or exotic locations
- Doing something forbidden
- Reliving a previous experience
- Being found irresistible
- Trying new sexual positions

See how women's fantasies include romantic destinations, being found utterly irresistible, new partners … Another very common female sexual fantasy is to be raped. NOT IN REAL LIFE. But being taken against her will is often arousing in a woman's fantasy, as it's a way to alleviate any residual guilt she might feel about being her sexual desires.

Men and women view acting out fantasies very differently. Men have more factual fantasies and so will interpret their partner's in the same way, feeling she is dissatisfied somehow if he's not doing her on a soft, sandy moonlit beach, against her will, coming within a nanosecond because she's so desirable. She can say, "It's just a fantasy!" but he won't understand as, to him, fantasies are definitely things he'd like to happen in real life. Similarly, if you whisper to your man, "What are your sexual fantasies?" and seem receptive to them, he will probably then start flipping through his diary saying, "So … threesome on Saturday, then?"

However, if you can manage to navigate the treacherous oceans of vulnerability and embarrassment, Fantasy Island can be a mind-blowing place to visit. So, as ever, this is the bit where I go all bossy and tell you what to do.

Bring up the subject in a sexy way

Sexpert Tracey Cox suggests that you tell your partner, "I had the sexiest dream last night," and then go on to describe your fantasy. If he rears back in horror, you know not to bother taking it farther because he's not interested. But if he seems turned on or intrigued, add that it's been a fantasy of yours for ages, and how would he feel about acting it out? This also gives him a very easy way to confess to any naughty fantasies that he's been harboring, too.

Find a couple of props

Visual props are good, like clothing, sunglasses, snap-on latex gloves for medical scenarios, etc.

Keep your sense of humor

If it all goes wrong, laugh about it. There's nothing worse than both of you grimly carrying on with something that lost all its sexiness two hours ago. Don't laugh at each other, laugh at the silliness of the situation. Then kiss and do something else.

Common sex problems

When good sex goes bad, it's not always down to boredom or emotional reasons. Sometimes the problems are medical, and need medical cures. Don't start looking up symptoms on the Internet—instead, read my guide to the most common sexual problems and how to fix them.

Men's problems

Premature ejaculation

Almost half of all men suffer from the problem of premature ejaculation (PE) at some point in their life. And you don't have PE just because you always come before your partner; you only have it when you can't control when you come at all. If this is a recent problem, see your primary care doctor to rule out any possible medical causes. Some conditions like a urinary infection or problems with your prostate can bring PE on suddenly.

If it is a common problem, and one that you've had for most of your life, then it's more likely that there are mental or emotional causes. For some reason, you haven't learned to recognize the moment just before you're about to orgasm—psychosexual therapist Paula Hall calls this point "the moment of inevitability." This might have been caused by your very earliest sexual experiences—for example, if you grew up in a home where masturbation was seen as "dirty," you probably would have rushed through masturbation as quickly as possible to lessen the risk of being discovered. This could have caused your penis to get accustomed to very sudden orgasms. Similarly, if your early screws were fast, furious affairs in dark alleyways, you won't have learned to take your time.

Men who don't have PE can recognize the "point of inevitability" and stop all stimulation and wait for their orgasm to recede (or just go with the flow then apologize). If you can't spot this point and your climax is usually an unwelcome surprise, then you need to take matters into your own hands. Here's my advice:

• Stop sex for a while and instead explore your partner's body with your mouth and hands. Take the pressure away.
• Practice the squeeze technique. Start masturbating (alone or with your partner) until just before you feel like you're going to orgasm. When it's imminent, either you or your partner uses their hand to squeeze the penis just under the head. You might lose some erection, that's normal. This squeeze should make your orgasm retreat. When it's all clear, try the technique again. After practicing this several times, you should be used to delaying your orgasm using this technique, and soon you should be able to delay your climax without using the squeeze.
• See your primary care physician if the problem is very serious. He might be willing to prescribe some antidepressants, which will have a side effect of delaying your orgasm.

Impotence

At some point in their life, according to research by the Sexual Dysfunction Association in the UK, one in 10 men will suffer from impotence. This means that almost 2.3 million men in the UK (where I live) are suffering now.

Experts used to believe that the causes were almost always mental, but new research points to their being a physical problem in 70 percent of cases. However, it's usually a mixture of mental and physical. If the problem comes on suddenly, or doesn't happen every time, it's much more likely to be a mental issue:

Common mental causes of impotence
- Stress, anxiety, or depression
- Relationship problems or sexual boredom
- Worrying about impotence

You can work on these issues yourself—for example by identifying any areas of stress in your life and removing them. Your partner can also help by taking away any pressure you might feel to "perform." Perhaps take sex completely off the menu for a month and use other ways to bring each other pleasure, like oral sex or mutual masturbation. Take steps to alleviate boredom in the relationship —follow the earlier tips on keeping things interesting; make proper "dates" with your lover; consider using toys in the bedroom. If the problem persists and you think you've done everything you can yourself, consider seeing a psychosexual counselor.

A longer-term problem, where the male impotence very rarely or even never improves, points to a physical reason:

Common physical causes of impotence
- High cholesterol
- Prescribed drugs
- Smoking
- Alcohol or party drugs
- Surgery or illness
- Diabetes
- High blood pressure, and poor circulation
- Kidney problems
- Multiple sclerosis or other neurological diseases

Some of these you can cure yourself, for example by stopping smoking, drinking, and taking drugs, and adopting a healthier lifestyle. For the other issues, it's worthwhile consulting your doctor. There have been many medical advances in this area in the last ten years, so your chances of finding a cure are better than they've ever been, whether that cure is psychosexual counseling, implants, Viagra, vacuum pumps, or surgery.

Women's problems

Penetration hurts you
If it hurts when he enters you, the most likely reason is that you don't want him there. Either you're not yet aroused enough for the vagina to have lubricated and lengthened—your vagina increases in size during the arousal process, to accommodate his penis—or you're just in a mood with him. For emotional cures, see my tips in the Bathroom chapter.

If you're not aroused enough yet, back off from penetration and have more foreplay until you're naturally wet, and consider adding a drop or two of artificial lube. Often the wetter you feel, the wetter you'll naturally become.

Possible medical causes
If the pain is lower down, or to one side, see your doctor to rule out an underlying condition, like endometriosis, cysts, fibroids, a prolapse, or pelvic inflammatory disease. Another possible cause is uterine retroversion, where the womb tilts toward the back of the pelvis. All these conditions can mean that wild, abandoned deep thrusting can hurt you, but sex isn't off the menu forever; you might just feel comfier switching to a more shallow position, like the spoons or missionary positions.

Outdoors

What's the secret of great sex? Location, loction, location! So get outside and start making the **earth move.** The easiest way to put the spark back into your lovemaking is simply to **switch the venue.** Outdoor sex boosts adrenaline (through the fear of possibly being caught), which can **heighten arousal**, and having sex in new places forces you to try new positions. But don't just take my word for it, get out there and see for yourself. You'll soon find that **everything in the garden is lovely**—and the parking lot, the shopping mall, the swimming pool …

Location, location, location

I've got some good news and some bad news. The bad news is I'm slapping a ban on bedroom sex for one month. No cozy, duvet-shrouded romps for four whole weeks. I don't care how bouncy and supportive the marital mattress may be, you're not allowed to hump on it. The good news is this will revitalize your sex life. The problem with bedroom romping is that it's too comfortable, and comfort is not synonymous with passion.

Think of the greatest sex scenes in literature—how many of them take place after the heroine plumps up her pillows and curls up with a hot-water bottle? No, the real action always occurs outside: in barns, meadows, steamed-up cars, and alleyways. Forget the main reason for this (that the couple didn't have a marital bedroom, or if they did, their legal partner was sleeping in it) and concentrate on the outcome: passionate, desperate sex.

This is a situation where mood follows action. When your partner finds you grappling with him furiously in the vegetable patch, he surmises that you must be overcome with lust for him, and responds in kind. The risk of being caught makes your body produce adrenaline, which increases your heartbeat and heightens your senses. Danger actually boosts people's attraction for each other, along with their dopamine levels, which adds to the arousal process.

In short, outdoor romping is great for your sex life. Don't worry about choosing a romantic spot. Obviously a beautiful hillside overlooking a spectacular lake would be best, but anywhere will do as long as it's far away from the marital bed. I know of couples who use their garden shed as a hump hideaway and others who reignite the spark by pretending to change the spark plugs in the garage.

The easiest location is your own backyard, if you have one. You may feel self-conscious if it's overlooked by neighbors. But if not; you don't need my advice as you're probably happily humping among the rose bushes. (Just one word if that's you: it's still against the law to have sex within sight of other people, so be careful.) If you are a shyer seductress, find or create an area in your yard that combines discretion with passion. A garden shed is ideal; fill the space with hanging lanterns or votive candles in jam jars, and have sensuous-smelling plants potted up outside the door.

If you have kids, corrupt their innocent toys with lusty romps. Trampolines are especially good, as are playhouses. With a garage, you're laughing all the way to the shag: make passionate love on your car bonnet or grope each other's chest on your freezer.

Be prepared

Women take longer than men to go through the stages of arousal, so spend time beforehand getting as excited as possible. If you're driving without the kids in the car, play an erotic CD—one you have recorded of the two of you having sex, a spoken-word book of erotic fiction, or one that you usually have as your sex song. Then slip into the back seat and neck like teenagers—kissing is the best way to start your nether regions lubricating and expanding in readiness for sex.

Cunning lingo

While men are more visual, women are aroused by sounds so another route to outdoor nookie is talking—tell your man exactly what you'd like to do to him. Indulge in this while on vacation in a foreign country, where nobody can translate phrases like, "I want to chew your panties off with my teeth." If you try this at home, agree beforehand some code words for your private parts, then you could chat away in public.

Gardener's erection time

You can create a total sex den in your yard, but so discreetly that elderly aunts won't faint if they go outside to smell the roses. I'm married to a landscape gardener, so with his years of expertise in this area, he knows exactly how to turn a garden into a seductive, sexy, and, most importantly, private space. Here are his ideas.

Privacy

Firstly you need to create a private space in which you can hump unobserved. You could use your shed for rough and ready romps, but for a more picturesque atmosphere, invest in a pergola or a gazebo. If you have one but it's open sided, plant climbers (see below for plant tips) around the edges to block off the neighbors' view. Or consider installing overhead beams in the yard, like huge curved arches. When you grow climbers up these, they create a completely natural roof over your sex den, under which you can merrily get up to all kinds of filth without anyone spotting a thing.

Lighting

There are many ways to light your sexy shag-space. The most economical way is to place candles or lanterns everywhere, but when the mood strikes, you don't want to have to rummage around for a box of matches. (Do invest in a citronella candle, though, to help keep mosquitoes away from your tender naked bottoms.) Invest in some garden lights—sequential ones are especially attractive—and ones that can be put inside a water feature give off a very romantic glow. Or, build a fire (see below).

Heating

You'll need to find a way to heat the space. If your neighbors do catch a glimpse of you both, your man won't want them to see him shriveled by the cold. The sexiest heat is an open fire: sink a fire pit into your yard to romp beside. Less permanently, you can buy an outdoor fire-bowl, wood-burner, or just build a huge wood fire in your barbecue.

Sexy plants

To get you in the mood, grow sweetly fragranced plants around your sex den. Jasmine is a renowned aphrodisiac, and its scent is said to stimulate the production of endorphins in the body, boosting your libido and inducing mild feelings of euphoria. Get in there! Combine privacy and aromatherapy by planting a climbing jasmine, like *Jasminum humile* (a summer flowering climber), *Trachelospermum jasminoides* (a late-summer flowering climber), or the appropriately named *Jasminum nudiflorum* (winter flowering climber).

Other good choices would be plants that smell like chocolate. Did you know about these? How cool are they! Try *Clematis* 'Jan Fopma' (a purple-flowered clematis), or *Akebia quinata* (climber), both of which smell like Willy Wonka's factory. Finally, what about a bush? I'm sure your man likes bushes, how about you? Try *Daphne odora* 'Aureomarginata' (a small evergreen shrub with a very sexy smell).

Sexy furniture

Don't even attempt to get down and dirty on a fold-up garden chair, unless you want to literally get down and dirty on the ground when it collapses. Buy your partner a love seat instead, where you can both sit and neck wildly while your children almost drown in the wading pool.

For extra seduction, give the chair on your anniversary (aww) and have it engraved with something romantic but arousing, translated into a foreign language—perhaps the language of the country where you honeymooned or had your first vacation together?

Nought to sexy in seconds

Remember those steamy back-seat sessions in the car when you were 16 years old, and desperate to pass your driving test any way you could? We are going to relive those happy, vaguely uncomfortable, times. The best thing about car-sex when you're older is that you've probably got a bigger car, a license, and a garage. The bigger car means you're not in quite so much danger of giving yourself an accidental hysterectomy with the stick shift, the license means you can park you car anywhere before you romp, and the garage means you can have warmer—but slightly less thrillingly risky—vehicular nookie whenever you like. Any of the following ideas can be done in the privacy of your garage or driveway, or outside in more "dangerous" places like parking lots, by the side of the road, or even in a mad rush while you go through a car-wash. Don't be tempted to try them out while either of you is driving, however.

Flirty foreplay

• Slip a dirty note under the sun visor of your man's car. Make it explicit and include lots of man-friendly words like "big," "manly," "strong," and "powerful." "When you get home tonight, I can't wait to feel your big, manly hands stroking all over my soft, firm breasts before you powerfully fuck me," for example.

• Buy some of the audio porn recommended in the Living Room chapter (see page 42), and slip the CD into your fella's car stereo in secret. Either leave it there as a surprise, or put up a sticky note saying "Turn me on" on the stereo as a hint (or a warning, if he sometimes drives the kids to school).

• Secretly record a lovemaking session between the two of you, and burn it onto a CD and leave that in his car, as above. Make sure it's a sexy one, and not full of tutting and apologizing.

• Save the scary envelope from a parking ticket, and slip a sexy message inside and leave it on his car. "Warning: you have exceeded the recommended levels of sexiness" would be appropriate, if incredibly cheesy.

• When you're sitting next to him in the passenger seat, wear a short skirt and no underwear. During the drive, let him "accidentally" get a glimpse of your naked Lady Garden.

Red-light district

While I don't ever advise doing sexy stuff when the car is in motion, you do occasionally have to stop at a red light. And then you can …

• Neck wildly and passionately, until you can no longer pretend the incensed beeps from the car behind you are harp music.

• Take it in turns to describe a sexual fantasy while the lights are red—you do one, he does the next. (Check the back seat first for any stunned and revolted children.) This can just be a naughty game, or you can use it to hint at an activity you'd secretly love to try.

• Also at alternating red lights, take turns to create an erotic story with your man. On your turn, you must describe a sexy scenario until the lights change to yellow. When you next stop, your partner takes over and carries the story on. Rules: no hesitation! No deviation (unless sexual)! And you must carry on talking till the lights change, then immediately stop. Try to leave it on a cliffhanger. "Just as he was about to rip aside her tiny silver thong, he noticed that her …" etc.

• Lick his ear, swirling your tongue around the outside and plunging it into the middle. Most men are very sensitive in this area.

• Study the couple in the car in front of you, and speculate what kind of things they get up to in bed. Make them as explicit as you can.

• Ram your hand inside his pants and stroke and fondle him till the lights change, then remove your hand in a ladylike fashion and say no more about it, until you get to the next red light …

• Ram his hand inside your pants and let him fondle you until the lights change. Warning: if you're driving, he might take some persuading to stop this when you pull away.

Sex in the car

Whether you're lurking in the garage at home, or doggedly dogging in a public parking lot, there's no denying that sex in a car is difficult. It's cramped and restricting. However, it's also intimate, novel, and the very confined nature of the space gives you lots of things to brace your feet against, giving you more leverage. These are good positions to try:

Back-seat rider

The missionary position also works relatively well on the back seat of a car. But slightly more adventurous is the reverse-cowgirl position. Start by moving both front seats as far forward as they'll go, then hop in the back with your fella. Have him sit down, with his back against the door and his legs flat along the seat. Climb on top of him, facing toward his feet. Hold onto the handrail above the door as you grind against him, or hold onto the headrests. You could squat over him, feet flat on the seat, for maximum penetration, but not if you're very tall.

Good for: Fast, furious frolicking.
Bad for: Comfort.

Paradise by dashboard light

Get him into the front passenger seat and ask him to recline the seat right back. Then straddle him and lower yourself onto his "stick shift." In this position, you're relatively comfy as your knees can rest on the padded upholstery. Also, you can try this position in reverse, with you facing outward, looking through the windshield into the horrified faces of everyone else in the library parking lot.

Good for: Passing your driving test; G-spot action.
Bad for: Sustained sex.

Public romping

It's against the law to have sex in a public place, just like it is to indulge in a post-coital cigarette. So in the following tips, I by no means advocate that you have sex where anyone else could see you, OK? That would be the truth even without the law, though, I must admit. It's the thrill of being seen that's erotic—not actually being stared at by a busload of seniors.

• Go to a big, anonymous department store that offers late-night shopping. Find a quiet changing room, grab an armful of clothes and your partner, and ravish each other up against the full-length mirror.

• Swimming pools are a good venue for an evening date with your mate. Break all the "no petting" rules in the shallow end, canoodle in the jacuzzi, then finish it all off with a satisfying, lusty, damp banging in the big, lockable family changing room.

• Find a remote, unused disabled toilet and drag your partner in there for a quickie. They are especially good if they have a light you can turn off—you'll be shagging in absolute pitch blackness.

• Take him to the darkest corner of the movie theater and place a coat over your laps, underneath which you can do all manner of filthy things to one another. When it all gets too much, rush out of there and ravish one another in the toilet or the parking lot.

• Book a small, private box at the opera, and see how much naughtiness you can get up to without anyone realizing. When I did this, it was quite a lot! You can also try this at the races or the theater, but there's something especially passionate and rousing about opera music …

• Spas are very sexy. Go to a big, posh one that offers lots of different sensory rooms, with aromatherapy, heat, and steam. Some vacation resorts are great for having swanky spas and they also have child care for the kids. Book a day-pass for the two of you, and spend the morning wafting around the different spa rooms, then head back to your room and finish the job.

Positions for the great outdoors

Expect the fast and the furious. Having sex outside means having passionate nookie without any of the niceties of bedroom humping. Don't expect it to be a romantic experience: the idea is to get to the climax as fast as possible, so the sweet-nothing whispering and slow undressing has to go. If he manages not to ram your face into the barbecue pit, that's just a bonus. The secret is to concentrate on positions that deliver maximum stimulation in the minimum time.

Girl on top

This is a great bet for al fresco fornicating as it can be stimulating and discrete at the same time. If you have dressed appropriately in no panties, a long, loose skirt, and a top that buttons up at the front, you could enjoy amazing sex in the middle of a outdoor party and nobody would know. Start by massaging your man through his trousers to get him aroused—this is easiest if you sit on his lap, and use one hand to slide under his waist band and grab his nether regions. Once he is hard, undo his trousers then sit astride him. Your skirt should cover the big moment as you slide him inside you, and then he can unbutton your top so he can see your breasts bouncing with every thrust.

When you're on top, sit up straight and make your man support his weight on his elbows as he lies on his back. This will shift the position of his penis slightly so it rubs directly against your G-spot. Then he can slip one hand under your skirt to massage your clitoris as you ride him.

Good for: Maximum stimulation with minimum arrests.

Bad for: Making you want to be noisy and unbridled—try to keep it down if you're in the park, thanks.

Doggy style

No, not dogging-style, although the classic canine position is perfect for boffing outside. Try it up against a lamppost, if you like. Make sure your man is wearing a jacket that reaches his hipbones. You should be in your obligatory long skirt.

Find somewhere secluded and romantic. The best place is in the woods, where you can find a tree with a branch at exactly the right height to lean against. (Ideally, you'd be leaning up against a branch that is the same height as your knees—bent over in this position, your G-spot will be at the perfect angle to receive his thrusts.) Then bend over, brace yourself, and enjoy a fast, furious quickie.

Good for: Bringing back the "just-met" passion.
Bad for: Clitoral stimulation. Ideally, you'd have worked yourself up a bit first by having a crafty fiddle in the gift-shop toilet.

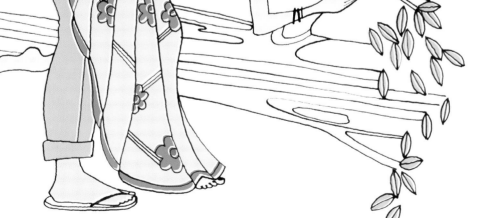

Naughty by nature

Forget tree-hugging—they never call you afterward. Instead, embrace nature more passionately with your partner, by romping up against the bark of a tree. I have done this several times in my marriage, and each time it's turned a dull "Are we there yet?" stroll through the woods into a saucy encounter that sticks in both our minds, even as we're still pulling twigs out of our hair months later.

So, here's what to do. If you're the same height as your man, you can have standing-up sex on any flat surface as your bits will be at the right heights. But if he's taller than you, you'll need to find a tree that has roots growing out through the soil at its base—you can then stand on these, and raise yourself up to your man's level. If you're a lot shorter than your man—anything over 5 inches shorter—he will need to lift you up slightly.

Anyway, lean back against the tree and part your legs. Your partner (or lucky gamekeeper) then stands in front of you with both of his legs inside yours, and grasps your rear. He then enters you, and, if you're petite, supports your weight as you wrap both legs around his waist. If you're the same height or very close, you can simply raise one of your legs— bending it at the knee—as you have sex. This changes the angle of your vagina and makes the penetration deeper.

Good for: Relatively "romantic" public sex, and lots of kissing.

Bad for: Long sex—his arms will get tired.

Buckle up

Push the passenger seat back as far as it can go, and recline it as much as possible. Lie on the seat and invite your man to climb aboard you, missionary style. When he's inside you, brace your feet up against the dashboard. This means you can thrust your hips against his more than you usually can, giving him a deeper penetration which makes up for his limited movement.

Good for: Clitoral stimulation, if you really grind yourself against him. Angle your hips upward as much as possible for maximum clitoral stimulation.

Bad for: Much variation. Once you're in this position, you're pretty much there for the duration.

Sex and the city center

A very sexy way to spend time with your man is shopping for sex toys. This is the one kind of shopping that he might even be enthusiastic about. There are more retailers now than ever, both on Main Street and on the Internet. There are also Erotica exhibitions that take place every year in various big cities (you can find these by searching the Internet).

Where you go is up to you. I'm not going to send you straight to the Internet, as shopping in person can be very sexy. Don't imagine that today's sex stores are anything like they used to be: gone are the blacked-out windows, scruffy-looking store owners, and seedy-looking customers licking their lips in front of magazines like *Obese and Up For It* or *Barely Legal*. The buzzwords in sex stores these days are "female friendly." Most stores are more like large chains of coffee shops—StarFucks, perhaps—brightly lit, well laid out and staffed with young, attractive salesclerks.

Some are designed to be totally women friendly, but are open to people of both genders. Others are split over two levels, and to attract more women, they keep the street-level floor unlicensed. This means they're not allowed to sell X-rated merchandise here. Men usually only bother with the licensed, hardcore materials, so they go straight to the licensed floor, leaving you in a nonthreatening environment.

The merchandise has improved, too. Many stores carry attractive, good-quality lingerie and some stores specialize in sexy fitting rooms, with chairs where your partner can sit and watch you slip into something uncomfortable.

There are toys of every description, with walls of vibrators and countless gadgets you can use as a couple. Some of the higher-end stores also include designer sex toys. Think *Objets d'Tart*—beautifully sculpted out of semi-precious stones, they look more like an elegant table centerpiece than something you'd shove up your what's-it.

If you prefer Internet shopping, the world is your remote-controlled oyster. Again, the online stores are female friendly, informative, and deliver in unmarked packages. You can order online or over the phone—and some offer a 24-hour order line so if the urge for a Jessica Rabbit vibrator hits you at 3 o'clock in the morning, you can place your request there and then.

Main street and online

EARLY TO BED, Chicago
early2bed.com
This women-owned establishment sells a array of high-quality sex toys and accessories, and erotic gifts, both online and in the Chicago store. The store was opened in 2001 to provide a safe, welcoming place where women could shop for sex toys, books, accessories, and information. It is very women-oriented but has a guy-friendly atmosphere, so is a good place for couples to shop.

BABELAND, Seattle and New York
www.babeland.com
The first Babeland store was opened in 1993 in Seattle because of a lack of women friendly sex stores there. Since then it has opened two stores in Manhattan and one in Brooklyn. Run by women, the stores are popular with women and couples. They sell a wide range of sex toys, accessories, and books, and run a well-known online store. Their website provides very good links to other women friendly sex sites and lists events. A good site to start with if you are going online to look at sex toys for the first time.

GOOD VIBRATIONS, San Francisco and Boston

www.goodvibes.com

This store was established in San Francisco in 1977 to provide a comfortable, safe environment for sex-positive products and educational materials for women and couples. The stores and the website sell high-quality sex toys, books, and adult movies, and give sex and health advice.They also host sex education workshops and community events.

SH!, London

www.sh-womenstore.com

I love this shop. The company put all its efforts into making itself girl-friendly, to the extent that men can't come in here alone, and you'll instantly feel you've walked into a place of safety. Staff are informative and excel at minimizing your embarrassment. You'll be discussing your vaginal needs and tilted cervix within seconds. Good range of products, too. This store is good for advice and customer service, but bad for your man going in to buy you a secret gift, because he must be accompanied by a female.

MYLA

www.mylausa.com

Myla has stores throughout London, Ireland, and Germany, and is about to open a store in New York. You can also buy their exclusive products online. It is the home of the Bone—the iconic sex toy by Tom Dixon (see pages 96–97). Myla is like "Vaginal Vogue," stocking chic designer accessories for your nether regions, from genuinely beautiful lingerie to vibrating cock rings that wouldn't look out of place in Tiffany & Co. The stores are all well-lit and elegant. It is especially good for luxury lingerie but bad on your purse.

COCO DE MER, Los Angeles and London

www.coco-de-mer.com

This upmarket boudoir-boutique is run by Sam Roddick (the daughter of Body Shop founder Anita Roddick) and is gorgeous. I visited the store in London's Covent Garden, and its red walls and crushed-velvet upholstery gave it the darkly sensual look of a nineteenth-century bordello—no sign of a willy ice-cube tray here—and the products are at the upper-upper end of the market. Crystal and glass hand-crafted dildos promise to be the poshest thing you ever stuff up your what's-it, the lingerie is well-made and deeply sexy, and the accessories are amazing. It is good for designer sex toys and lingerie with a feeling of old-fashioned glamour, but like MYLA it is pricey.

EROTICA EXHIBITION, annual exhibition at Olympia, London

www.erotica-uk.com

The Erotica Exhibition is held every year in the Olympia exhibitions halls in London. Its massive square footage is filled with exhibitionist-exhibitors selling everything from handbag-sized vibrators to bespoke bondage beds. Erotic sculpture, costumes, fetish-wear, pornography … Everything you've ever wanted to know about sex but were afraid to Google. It runs for three days every November. It's not as pink and fluffy as the new breed of sex shop, it does have a definite hardcore edge, but if you can cope with meeting porn stars in the flesh and seeing couples experimenting with bullwhips, it's worth a visit. You can steer clear of the more extreme areas and just stick to browsing the sex-toy stalls. If either of you has any kind of fetish, you'll be able to see all its related equipment here, and most of the equipment is available to buy on the day. It is interesting for the sheer volume of different merchandise all under the same roof. When you go to a large erotica exhibition like this, after the initial shock, where you don't know where to look, you soon adjust and know exactly where to look. If London is too far for you to go, look online for similar exhibitions in a big city near you.

Internet directory

If you and your man often flake-out in front of your laptops in the evening, snuggle up together and make it a browse to remember by visiting erotic sites. The following are worth a bookmark.

Amateur Porn
Red Tube
www.redtube.co.uk
This is like an X-rated version of You Tube, so if you don't enjoy porn, step away from this site. If you do, this site is worth a look as it offers free, explicit videos that people have uploaded themselves. There are men and women masturbating, couples having sex, but nothing illegal or disturbing.

Aroma Patches
Scentuelle Libido Patches
www.scentuellepatch.com
Patches designed to stimulate sex drives. Visit their very nonthreatening website for full information about the products.

Erotic Audio
Erotic Audio Stories for Women
www.redwordsaid.com
Eroticast
www.eroticast.net
Literotica
www.literotica.com

Erotic Fiction and Magazines
For the Girls
www.forthegirls.com
Sssh.com
www.sssh.com
Cliterati
www.cliterati.co.uk
Scarlet
www.scarletmagazine.co.uk

Lingerie
Eden Fantasys
www.edenfantasys.com/sexy-lingerie

Sex Advice
The following are sexperts, sex educators, and lecturers. All have their personal sex-positive approaches to women's sex—some are young, bold, and brazen and others are older and less so. Most give advice online.
Em & Lo
www.emandlo.com
Tracey Cox
www.traceycox.com
Tristan Taormino
www.puckerup.com
Betty Dodson and Carlin Ross
dodsonandross.com
Annie Sprinkle
www.anniesprinkle.com

Sex Blogs
Susie Bright
http://susiebright.blogs.com
Girl with a One-track Mind
http://girlwithaonetrackmind.blogspot.com
Belle du jour
http://belledejour-uk.blogspot.com

Sex Furniture
There are two kinds of sex furniture: the blatant, out-and-out "look at me, I'm a kinky couch" type of equipment that is covered in black vinyl, has built-in dildos and means you can never invite people round ever again, or the more discreet kind. I prefer the more discreet, but it's your house. Here are some sites:
Tantra Chair
www.tantrachair.com
Liberator
www.liberator.com
Amazon
www.amazon.com

Sex Toys
See the stores listed on pages 136–137 for sex toy sites, plus the following:
Blissable
www.blissable.com
MyPleasure
www.mypleasure.com
Discreet Romance
discreet-romance.com
Amazon
www.amazon.com

Tantric Sex
Sacred Loving
www.sacredloving.net
Institute for Ecstatic Living
www.ecstaticliving.com
Val Sampson
www.valsampson.co.uk

Index

A FIREFLY BOOK

Published by Firefly Books Ltd. 2009

First printing

Publisher Cataloging-in-Publication Data (U.S.)
Taylor, Kate.
   Domestic sex goddess / Kate Taylor
[144] p. : col. photos., col. ill. ; cm.
Includes index.
Summary: Realistic advice for couples on intimacy
and sexual pleasures, with photographs and artwork
to illustrate sexual techniques. Quizzes and other
interactive elements are included.
ISBN-13: 978-1-55407-536-2 (pbk.)
ISBN-10: 1-55407-536-X (pbk.)
1. Sex. 2. Sex instruction. 3. Sexual excitement.
I. Title.
613.96 dc22   HQ31.T39 2009

A CIP record for this book is available from Library
and Archives Canada.

Published in the United States by
Firefly Books (U.S.) Inc.
P.O. Box 1338, Ellicott Station
Buffalo, New York 14205

Published in Canada by
Firefly Books Ltd.
66 Leek Crescent
Richmond Hill, Ontario L4B 1H1

Printed in Hong Kong